90 0956457 0

INSTRUCTIONAL PRACTICES WITH AND WITHOUT EMPIRICAL VALIDITY

ADVANCES IN LEARNING AND BEHAVIORAL DISABILITIES

Series Editors: Bryan G. Cook, Melody Tankersley and Timothy J. Landrum

Recent Volumes:

ADVANCES IN LEARNING AND BEHAVIORAL
DISABILITIES   VOLUME 29

INSTRUCTIONAL PRACTICES WITH AND WITHOUT EMPIRICAL VALIDITY

EDITED BY

BRYAN G. COOK
University of Hawaii at Manoa, Honolulu, HI, USA

MELODY TANKERSLEY
Kent State University, Kent, OH, USA

TIMOTHY J. LANDRUM
University of Louisville, Louisville, KY, USA

United Kingdom − North America − Japan
India − Malaysia − China

Emerald Group Publishing Limited
Howard House, Wagon Lane, Bingley BD16 1WA, UK

First edition 2016

Reprints and permissions service
Contact: permissions@emeraldinsight.com

British Library Cataloguing in Publication Data
A catalogue record for this book is available from the British Library

ISBN: 978-1-78635-126-5
ISSN: 0735-004X (Series)

Printed and bound by CPI Group (UK) Ltd, Croydon, CR0 4YY

ISOQAR certified
Management System,
awarded to Emerald
for adherence to
Environmental
standard
ISO 14001:2004.

ISOQAR
REGISTERED
Certificate Number 1985
ISO 14001

INVESTOR IN PEOPLE

CONTENTS

LIST OF CONTRIBUTORS

Alyson A. Collins	Texas State University, San Marcos, TX, USA
Lauren W. Collins	University of Hawaii, Honolulu, HI, USA
Bryan G. Cook	University of Hawaii, Honolulu, HI, USA
Lysandra Cook	University of Hawaii, Honolulu, HI, USA
Robin Parks Ennis	University of Alabama-Birmingham, Birmingham, AL, USA
Jiwon Hwang	The Pennsylvania State University, University Park, PA, USA
Christina Keaulana	Leeward Community College, Pearl City, HI, USA
Kimberly M. Landrum	Department of Special Education, University of Louisville, Louisville, KY, USA
Timothy J. Landrum	University of Louisville, Louisville, KY, USA
Mickey Losinski	Kansas State University, Manhattan, KS, USA
Kent McIntosh	University of Oregon, Eugene, OR, USA
Stephanie Morano	The Pennsylvania State University, University Park, PA, USA
Rhonda N. T. Nese	University of Oregon, Eugene, OR, USA
Paul J. Riccomini	The Pennsylvania State University, University Park, PA, USA
Amy Gillespie Rouse	Southern Methodist University, Dallas, TX, USA

Amy E. Ruhaak   University of Hawaii, Honolulu, HI, USA

Richard L. Simpson   University of Kansas, Lawrence, KS, USA

Melody Tankersley   Kent State University, Kent, OH, USA

Julie L. Thompson   Michigan State University, East Lansing, MI, USA

Matt Tincani   Temple University, Philadelphia, PA, USA

Jason C. Travers   University of Kansas, Lawrence, KS, USA

CHAPTER 1

INSTRUCTIONAL PRACTICES WITH AND WITHOUT EMPIRICAL VALIDITY: AN INTRODUCTION

Bryan G. Cook, Melody Tankersley and
Timothy J. Landrum

ABSTRACT

Educators' decisions regarding what instructional practices they use have significant consequences for the learning and life outcomes of their students. This is especially true for students with learning and behavioral disabilities, who require highly effective instruction to succeed in school and achieve their goals. In this volume of Advances in Learning and Behavioral Disabilities *chapter authors provide readers with accessible information on theory, critical elements, and research for instructional practices that are and are not supported by bodies of scientific research as effective in critical outcome areas. Educators can use this content to inform and enhance their instructional decision making. To contextualize subsequent chapters, in this introductory chapter we discuss the research-to-practice gap in special education, the importance of considering scientific research when making instructional decisions and considerations for interpreting and applying research findings*

Instructional Practices with and without Empirical Validity
Advances in Learning and Behavioral Disabilities, Volume 29, 1–16
Copyright © 2016 by Emerald Group Publishing Limited
All rights of reproduction in any form reserved
ISSN: 0735-004X/doi:10.1108/S0735-004X20160000029001

on instructional practices. We conclude with a preview of the chapters in the volume.

Keywords: Empirical validity; research evidence;
research-to-practice gap

Although educational stakeholders may not always agree on which outcomes are the most critical, a fundamental goal of every educator is to provide effective instruction that supports students in attaining their goals and realizing their academic, behavioral, and social potentials. Of the many influences on student outcomes (e.g., genes, parent involvement, home environment, peer group, school, and community resources), instruction is the variable over which educators have the most control. Although it is not the sole influence on student performance, instruction makes a meaningful difference in how students learn (e.g., Hattie, 2003). Using highly effective instructional practices appears particularly important for students with learning and behavioral disabilities (Vaughn & Dammann, 2001). Although nondisabled students may be able to "fill in the gaps" and perform satisfactorily when provided mediocre instruction, students with learning and behavioral disabilities require highly effective instruction to reach their potentials. Indeed, contemporary multi-tiered frameworks (e.g., response to intervention, school wide positive behavior supports; Fletcher & Vaughn, 2009; Sugai & Horner, 2009) reflect the widespread belief in the importance of effective instruction for all learners, but especially for students with and at risk for learning and behavioral disabilities.

Despite general agreement on the importance of effective instruction in education, considerable disagreement exists about which instructional practices are in fact effectual. Indeed, the history of special education abounds with practices that are believed by many to be effective and widely applied, yet actually have little effect − and sometimes have an inverse effect − on learner outcomes (e.g., Foxx & Mulick, 2016; Kavale & Mostert, 2004). Such ineffective instruction is consequential, as the effects of learning compound over time and can exacerbate the effects of a disability. The Matthew effect, in which the rich get richer and the poor get poorer, seems to apply in education (Stanovich, 1986). Effective instruction enables students to succeed in learning, which engenders future success and learning. In contrast, when children fall behind in school because of poor instruction, they are less likely to understand future instruction, and more likely to develop negative attitudes toward schooling and to act out. Moreover, by definition, students with learning and behavioral disabilities experience unique and serious learning challenges. The negative and cumulative effects of ineffective instruction will, then, be particularly strong for these learners.

Given the importance of implementing highly effective instruction and avoiding instructional approaches that are ineffective, the purpose of this volume is to identify and describe effective and ineffective practices for students with learning and behavioral disabilities in critical areas (i.e., reading, problem solving in math, writing, communication, student choice, physical movement, classroom behavior, school discipline, stereotypical behavior). To this end, the authors of chapters in this volume review research findings related to the highlighted practices, discuss the theory underlying the practices, and overview how to implement the effective practices. It is our hope that the information in these chapters will assist educators in making instructional decisions that will optimize, rather than impede, the outcomes and progress of students with learning and behavioral disabilities. In addition to previewing the topics addressed in the subsequent chapters of the volume, in this introductory chapter we provide a context for the chapters by discussing (a) the nature of the research-to-practice gap, (b) the critical role of scientific research in determining effective and ineffective practices, and (c) nuances in interpreting and applying research on the effectiveness of instructional practices.

THE RESEARCH-TO-PRACTICE GAP

A gap exists between the knowledge generated by research and what occurs in everyday practice in many fields, including special education. This research-to-practice gap has two sides, each with deleterious effects on learner outcomes. First, practices shown by research to have unreliable, trivial, or even negative effects on student outcomes are commonly used in classroom with students with and at risk for disabilities – including practices described in this volume (e.g., learning styles, suspensions, the keyword method, stand-alone grammar instruction, Brain Gym®, deep-pressure therapy). For example, special education service providers reported that they use some ineffective instructional practices more frequently than practices shown by sound research to be highly effective

(Burns & Ysseldyke, 2009). Secondly, many practices shown by sound research to reliably improve student outcomes are used infrequently. In fact, Borders, Bock, and Szymanski (2015) reported that 16 of the 25 evidence-based practices examined in their study were used by less than half of participating special education teachers. Similarly, a statewide survey indicated that teachers are neither well prepared in or commonly implement evidence-based practices for students with behavioral disabilities (Gable, Tonelson, Sheth, Wilson, & Park, 2012; see also Stormont, Reinke, & Herman, 2011). Given the recognized importance of using highly effective practices, both sides of the research-to-practice gap seem perplexing — why don't educators use the most effective instructional practices and why do they use less effective practices?

Although scientific research is a powerful tool, it is not an intuitive or straightforward approach for quickly addressing the myriad issues faced daily in our personal and professional lives. Pierce (1877) and others have proposed that people commonly use other ways of knowing such as tradition, authority, and personal experience to form the beliefs that are the basis for their decisions. These approaches can and often do result in valid conclusions. However, each has serious flaws that can lead educators to erroneous beliefs. For example, despite being "authorities," professors, professional development providers, curriculum developers, and other experts often promote practices that have been shown by research to have little, no, or negative effects on student outcomes. Indeed, many experts have professional and financial interests in the practices they promote, which should cause educators to be cautious of their advice. Likewise, though personal experience is a fundamental way people make sense of the world, it is interpreted in ways that lead to mistaken beliefs. For example, a teacher may mistakenly form a belief in the effectiveness of a practice by selectively focusing on a few students who seem to be responding positively to it. However, the teacher may be ignoring the negative reactions of other students or not systematically assessing students' performance, which might reveal that the intervention is actually ineffective. Moreover, people's interpretations of their experience are influenced by their feelings and emotions (Heath & Heath, 2008). For instance, if a teacher is excited about a new program, s/he is more likely to pay attention to indications that it works (and ignore indications that it does not). The tendency of special educators, parents, and other stakeholders to want (sometimes very badly) practices to help improve the lives and outcomes of their children, though understandable, likely clouds their judgments as to whether those practices work.

The limitations of these common ways of knowing are exacerbated by the effects of confirmation bias. Confirmation bias involves individuals disproportionally seeking out, attending to, and finding convincing information that is consistent with their established beliefs and values (Nickerson, 1998). For example, if a teacher already believes that a practice is effective, even if it is actually ineffective, s/he will likely retain and strengthen the established belief by only talking about the practice with teachers s/he knows share similar views, visiting websites that support the practice, and discounting any evidence suggesting the practice doesn't work. Indeed, confirmation bias is so strong that, rather than resulting in changed minds, scientific evidence that disputes previously held beliefs may actually increase the strength of erroneous beliefs (i.e., the backfire effect; Nyhan & Reifler, 2010). Thus, the typical ways in which people, including teachers, reason and come to believe that instructional practices work are highly fallible. Moreover, once a belief is formed, it is very difficult to change.

Carnine (1997) examined possible causes of the research-to-practice gap in special education from the research side of the equation. He suggested that research findings are insufficiently trustworthy, useable, and accessible to be implemented on a broad scale. For example, teachers may not trust the work of a researcher who has not taught in the classroom for decades. Research findings are also likely to be perceived as unusable by teachers when they feature technical terms and statistics that many educators are not trained to understand or value. Additionally, teachers typically do not subscribe to or read the journals in which research findings are reported, making research findings inaccessible to most practitioners. Because research studies are perceived as untrustworthy, unusable, and inaccessible to most educators they seldom impact educators' instructional decision making. Despite the challenges posed by the stubborn nature of the research-to-practice gap, it is critical that the field continue to strive to base practice on sound science because, as we discuss in the next section, science provides the most valid basis for determining which instructional practices do and do not work.

USING SCIENTIFIC RESEARCH TO IDENTIFY EFFECTIVE AND INEFFECTIVE PRACTICES

Like other ways of knowing (e.g., tradition, authority, personal experience), science is an imperfect approach for approximating the truth.

Its limitations (Cook, 2014) notwithstanding, scientific research is designed to address threats to validity and represents an unparalleled approach for determining what does and does not work (Kauffman, 1999; Odom et al., 2005; Slavin, 2002). Although a full discussion of the merits of scientific research are beyond the scope of this chapter, here we briefly discuss two aspects of scientific research that make it the most reliable way of knowing that serve as a basis for effective instruction in special education: (a) features of experimental research that establish causality and (b) the scientific method.

Experimental research, which we use here to refer to both group experiments and single-case designs, features elements that reasonably establish causality (i.e., determine whether an instructional practice causes improved learning outcomes) (Cook, Cook, Landrum, & Tankersley, 2008; Tankersley, Harjusola-Webb, & Landrum, 2008). For instance, experimental research uses objective and reliable measures of observable outcomes. In contrast, others ways of knowing rely on one's own subjective impressions and the others' beliefs. Moreover, beliefs based on personal experience are often formed on one or a small number of experiences, whereas experimental studies involve a large number of individuals, studying individuals intensively over time, or both.

Experimental studies are also uniquely designed to control for alternative explanations to any observed improvements in participant outcomes (Cook et al., 2008; Tankersley et al., 2008). For example, in group experimental research participants are randomly assigned to either a group that receives the targeted instructional practice (experimental group) or a group that does not receive the targeted intervention (but may instead receive "business as usual" instruction; the control group). Researchers use random assignment to ensure that they have not introduced bias into group assignment. To the degree that everything except the presence of the instructional practice is the same between the two groups, if the outcomes of the experimental group improve markedly more than the outcomes of the control group, one can logically conclude that the instructional practice caused the differential improvement. Single-case studies use a similar logic, but rather than comparing the performance of groups who do and do not receive the intervention, they compare outcomes within individuals over time when they are and are not receiving the intervention. Thus, rather than taking someone else's word for it or basing beliefs based on one's emotions or subjective impressions, experimental research involves reliable, systematic, and logical observations and analyses to determine what does and does not work.

Despite the many strengths of experimental research, it is important to treat all knowledge claims, including those based on scientific research, with healthy skepticism. All research studies have flaws and limitations. Many of these limitations stem from the difficulties of conducting research in classroom and school settings. For example, it is difficult − sometimes impossible − to randomly assign students in classrooms to different groups, so researchers often use convenience sampling and try their best to make the treatment and control groups as similar as possible. In these quasi-experimental studies, it is possible that that unmeasured differences exist between the groups, which pose a threat to the study's validity. Moreover, researchers may introduce bias into their studies. That is, researchers are human beings, and they may make decisions when designing and conducting a study to help attain the findings they desire (Simmons, Nelson, & Simonsohn, 2011). Indeed, researchers sometimes even fabricate data to produce desired findings, as occurred with the study indicating a link between vaccinations and autism (Godlee, Smith, & Marcovitch, 2011).

Recognizing the limits of any single study, the scientific method entails that knowledge is formed by the accumulation of evidence across multiple studies that verify, disprove, or refine one another. Rather than draw firm conclusions from a single study, scientists use individual studies as the basis for subsequent studies that test the validity of the original findings (i.e., through replication; see Travers, Cook, Therrien, & Coyne, in press). After multiple, related studies have been conducted (and only then), research consumers can determine confidently that a practice works (i.e., when multiple studies consistently show positive effects for a population of learners), has mixed effects (i.e., when some studies show the practice has positive effects but other do not), or is generally ineffective (i.e., when the majority of studies show small, no, or negative effects). The process of ongoing replication uncovers erroneous findings over time, as when subsequent studies disproved initial and erroneous findings related to, for example, facilitated communication (Travers, Tincani, Thompson, & Simpson, 2016) and the effects of vaccinations and autism (Godlee et al., 2011).

Using bodies of scientific, experimental research to determine the effectiveness of practices and then (a) prioritizing application of practices supported as effective and (b) avoiding practices identified as ineffective (i.e., bridging the research-to-practice gap) seems imperative for broadly improving the outcomes of students with learning and behavioral disabilities. However, as discussed in the next section, interpreting and applying the findings of bodies of scientific research involves multiple and nuanced considerations.

INTERPRETING AND APPLYING RESEARCH FINDINGS

When interpreting and applying research findings, whether it be from literature reviews found in professional journals or the overviews in this volume's chapters, educators need to be savvy research consumers. Among other issues, it is important that educators understand that research support does not connote universal effectiveness, research support exists on a continuum, and identifying practices that are and are not supported by research is only the first step in a process of instructional decision making for improving student outcomes.

Causality in educational research applies generally rather than universally. That is, when research shows that a practice (e.g., self-regulated strategy development; Rouse & Collins, 2016) causes improved outcomes, it means that the practice resulted in improved outcome for most, but not all, study participants. Even in studies examining the most effective instructional practices, some students (often called non-responders) fail to respond positively to the intervention. That is the nature of individual differences – no single practice works for everyone. Therefore, educators should not expect any practice, even those strongly supported as effective by large bodies of experimental research, to work for everyone. Accordingly, it is important to formatively assess the performance of students regardless of what instructional practice is being used (Hosp, Hosp, & Howell, 2007). This caution notwithstanding, prioritizing practices shown by research to generally cause improved outcomes and avoiding practices shown to be generally ineffective is a sound and defensible starting point for instructional decision making that is likely (though not guaranteed) to result in improved student performance.

Additionally, rather than evaluate research support dichotomously (e.g., research either supports a practice as being effective or ineffective), educators should recognize that research support exists on a continuum with a lot of gray area between the poles. That is, frequently the research evidence is less than clear as to whether a practice is effective; and it is important that educators distinguish between different types and levels of research support. For example, relatively new practices with small research bases documenting their effects might be considered promising practices (Cook,

Cook, & Collins, in press). Although such evidence shouldn't elicit the same level of confidence as a larger research base, it can be used as a reasonable justification to implement a practice, especially when (a) no relevant empirically validated practice has been identified or (b) students did not respond to existing empirically validated practices. A lack of research evidence warrants considerable caution, but especially for practices that have been used for years. Developers and promoters are responsible for building a research base for their practice. A lack of evidence for long-standing practices should, then, be a cause of considerable concern. In contrast, it is predictable that little or no research has been conducted on new practices. Finally, a research base with mixed evidence (i.e., some studies show the practice works, others that it does not) needs to be examined in more detail. Do most studies show positive or no/negative effects? Do higher quality studies (e.g., studies with reliable and valid outcome measures, larger and representative samples, strong internal validity) tend to show positive or no/negative effects? Do studies with participants and settings that match those targeted by the educator show positive or no/negative effects? Answers to these questions will help to clarify how much confidence educators should place in a practice with mixed research support. Regardless, mixed findings should always warrant caution and practices supported by a research base with consistently positive findings should be prioritized over practices with mixed research findings. Though educators should value research evidence, it is important that it be considered as part of broader process for effective instructional decision making.

Considerable attention has been devoted to identifying specific practices supported as effective by bodies of rigorous research (i.e., evidence-based practices, Cook & Cook, 2013). Yet Spencer, Detrich, and Slocum (2012) suggested that this emphasis is misplaced. Reflecting the spirit of evidence-based practice reforms in other fields (Sackett, & Rosenberg, Gray, Haynes, & Richardson, 1996), Spencer et al. suggested that evidence-based practice should be conceptualized as a decision-making process that includes consideration of research support but involves much more. Specifically, when making instructional decisions aimed at optimizing learner outcomes, educators will have to use their professional judgment and expertise to select a practice, adapt and implement the practice, and evaluate the impact of the practice (see also Torres, Farley, & Cook, 2012).

When selecting a practice, educators should certainly consider the research supporting various instructional options, prioritizing those

shown to be generally effective and avoiding practices that are likely ineffective. However, they need to also assure that a selected practice aligns with the needs, goals, and values of relevant stakeholders (e.g., learner, teacher, family). Selecting a highly effective practice that addresses an outcome that isn't relevant for the learner or for which the teacher doesn't have the requisite resources does little good. After selecting a practice, educators should identify the critical elements in the practice that need to be implemented as designed, or with fidelity, for the practice to be effective. Then they should consider ways that they can adapt nonessential aspects of the practice to make it best fit their teaching style, their classrooms, and the student's needs and interests (Leko, 2015). To determine whether the practice is effective as implemented for targeted learners, educators should formatively assess learner progress. This ongoing data collection will enable educators to make decisions on whether the targeted learner(s) is responding well to the practice as implemented (and the practice should continue to be implemented in the same way), the practice is not resulting in a sufficient level of student progress (and therefore might be adapted in different ways or implemented with greater fidelity), or the practice appears to be ineffective (even after attempts to adapt and implement critical elements with high fidelity, and therefore should be discontinued).

In summary, a considerable research-to-practice gap exists in special education that has inhibited the outcomes of students with learning and behavioral disabilities. The findings of scientific research can provide important guidance for educators when making instructional decisions, but educators need information on research that is trustworthy, useable, and accessible to translate it into practice and bridge the research-to-practice. The aim of this volume is, therefore, to provide trustworthy, useable, and accessible information on prominent practices that are and are not supported as effective by bodies of scientific research, which educators can use to augment and enhance their instructional decision making. In the following section, we preview the chapters in this volume and the practices they describe.

PREVIEW OF CHAPTERS AND PRACTICES

In Chapter 2, B. G. Cook and Keaulana provide an overview of two instructional approaches that purport to improve reading outcomes,

especially reading fluency. After providing an overview of the importance of reading fluency, the authors describe repeated reading – its theoretical basis, how to implement it, and its research base. Although the research base is not without its limitations, a number of research reviews conclude that repeated reading positively impacts reading fluency, especially for students with and at risk for learning disabilities in reading. B. G. Cook and Keaulana also review the theory and research examining colored filters (e.g., colored lenses), which have been extensively used in the United States, the United Kingdom, and elsewhere for decades to improve reading performance. Yet multiple research reviews conclude that serious methodological problems exist in studies supporting the effectiveness of colored filters and the extant research suggests that colored filters do not reliably improve reading performance.

In Chapter 3, Riccomini, Hwang, and Morano discuss an approach for improving problem solving in mathematics for students with learning disabilities that is not supported as effective by research (the keyword strategy) and two instructional approaches that have been shown by reliable research to improve mathematics problem solving for this population (the heuristic approach and the semantic approach). In the heuristic approach, teachers provide learners explicit instruction in how to solve problems rather than looking for particular keywords. In the semantic approach, students are taught conceptual understanding as well as procedural knowledge – often using schematic images to represent the mathematical problem to guide problem solving procedures.

Rouse and A. A. Collins explore two approaches to teaching writing in Chapter 4. The authors explain that Self-regulated Strategy Development (SRSD) has been demonstrated to improve writing outcomes for students with learning and behavioral disabilities by an impressive body of research. SRSD involves learning and applying a six-step learning strategy, typically using a mnemonic (e.g., POW + TIDE: *P*ick my idea, *O*rganize my notes, *W*rite and say more; *T*opic sentence, at least three *I*mportant *D*etails, *E*nding). In contrast, the authors suggest that traditional, stand-alone grammar instruction (e.g., providing instruction through worksheets or workbooks on sentence diagraming and defining components of the English language), though commonly practiced, is not supported as an effective practice for improving quality of writing.

In Chapter 5, Travers, Tincani, Thompson, and Simpson contrast two approaches focused on improving communication for individuals with disabilities, facilitated communication and the Picture Exchange Communication System (PECS). PECS, which involves teaching communication

through a six-phase process involving picture symbols, is supported by sound theory and researchers have systematically developed an empirical base that establishes PECS as a validated instructional approach. In contrast, facilitated communication (sometimes also referred to as "supported typing" and "rapid prompting method") has been shown to be ineffective by a substantial research base. Travers et al. discuss how PECS and facilitated communication can be considered examples of sound science and pseudoscience, respectively.

Ruhaak and B. G. Cook examine two approaches for using movement-based techniques to improve the school-related behaviors of students with learning and behavioral disabilities in Chapter 6. Brain Gym® is used throughout the world and involves using specific movements to improve different outcomes, including student behavior. However, the authors report that the approach is based on outdated neurological principles and research supporting Brain Gym® is scarce and has been challenged as methodologically flawed. In contrast, antecedent bouts of exercise (engaging learners in short periods of exercise to improve subsequent behavior) appear to be a promising practice with growing empirical support. The authors provide research-based guidelines for using bouts of exercise to improve student behavior.

In Chapter 7, T. J. Landrum and K. M. Landrum describe three related approaches for improving the effectiveness of instruction: learning styles, learning preferences, and student choice. Learning styles, which involves assessing a student's preferred learning modality (e.g., visual, auditory, kinesthetic) and then delivering instruction through that modality, is one of the most popular learning theories in education and is purported to be a critical tool for effectively instructing students with and at risk for learning and behavioral disabilities. However, the authors report that research shows learning styles are not assessed reliably and instruction targeting particularly learning styles is ineffective. Though learning preferences, which are associated with differentiated instruction, have not been researched extensively, they are conceptually consistent with student choice (e.g., allowing students to choose which task to do, in what order to do tasks, where to complete to a task). In comparison to learning styles, student choice is supported as effective for increasing engagement and reducing problem behavior by an extensive research base.

L. W. Collins and L. Cook present effective and ineffective ways to deliver verbal reinforcement to improve classroom behavior for students with learning and behavioral disabilities in Chapter 8. The authors note that although behavior specific praise and feedback are both empirically

validated approaches for improving students' classroom behavior, the approaches are commonly misapplied, which renders them ineffective. Specifically, they recommend educators adhering to the following research-based principles when implementing praise and feedback: positive and nonjudgmental, specific and corrective, sincere and credible, immediate and with proximity, delivered with variety, and evaluate and adjust. The authors provide practical examples of how and how not to implement praise and feedback according to these principles.

In Chapter 9 Nese and McIntosh review two approaches for improving behavior at the school level: exclusionary practices (e.g., time-out, office discipline referrals, suspensions) and school wide positive behavioral interventions and supports (SWPBIS). The authors describe how exclusionary practices, despite being commonly used in schools, are not associated with improved behavior (in fact, they are often exacerbate problem behaviors), impair learning outcomes by removing the student from the instructional environment, are often applied for minor behaviors (e.g., disruption, defiance), and are applied disproportionately to students of color. SWPBIS – a three-tiered, systems-level, data-based approach that provides supports for preventing the occurrence of problem behavior for all students – represents a research-based alternative to exclusionary practices. The authors provide descriptions and examples of approaches used at each of the three tiers of SWPBIS.

In the final chapter of the volume (Chapter 10), Losinski and Ennis contrast two approaches aiming to reduce stereotypical behaviors (repetitive motor movements and vocalizations) of students with autism spectrum disorders. Although deep-pressure therapy (e.g., wearing weighted vests, therapeutic brushing) has become a popular intervention in some circles, especially among occupational therapists, the authors' critical review of the literature suggests that research on deep-pressure therapy and stereotypical behavior is sparse, is of low methodological quality, and inconclusive. Alternatively, function-based interventions have a strong theoretical basis and promising empirical support for reducing stereotypical behavior. Function-based interventions are based on functional behavior assessments that identify the function of the problematic behavior (e.g., positive reinforcement via sensory stimulation, negative reinforcement via escape from activities). The authors provide guidelines for conducting a functional behavior assessment and designing a function-based intervention that addresses the same function as the problem behavior, which obviates the need for students to engage in the problem behavior.

CONCLUSION

In this volume, chapter authors provide non-technical discussions of the research bases for prominent practices that are and are not supported as effective. Based on the descriptions of these research bases, the theories underlying the practices, and the essential elements of the research-based practice featured in the following chapters, it is our hope that this volume will help educators begin to bridge the research-to-practice gap. Though providing trustworthy, useable, and accessible information on research findings appears to be a critical first step, we recognize that improving outcomes for students with learning and behavioral disabilities will require much more, including engaging in a valid process of instructional decision making and the provision of ongoing training and support.

REFERENCES

Borders, C. M., Bock, S. J., & Szymanski, C. (2015). Teacher ratings of evidence-based practices from the field of autism. *Journal of Deaf Studies and Deaf Education, 20*(1), 91−100. doi:10.1093/deafed/enu033

Burns, M. K., & Ysseldyke, J. E. (2009). Reported prevalence of evidence-based instructional practices in special education. *Journal of Special Education, 43*, 3−11. doi:10.1177/0022466908315563

Carnine, D. (1997). Bridging the research-to-practice gap. *Exceptional Children, 63*, 513−521.

Cook, B. G. (2014). A call for examining replication and bias in special education research. *Remedial and Special Education, 35*, 233−246. doi:10.1177/0741932514528995

Cook, B. G., & Cook, S. C. (2013). Unraveling evidence-based practices in special education. *Journal of Special Education, 47*, 71−82. doi:10.1177/0022466911420877

Cook, B. G., Cook, S. E., & Collins, L. W. (in press). Terminology and evidence-based practice for students with EBD: Exploring some devilish details. *Beyond Behavior, 25*(2).

Cook, L., Cook, B. G., Landrum, T. J., & Tankersley, M. (2008). Examining the role of group experimental research in establishing evidenced-based practices. *Intervention in School & Clinic, 44*(2), 76−82. doi:10.1177/1053451208324504

Fletcher, J. M., & Vaughn, S. (2009). Response to intervention: Preventing and remediating academic difficulties. *Child Development Perspectives, 3*(1), 30−37. doi:10.1111/j.1750-8606.2008.00072.x

Foxx, R. M., & Mulick, J. A. (Eds.). (2016). *Controversial therapies for autism and intellectual disabilities: Fad, fashion, and science in professional practice.* New York, NY: Routledge.

Gable, R. A., Tonelson, S. W., Sheth, M., Wilson, C., & Park, K. L. (2012). Importance, usage, and preparedness to implement evidence-based practices for students with emotional disabilities: A comparison of knowledge and skills of special education and general education teachers. *Education & Treatment of Children, 35*, 499−519.

Godlee, F., Smith, J., & Marcovitch, H. (2011). Wakefield's article linking MMR vaccine and autism was fraudulent. *British Medical Journal, 342,* c7452. doi:10.1136/bmj.c7452

Hattie, J. (2003). *Teachers make a difference: What is the research evidence?* Melbourne: Australian Council for Educational Research. Retrieved from http://start.sd34.bc.ca/innovation/wp-content/uploads/2014/01/Hattie_TeachersMakeADifference.pdf

Heath, C., & Heath, D. (2008). *Made to stick: Why some ideas survive and others die.* New York, NY: Random House.

Hosp, M. K., Hosp, J. L., & Howell, K. W. (2007). *The ABCs of CBM: A practical guide to curriculum-based measurement.* New York, NY: Guilford Press.

Kauffman, J. M. (1999). How we prevent the prevention of emotional and behavioral disorders. *Exceptional Children, 65,* 448–468.

Kavale, K. A., & Mostert, M. P. (2004). *The positive side of special education: Minimizing its fads, fancies, and follies.* Lanham, MD: Scarecrow Education.

Leko, M. M. (2015). To adapt or not to adapt. *Teaching Exceptional Children, 48*(2), 80–85. doi:10.1177/0040059915605641

Nickerson, R. S. (1998). Confirmation bias: A ubiquitous phenomena in many guises. *Review of General Psychology, 2,* 175–220.

Nyhan, B., & Reifler, J. (2010). When corrections fail: The persistence of political misperceptions. *Political Behavior, 32,* 303–330. doi:10.1007/s11109-010-9112-2

Odom, S. L., Brantlinger, E., Gersten, R., Horner, R. H., Thompson, B., & Harris, K. R. (2005). Research in special education: Scientific methods and evidence-based practices. *Exceptional Children, 71,* 137–148.

Pierce, C. S. (1877). The fixation of belief. *Popular Science Monthly, 12,* 1–15.

Rouse, A. G., & Collins, A. A. (2016). Effective and ineffective writing practices for students with disabilities. In B. G. Cook, M. Tankersley, & T. J. Landrum (Eds.), *Instructional practices with and without empirical validity* (Vol. 29) Advances in Learning and Behavioral Disabilities. Bingley, UK: Emerald Group Publishing Limited.

Sackett, D. L., Rosenberg, W. C., Gray, J. A. M., Haynes, R. B., & Richardson, W. S. (1996). Evidence based medicine: What it is and what it isn't. *British Medical Journal, 312*(7023), 71–72. doi:10.1136/bmj.312.7023.71

Simmons, J. P., Nelson, L. D., & Simonsohn, U. (2011). False-positive psychology: Undisclosed flexibility in data collection and analysis allows presenting anything as significant. *Psychological Science, 22,* 1359–1366. doi:10.1177/0956797611417632

Slavin, R. E. (2002). Evidence-based education policies: Transforming educational practice and research. *Educational Researcher, 31*(7), 15–21. doi:10.3102/0013189X031007015

Spencer, T. D., Detrich, R., & Slocum, T. A. (2012). Evidence-based practice: A framework for making effective decisions. *Education and Treatment of Children, 35,* 127–151. doi:10.1353/etc.2012.0013

Stanovich, K. E. (1986). Matthew effects in reading: Some consequences of individual differences in the acquisition of literacy. *Reading Research Quarterly, 21,* 360–407.

Stormont, M., Reinke, W., & Herman, K. (2011). Teachers' knowledge of evidence-based interventions and available school resources for children with emotional and behavioral problems. *Journal of Behavioral Education, 20,* 138–147. doi:10.1007/s10864-011-9122-0

Sugai, G., & Horner, R. H. (2009). Responsiveness-to-intervention and school-wide positive behavior supports: Integration of multi-tiered system approaches. *Exceptionality, 17,* 223–237. doi:10.1080/09362830903235375

Tankersley, M., Harjusola-Webb, S., & Landrum, T. J. (2008). Using single-subject research to establish the evidence base of special education. *Intervention in School & Clinic, 44,* 83–90. doi:10.1177/1053451208321600

Torres, C., Farley, C. A., & Cook, B. G. (2012). A special educator's guide to successfully implementing evidence-based practices. *Teaching Exceptional Children, 45*(1), 64–73. doi:10.1177/004005991204500109

Travers, J. C., Cook, B. G., Therrien, W. J., & Coyne, M. D. (in press). Replication research and special education. *Remedial and Special Education, 37*(4).

Travers, J. C., Tincani, M., Thompson, J., & Simpson, R. L. (2016). Picture exchange communication system and facilitated communication: Contrasting an evidence-based practice with a discredited method. In B. G. Cook, M. Tankersley, & T. J. Landrum (Eds.), *Instructional practices with and without empirical validity* (Vol. *29*). Advances in Learning and Behavioral Disabilities. Bingley, UK: Emerald Group Publishing Limited.

Vaughn, S., & Dammann, J. E. (2001). Science and sanity in special education. *Behavioral Disorders, 27,* 21–29.

CHAPTER 2

TWO APPROACHES FOR IMPROVING READING FLUENCY: RESEARCH SUPPORTS REPEATED READING BUT NOT COLORED FILTERS

Bryan G. Cook and Christina Keaulana

ABSTRACT

Reading fluency, which is critical for developing reading comprehension, is a fundamental skill in both school and life. However, many students with learning and behavioral disabilities are disfluent readers. To improve reading performance for these learners, educators should implement practices shown by reliable research to cause improved reading fluency. In this chapter, following a discussion of reading fluency and its importance, we describe two instructional practices that educators might use to improve students' reading fluency: colored filters and repeated reading. The research on the colored filters is, at best, inconclusive, whereas the research literature suggests that repeated reading is an effective practice. To bridge the gap between research and practice and improve the reading fluency of students with learning and behavioral disabilities, educators

Instructional Practices with and without Empirical Validity
Advances in Learning and Behavioral Disabilities, Volume 29, 17−38
ISSN: 0735-004X/doi:10.1108/S0735-004X20160000029002

and other stakeholders should prioritize the use of research-based practices (e.g., repeated reading) but avoid practices without clear research support (e.g., colored filters).

Keywords: Reading fluency; repeated reading; colored filters

Reading, and specifically reading fluency, is a critical skill in contemporary society and a major focus in schools and classrooms. However, students with learning and behavioral disabilities often experience problems with reading fluency. Given the importance of students with learning and behavioral disabilities attaining proficiency in reading, educators should only use highly effective instructional approaches when providing reading instruction to these learners. In this chapter, following an overview of reading fluency, we discuss two different approaches for teaching reading fluency to students with learning and behavioral disabilities, one that is supported by research as effective (i.e., repeated reading) and one that is not (i.e., colored filters).

READING FLUENCY

Reading is one of the most important skills taught in schools and can be considered a gateway skill for other academic, social, and post-school outcomes. Reading is used to access information and learning in virtually every academic content area and reading performance is associated positively with pro-social behavior, graduation, and college attendance, but correlates negatively with aggression, dropping out of school, and suicidal ideation/attempts (Daniel et al., 2006; Hernandez, 2012; Lesnick, Goerge, Smithgall, & Gwynne, 2010; Miles & Stipek, 2006). Moreover, reading is related to an individual's job opportunities and earning potential after school and to productivity at the societal level (Annie E. Casey Foundation, 2010; National Endowment for the Arts, 2007). In short, "Reading correlates with almost every measurement of positive personal and social behavior surveyed" (National Endowment for the Arts, 2007, p. 6).

Although traditionally neglected, fluency has received considerable attention as a critical area of reading in recent years, in large part due to its prominence in the influential Report of the National Reading Panel (NRP; National Institute of Child Health and Human Development [NICHD], 2000). Based on their comprehensive review of experimental and quasi-experimental research on reading, the NRP recommended that the most effective approach for teaching children reading includes a combination of instruction in phonemic awareness, phonics, fluency, comprehension, and vocabulary. Fluent readers read accurately (correctly identifying the vast majority of words), automatically (quickly, effortlessly), and with prosody (with appropriate expression consistent with meaning) (Kuhn, Schwanenflugel, & Meisinger, 2010; NICHD, 2000). Although fluent reading may be desirable in its own right, fluency is typically targeted as a critical area of intervention because of its empirical and theoretical link to reading comprehension (i.e., understanding what is read). Consistent with the NRP's perspective, fluency is the bridge between word recognition and reading comprehension (Pikulski & Chard, 2005; Rasinski, 2012). This connection to comprehension is apparent in Kuhn et al.'s (2010) definition of reading fluency:

> Fluency combines accuracy, automaticity, and oral reading prosody, which, taken together, facilitate the reader's construction of meaning. It is demonstrated during oral reading through ease of word recognition, appropriate pacing, phrasing, and intonation. It is a factor in both oral and silent reading that can limit or support comprehension. (p. 240)

Accuracy is perhaps the most obvious aspect of fluency underlying comprehension. If one is not able to accurately read a very high proportion of the words in text, meaningful comprehension is unlikely. Automaticity, the quick and effortless reading associated with fluency, also supports comprehension. That is, slowly and laboriously identifying words requires significant cognitive effort from disfluent readers, which leaves insufficient attention to devote to comprehending the text. Finally, prosody, or reading with appropriate expression, is an important indicator of comprehension. Emphasizing the wrong word in a sentence, for example, can interfere with meaning even if all the words are read accurately and effortlessly.

Empirical evidence also indicates a strong correspondence between reading fluency and reading comprehension (Klauda & Guthrie, 2008). For example, Fuchs, Fuchs, and Maxwell (1988) reported that a measure of reading fluency (i.e., number of words read correctly in one minute) was a more accurate predictor of scores on a standardized test of reading comprehension than other commonly used assessments of reading compre-hension (i.e., answering comprehension questions, passage recall, and cloze measures) for 70 middle school boys with high-incidence disabilities. Although reading experts have traditionally focused on the importance of fluency in developing comprehension, Klauda and Guthrie (2008) reported a bi-directional relation between reading fluency and comprehension (see also Pikulski & Chard, 2005). That is, while improved fluency facilitates comprehension, improved comprehension also increases fluency (e.g., read-ers who comprehend the text can better anticipate words coming next and therefore can read more quickly and accurately).

Difficulties with reading are commonly experienced by students with learning and behavioral disabilities. Reading deficits are the most common reason for children being identified as learning disabled (Fletcher, Lyons, Fuchs, & Barnes, 2007), with approximately 80% of students with learning disabilities experiencing reading problems (Lyons, Shaywitz, & Shaywitz, 2003). Although not a defining characteristic, students with emotional and behavioral disorders (EBD) also typically experience low reading perfor-mance. For example, in their meta-analysis of 25 studies, Reid, Gonzalez, Nordness, Trout, and Epstein (2004) found an effect size (d) of -0.61 for the reading performance of youth with EBD in comparison to nondisabled peers. Specific to reading fluency, Wanzek, Al Otaiba, and Petscher (2014) reported that 2nd graders with LD and EBD read significantly fewer words per minute on average than nondisabled peers. These differences were main-tained throughout 2nd and 3rd grade. Problems in reading fluency in early grades are especially consequential, as a Matthew effect appears to exist in reading in which strong reading begets stronger reading and reading strug-gles continue to worsen over time (Stanovich, 1986). Thus, reading fluency appears to be a major obstacle for students with learning and behavioral dis-abilities that needs to be addressed by highly effective, research-based instructional practices; these students who are highly at-risk for reading fail-ure cannot spare precious instructional time on ineffective practices.

In the following sections we provide an overview of two instructional approaches for reading fluency — one supported as effective by a consider-able research base (i.e., repeated reading) and one that the research does not collectively support as effective (i.e., colored filters). For each practice, we describe what the practice is, summarize its theoretical basis, and review the empirical literature regarding its effectiveness. Based on our review of the literature, we recommend that educators implement repeated reading to improve reading fluency for students with learning and behavior disabil-ities, but not use colored filters.

COLORED FILTERS

Using colored filters to improve reading fluency and other reading outcomes became popular in the 1980s based in part on the media's coverage
of the early work of Helen Irlen and others (e.g., Irlen, 1983). Colored filters continue to be used throughout the world (The Irlen Institute, n.d.,
claims that their approach has been used with over 1,000,000 individuals)
and anecdotal accounts of their success are common in the popular press
(e.g., CBS Los Angeles, 2014; Zimmerman, 2014). In this section, we discuss what colored filters are, their theoretical basis, how they are used, and
the research investigating their effectiveness.

What Are Colored Filters?

Colored filters can take many forms: plastic transparencies or overlays
(placed on reading material), lenses in specially made glasses and contact
lenses, and as an "app" to customize the color of one's smartphone and
tablet screens. Although often referred to as colored overlays or lenses, in
this chapter we collectively refer to these devices as colored filters. The color
or tint of the filter varies by individual (Irlen Institute, n.d.; Wilkins &
Evans, 2010). In theory, colored filters allow individuals with visual stress
syndrome (as described in the following section, visual stress syndrome is a
perceptual processing disorder proposed by advocates of colored filters) to
read more comfortably and fluently as well as improve a host of other outcomes. Colored filters can be relatively expensive. For example, the Irlen
Visual Learning Center (n.d.) states that screening costs $295, diagnostic
testing costs $595, and a package that includes diagnostic testing and spec-
tral filters (overlays) costs $990.

Underlying Condition and Theoretical Basis

Visual stress syndrome (though it has been referred to by other names such
as Irlen syndrome, Meares-Irlen syndrome, and scotopic sensitivity syndrome, we generically use the term visual stress syndrome in this chapter) is
a condition with a wide range of symptoms such as sensitivity to light and
glare, poor reading comprehension, problems with attention and concentration, eye strain, fatigue, headaches, sleepiness, poor depth perception,
and poor reading fluency (Irlen Institute, n.d.; Irlen & Lass, 1989).

The Irlen Institute (n.d.) emphasized that the syndrome is a "perceptual processing disorder" related to problems with the brain processing visual information. Some have posited that pattern glare, which causes visual discomfort and distortion when viewing striped patterns such as rows of words in a text, underlies visual stress syndrome (e.g., Evans et al., 1996; Kriss & Evans, 2005; Wilkins & Evans, 2010). Individuals with visual stress syndrome reportedly experience discomfort, distortions, and reading problems especially under bright and fluorescent lighting (as is often present in classroom settings) and with black and white contrasts (e.g., black letters on a white page) (Irlen Institute, n.d.; Irlen & Lass, 1989). The Irlen Syndrome Foundation (2015) claimed that 46% of people with learning and reading problems, 33% of individuals with ADHD and autism, and 15% of the general population have the syndrome.

Visual stress syndrome is the theoretical foundation of colored filters because colored overlays/lenses are intended to resolve the symptoms associated with the syndrome. In theory, the Irlen method (Irlen Institute, n.d.) and other, related approaches (e.g., ChromaGen, n.d. and Intuitive Overlays [Wilkins, n.d-a]) and products (e.g., Reading Rulers; Crossbow Education, n.d.) involve using colored filters to filter out "offensive light waves, so the brain" of individuals with visual stress syndrome "can accurately process visual information" (Irlen Institute, n.d.). The "parts of the light spectrum" (Irlen & Lass, 1989, p. 416) that need to be excluded vary across individuals with visual stress syndrome. Wilkins and Evans (2010) further hypothesized that individualized colored filters may reduce excitation in the visual cortex – which is associated with visual fatigue, discomfort, and illusions/distortions – among individuals with visual stress syndrome.

Reflecting the importance of visual stress syndrome in understanding how colored filters work, the first stage of the Irlen Method is determining whether one has the syndrome and can therefore benefit from their colored filters (Irlen Institute, n.d.; Irlen & Lass, 1989). However, the existence of visual stress syndrome is controversial (Uccula, Enna, & Mulatti, 2014). Critics have suggested that visual stress syndrome is a vague and imprecise condition with (a) little or no objective evidence supporting its existence as an independent condition and (b) procedures for identification that are vulnerable to the placebo effect and do not directly measure the presence of an underlying condition (Handler & Fierson, 2011; Hyatt, Stephenson, & Carter, 2009; Kavale & Mostert, 2004). Reflecting the lack of evidence supporting the syndrome, in a joint policy statement from the American Academy of Pediatrics, American Academy of Ophthalmology, American Academy of Pediatric Ophthalmology and Strabismus, and American Association of Certified

Orthoptists, Handler and Fierson (2011) noted that "although Irlen and proponents of her method routinely refer to [scotopic sensitivity syndrome] as though it were an accepted medical syndrome, many experts question its validity" (p. e838). Uccula et al. (2014) summarized that visual stress syndrome may just be a collection of symptoms associated with dyslexia. Moreover, Henderson, Tsogka, and Snowling (2013) indicated a tautological aspect to visual stress syndrome, in that it is defined and diagnosed by its treatment. That is, visual stress syndrome is often diagnosed by responding positively to colored filters. Indeed, visual stress syndrome cannot be diagnosed using available standardized medical or educational assessments (Albon, Adi, & Hyde, 2008; Irlen Institute, n.d.; Irlen & Lass, 1989).

Procedures for Using Colored Filters

The first step in using colored filters is determining whether an individual has visual stress syndrome and will, in theory, benefit from the devices. The Irlen Institute (n.d.) does not specify the procedures it uses to diagnose visual stress syndrome, but indicates that it must be done by a certified Irlen screener or diagnostician. One initial indication of visual stress syndrome and candidacy for benefiting from colored filters is an observed improvement in reading speed (or reduction of related symptoms) when using a self-selected filter (Irlen & Lass, 1989).

The next step involves specifying the exact color to be used in one's filter. Again, the Irlen Institute (n.d.) does not specify their procedures beyond stating that, "we target the precise wave lengths of light causing your problems by using a limitless number of color filter combinations." Wilkins and Evans (2010) described using the Intuitive Colorimeter as part of the Intuitive Overlays system. This machine systematically adjusts hue and saturation to allow the individual to select the specific chromaticity that optimizes their visual perception. Colored overlays and/or lenses with this specific color are then ordered and produced. Wilkins (n.d-b) also described a procedure that could be carried out by educators with access to a range of colored overlays. In essence, an individual compares effects of reading with the different colored overlays to one another to identify the optimal color for the individual. Wilkins recommended, because children's responses may be equivocal and inconsistent, affirming the student's final choice by (re-)comparing the selected overlay to other preferred overlays. The optimal color may also be validated by examining whether its use improves reading rate or if the individual elects to continue using it (Kriss & Evans, 2005).

Once an optimal color is identified, the individual should consistently use devices of that color when reading and in other contexts (e.g., placing overlays on reading material, wearing glasses or contact lenses). Wilkins and Evans (2010) recommended using colored lenses rather than overlays because the color for the former can be selected more precisely and because lenses are more versatile and can be worn in any context, not just applied to reading material. Although using colored filters is purported to result in immediate gains in reading rate (and improvements in other symptoms), they will not correct all reading problems (Irlen Institute, n.d.; Irlen & Lass, 1989). That is, colored filters are claimed to improve the processing of visual stimuli (e.g., written text), but not help children learn to decode text. Thus, it is important that children receive appropriate reading instruction even when using colored filters. Moreover, in addition to using colored filters, Irlen and Lass (1989) recommended that teachers take further steps to optimize instructional conditions for students with visual stress syndrome, such as reducing lighting, using colored paper, using a bookstand or wearing a visor to reduce glare, and placing reading material directly in front of students.

Reviews of Research on Colored Filters

Researchers have conducted studies examining the effects of colored filters on reading outcomes for decades. Rather than attempt to review the body of research study by study, in this chapter we will summarize the many reviews conducted on this research base.

Evans and Drasdo (1991) reviewed the early research on colored filters. In addition to other areas, the authors reviewed the available research examining the effects of colored filters on reading performance. Five studies published in refereed journals were reviewed. Three of those studies showed that colored filters had no meaningful effect on reading performance. Findings were similarly mixed for other forms of evidence reviewed (e.g., studies published in non-refereed journals, anecdotal reports). The authors highlighted methodological problems with many of the studies reviewed, including lack of a meaningful control groups and not controlling for the placebo effect. Based on their review, the authors concluded that, "there is no conclusive proof from rigorous scientific studies that tinted lenses can help poor reading performance" (p. 215).

Kavale and Mostert (2004) reported the results of a meta-analysis on the effects of colored filters on reading outcomes. The meta-analysis involved 24 studies with over 1,000 participants. The authors reported a very small and negative average effect size for reading outcomes (−0.02), indicating that across studies the colored filters had no discernible effects on reading. The authors reported a very small effect specific to reading rate (0.13), but very small and negative effects for word recognition (−0.09) and reading comprehension (−0.11). Based on their findings, the authors suggested that colored filters "do not work" as a treatment for reading disabilities and "need to take their place in the history of interventions that have been tried in the name of special education but failed" (p. 173).

Albon et al. (2008) conducted a systematic search of the literature for experimental studies investigating the effects of colored filters on individuals with reading difficulties and disabilities. They identified eight randomized trials and 15 quasi-experimental (i.e., non-randomized studies). The authors summarized that the randomized trials indicated that "the intervention [colored filters] was no better than the control, and that preferred filters were no better than vision therapy, or blue filters, at improving reading speed" (Albon et al., 2008, p. 66). Similar findings were reported for reading accuracy and reading comprehension. The authors further noted that all randomized trials were considered to be of less than adequate quality with multiple threats to validity present. The results of the 15 non-randomized studies varied considerably and the authors noted that these studies were of poor quality and should therefore not be used to determine the effectiveness of colored filters. "In summary, there does not appear to be evidence to support the hypothesis that individually prescribed coloured filters can be effective in improving reading performance ... in subjects with reading disability" (p. 80). Finally, the authors noted that individuals with commercial interests in the approaches conducted some of the studies reviewed, thereby introducing another source of potential bias to the research base.

Hyatt et al. (2009) conducted a non-systemic, narrative review of 17 studies of colored filters. They emphasized the varied and often conflicting results in the research, as well as the methodological shortcomings of many studies (e.g., not controlling for placebo effect, lack of control groups, not establishing pre-test equivalency between groups, the possibility of experimenter bias, inappropriate outcome measures). The authors concluded that, "the research conducted on tinted lenses has failed to demonstrate the efficacy of the practice" (p. 329).

In a joint technical report issued by the American Academy of Pediatrics, American Academy of Ophthalmology, American Academy of Pediatric Ophthalmology and Strabismus, and American Association of Certified Orthoptists, Handler and Fierson (2011) conducted a narrative review of research related to a number of vision-related treatments for learning disabilities and dyslexia, including colored filters. Consistent with previous reviews, the authors noted that findings were mixed and that the studies, both older and more recent, suffered from a number of important methodological limitations. "Overall, study results have been inconsistent; many studies have shown that colored overlays and filters are ineffective, but a few studies have reported partial positive results" (p. e841). The reviewers emphasized that a placebo effect and other threats to validity might account for some or all of the positive effects reported in some studies.

Galuschka, Ise, Krick, and Schulte-Körne (2014) recently conducted a meta-analysis of randomized controlled trials evaluating the effects of treatments for children and adolescents with reading disabilities. Among the four randomized trials they identified, colored filters had, on average, a small and non-significant effect (Hedges' $g = 0.32$) on reading outcomes. The authors noted that small but positive effects were observed in the two studies with no-treatment control groups, but that effects were negligible in the two studies with control groups that received a placebo treatment (e.g., using a transparency with a different color), suggesting that any observed effects may be due to placebo effects.

In conclusion, it is important to recognize that a number of studies have shown positive effects of colored filters on reading fluency and other reading outcomes. However, the reviews indicate that (a) many studies showing positive effects of colored filters for some outcomes showed that they did not positively impact other outcomes measures, (b) many of the studies showing positive effects involved multiple and serious threats to the validity of the findings, and (c) many studies conducted by independent researchers have shown that colored lenses do not cause improved reading performance. Given the conclusions reached by reviewers of this research base, we recommend that educators prioritize instructional approaches with stronger research support, such as repeated reading.

REPEATED READING

In this section we provide an overview of how to implement repeated reading, briefly describe the theoretical basis for the intervention, and review the research related the effectiveness of repeated reading.

What Is Repeated Reading?

Repeated reading is a research-based instructional technique for improving the reading fluency of students with learning and behavioral disabilities that educators are likely to find appealing because of its straightforward implementation, flexibility, brevity, and low cost. As described by Samuels (1979) and Therrien and Kubina (2006), we provide some basic guidelines for implementing repeated reading. It is important to note that repeated reading is not appropriate for improving outcomes for readers at all levels. If students have not mastered foundational reading skills (e.g., phonological decoding), they are unlikely to benefit from repeated reading. That is, it is unlikely that repeatedly failing to read passages will improve fluency or other reading outcomes. Similarly, if a student is already a fluent reader, repeated reading is probably not needed.

In essence, repeated reading involves reading specific passages multiple times to a tutor/instructor. The passage should be at the student's instruction reading level (not their age level) and should be long enough that it will take the student at least one minute to read, but not more than about two minutes (typically 50–200 words). Ideally, the passage should be meaningful and culturally relevant to the student. Instructors can select passages from grade level texts or can obtain grade level reading passages commercially and on the internet. If students struggle and read selected passages very slowly, it may be appropriate to reselect passages at a lower reading level. Conversely, if students read quickly and fluently through passages on their first reading, passages at a higher reading level should probably be used.

The tutors or instructors should be fluent readers at the reading level of the passages. It is important that they be able to recognize errors and provide correct words when the student gets stuck. Both the student and the instructor (or tutor) should have a copy of the reading passage. The instructor tells the student when to begin reading the passage aloud and starts a stopwatch/timer as soon as the first word is read. The instructor listens carefully to the student read the passage, providing the word if the student gets stuck/pauses for three seconds. To keep track of the student's performance, the instructor marks his or her own copy when errors are made (i.e., mispronounced words, skipped words). At the end of the passage, the instructor records how long it took the student to complete the reading and the total number of errors. From this information, words read correctly per minute, which is the most common measure of reading fluency, can be calculated ([total words read correctly/seconds] x 60). Therrien (2004) found that using adults as instructors was significantly more effective than peers. Because repeated reading is relatively straightforward, paraprofessionals and parent volunteers can deliver the intervention.

After a short break, the student reads the same passage aloud again following the same procedures. The passage may be read a specific number of times (Lee & Yoon, 2015; found that reading passages four times was significantly more effective than reading passages two or three times) or until a predetermined criterion is met (e.g., 60 words per minute; Therrien, 2004; found that using a performance criterion was significantly more effective than repeating reading a set number of times). See Hasbrouck and Tindal (2006) for grade level fluency norms that can be used to set criteria. Depending on how many times the student reads the passage, repeated reading should only take approximately ten to fifteen minutes per session. Therrien and Kubina (2006) recommended that repeated reading be implemented at least three times per week.

Repeated reading can be delivered in a variety of instructional settings. It can be implemented for the whole class/large groups if students are matched appropriately and peer tutors are used. It can be used in small group settings with multiple adults (e.g., teacher, paraprofessional, parent volunteer) implementing repeated reading with selected students. Or it can be used in 1:1 situations. Repeated reading has been shown to be effective with students without disabilities, with students at-risk for reading problems, and students with a variety of disabilities (Therrien & Kubina, 2006). Repeated reading can also be easily combined with other reading and behavioral interventions. Depending on the student's needs, teachers may wish to use a number of potential adaptations to repeated reading, including providing a fluent preview of the passage, previewing specific words, providing feedback on errors after the reading is completed, charting progress, and providing additional reinforcement.

Theoretical Basis of Repeated Reading

Repeated reading is theorized to help bridge accurate but disfluent reading (e.g., reading slowly and with low prosody, but with few errors) and fluent reading by providing the repetitive practice needed to achieve automaticity (LaBerge & Samuels, 1974; Samuels, 1979). That is, by practicing reading words multiple times during repeated reading, students learn to read the practiced words more quickly and automatically (i.e., without effortful decoding) when they encounter them in the future. Rashotte and Torgesen (1985) provided empirical support for this theory. Participants in their study engaged in repeated reading under two conditions. In both conditions, repeated reading occurred over seven days by participants reading a different passage each day, four times each. In the first condition, passages were constructed so that they had very little overlap in words (i.e., almost all of the words were different). In the second condition, the different passages had a high degree of word overlap (i.e., contained many of the same words). Results showed that fluency (as measured by reading rate) improved at a significantly higher rate in the second condition than the first. Thus, it appears that repeated reading helps students become automatic at reading specific words through repeated practice, which they can then read fluently when the same words appear in future readings. Samuels (1979) suggested that repeated reading functions like practice in sports and music: reaching a high level of performance requires considerable and repeated practice to attain automaticity.

Reviews of Research on Repeated Reading

A substantial body of research has investigated the effectiveness of repeated reading for learners with and at-risk for learning and behavior disabilities, and researchers have conducted multiple reviews and meta-analyses to synthesize these studies' findings. As with the research on colored filters, we provide a review of the reviews in this chapter. Although earlier reviews on repeated reading were conducted (e.g., Dowhower, 1989; Meyer & Felton, 1999 — both of which concluded that repeated reading was generally effective), due to space considerations we focus on reviews conducted since 2000.

National Reading Panel (NICHD, 2000)
In response to Congress's charge to examine the effectiveness of different methods to teach children to read, the NRP formed subcommittees to review the research in various areas aspects of reading (e.g., alphabetics, phonics, comprehension, teacher education, computer technology). Each subcommittee searched for experimental studies published in peer-reviewed journals from 1990 to 2000 that investigated the effects of instructional interventions in the different areas of reading for kindergarten through 12th grade students (NICHD, 2000). The fluency subcommittee examined the research for two interventions, one of which was repeated and guided

repeated oral reading. Fourteen studies were identified that investigated immediate effects. That is, these studies addressed the question of whether a group of learners improved in fluency on a given passage after repeated readings. Most, but not all, of these studies involved students with or at-risk for reading disabilities. Perhaps not surprisingly, all studies reported positive results with "clear improvements across multiple readings regardless of students' reading levels or age levels although greater gains were sometimes attributed to poor readers" (pp. 3–15). Although it is not unimportant that repeated reading appears to improve fluency on reading passages that have been practiced, determining whether improved reading transfers to novel passages represents a more meaningful test of the effectiveness of repeated reading.

The panel meta-analyzed 14 group studies that compared changes in reading on novel reading passages between a group receiving repeated reading intervention and a control or comparison group. All but two of the studies reported significant effects favoring repeated reading. Nine of the studies involved "poor readers" (pp. 3–17) and five involved typical readers. Fluency outcomes (e.g., reading rate, reading accuracy) were measured in 10 studies, with an average effect size (d) of 0.44. The effect for word recognition (from eight studies) was slightly higher ($d = 0.55$), whereas the effect on reading comprehension (measured in 12 studies) was slightly lower ($d = 0.35$). The subcommittee also identified 12 single-case design studies that examined the effects of repeated reading and involved a measure of transfer to novel reading material. All of the single-case studies involved elementary students with "learning problems" (pp. 3–18). Eleven of the 12 studies "found clear and substantial improvements in reading accuracy, speed, or comprehension" (pp. 3–19). The NRP summarized, based on their review of the research, that repeated oral reading "had a consistent, and positive impact" (pp. 3–3) on reading fluency, as well as word recognition and comprehension.

Chard, Vaughn, and Tyler (2002)
Although the NRP's review involved many studies involving students with and at-risk for reading disabilities, it also included studies with only typical readers. Therefore, Chard, Vaughn, and Tyler (2002) meta-analyzed the research on repeated reading specifically for elementary students identified as having learning disabilities. The researchers identified 24 studies (eight group studies with a control/comparison group, five single group studies, and 11 single-case and case study designs) that met their inclusion criteria: participants were elementary-aged students with learning disabilities,

reading fluency was measured, and the study was published from 1975 to 2000. Twenty-one studies (involving 128 participants) examined the effect of repeated reading without a model. Across studies, the average effect (d) on fluency (rate and accuracy) was 0.68. The authors also indicated that using a model during repeated reading, controlling difficulty of text, and providing feedback for missed words appear to be associated with stronger effects for repeated reading in the studies reviewed. Similar to the conclusions of the NRP (NICHD, 2000), Chard et al. concluded that, "repeated reading interventions for students with LD are associated with improvements in reading rate, accuracy, and comprehension" (p. 402).

Therrien (2004)

Therrien (2004) reviewed 18 studies on repeated reading that were published between 1977 and 2001, reported quantitative experiments, and involved children and youth from 5 to 18 years of age. In addition to calculating non-transfer (i.e., practiced passages) and transfer (i.e., novel passages) effects on reading outcomes, Therrien examined the effects of various aspects of repeated reading practices. Across 16 effects, the average non-transfer effect of repeated reading on fluency was positive and large ($d = 0.83$; $d = 0.67$ for comprehension). Perhaps more importantly, positive moderate effects were observed for fluency across 27 transfer effects ($d = 0.50$; average non-transfer effect for comprehension was 0.25). Therrien reported that repeated reading had a significantly higher effect on fluency for transfer passage when conducted by an adult ($d = 1.37$) than by peers (0.36). Similarly, interventions that required participants to reach a performance criterion before advancing to the next passage had a greater effect on transfer fluency ($d = 1.70$) than did intervention that involved a set number of rereading per passage ($d = 0.38$). Transfer effects in fluency were not strongly influenced by using peer models of fluent reading, receiving corrective feedback from peers (though receiving corrective feedback from adults was associated with large effects), reading a passage three (rather than two) times, including a comprehension activity (comprehension questions, paragraph summary), or charting progress. Therrien also reported effect sizes specific to students with learning disabilities. For students with learning disabilities, the effect of repeated reading on fluency for non-transfer passage was $d = 0.75$ ($d = 0.85$ for nondisabled participants), whereas the effect for transfer fluency was $d = 0.79$ ($d = 0.59$ for nondisabled participants). Therrien summarized that repeated reading can, "improve students' ability to fluently read and understand a particular passage and ... improve students' overall reading fluency and comprehension ability" (p. 259).

Lee and Yoon (2015)
Lee and Yoon (2015) sought to provide an updated meta-analysis on the effects of repeated reading specifically on fluency as well as to examine intervention components that may moderate effects. The authors identified 34 studies that met their inclusion criteria: published from 1990 to 2014 (in peer-reviewed journals, conference proceedings, and dissertations), used an experimental research design to examine the effects of repeated reading on school age (K-12) students with or at-risk for reading disabilities, and measured fluency outcomes in correct words read per minute. Across all effects, repeated reading had a large effect (Hedges' g = 1.41). Lee and Yoon reported that while large effects were found for both groups, significantly larger effects were associated with elementary (g = 1.63) than secondary (g = 0.86) students. Moreover, listening to a passage preview (g = 1.95; g = 0.94 with no listening preview) and reading the passage four times (g = 1.73) were also associated with significantly larger fluency effects. Previewing words, systematic error correction, goal setting, extrinsic rewards, and peer-mediated reading did not significantly influence fluency effects. As might be expected, generalized transfer effects (g = 0.97) were significantly smaller than non-transfer fluency effects (g = 1.94), though the transfer effects are still considered large. The authors concluded that, "the results of this study are consistent with prior findings supporting the effects of [repeated reading] interventions on reading fluency for students with [reading disabilities]" (p. 12).

Repeated Reading and Students with Behavioral Disabilities
We did not identify any reviews of research conducted specifically on the effects of repeated reading for students with or at-risk for behavioral disabilities. However, multiple studies have investigated the impact of repeated reading on this population, many of which are included in the reviews previously summarized. For example, we identified two single-case studies that included students with behavioral problems in the Lee and Yoon (2015) review. Ardoin, Williams, Klubnik, and McCall (2009) used an alternating treatment design to examine the effects of a daily intervention involving three and six repeated readings for four elementary-aged boys being educated in a residential facility for troubled youth. Results indicated that both forms of repeated reading resulted in improved fluency (measured by words read correctly per minute) on both practiced and novel

passages for all participants. Valleley and Shriver (2003) examined the effectiveness of repeated reading for four high-school students living at a residential treatment center because of behavior and learning problems using a multiple baseline design. Due to their behavioral issues, the researchers provided participants points for participation and effort that they could use in the token economy used at the residential facility. The researchers also used immediate, tangible reinforcers for one student. Results indicated that repeated reading (plus reinforcement) resulted in improved fluency on novel fourth-grade reading passages (except for one participant), novel fifth-grade reading passages (for all participants), novel ninth-grade reading passages (for all participants), and generalization passages from English and science classes (for all participants).

The What Works Clearinghouse (2014) review (see below) identified, but did not review (their review targeted studies that involved students with learning disabilities and that used repeated reading in isolation), at least two studies examining the effects of repeated reading on the fluency outcomes of students with behavioral disabilities. Strong, Wehby, Falk, and Lane (2004) used a multiple baseline design to investigate the effects of (a) direct instruction and (b) a repeated reading intervention on six middle school students identified with emotional and behavioral disorders. After collecting baseline data, the researchers implemented the direct instruction intervention, and added the repeated reading intervention in the final phase. The direct instruction intervention improved reading fluency for all students. The addition of the repeated reading intervention resulted in further improvement in fluency for four of the six participants. The authors speculated that the lack of further improvement associated with repeated reading for two students may have been due to ceiling effects; those two students were already reading proficiently when the repeated reading intervention was introduced. Finally, Cook et al. (2012) used a multiple baseline design to examine the effects of (a) repeated reading and (b) a behavioral intervention (Check In/Check Out combined with self-monitoring) in isolation and in combination on reading and behavioral outcomes for six middle school students exhibiting problem behaviors and low reading performance. Repeated reading in isolation improved reading fluency for all participants and behavior for most participants. However, the greatest gains in both outcome areas occurred when repeated reading was combined with the behavioral intervention. Additional studies not cited in the reviews described in this chapter provide further support for the positive effects of repeated reading on students with and at-risk for behavior disabilities (e.g., Alber-Morgan, Ramp, Anderson, & Martin, 2007; Escarpio & Barbetta, 2015; Scott & Shearer-Lingo, 2002; Staubitz, Cartledge, Yurick, & Lo, 2005).

Evidence-Based Practice Reviews

In recent years, special education – like many other fields – has begun to identify evidence-based practices to guide practice and policy (Cook et al., 2015; Odom et al., 2005). To be identified as evidence based, practices must be supported as effective by a minimum number of high-quality studies from which causality can be inferred. For example, the Council for Exceptional Children (2014) recommended that evidence-based practices in special education be supported as effective by two high-quality randomized group experiments, four high-quality non-randomized group quasi-experiments, or five high-quality single-case design studies. Reviews have been conducted to determine whether repeated reading should be considered an evidence-based practice (Chard, Ketterlin-Geller, Baker, Doabler, & Apichatabutra, 2009; Institute of Education Sciences, 2014; O'Keeffe, Slocum, Burlingame, Snyder, & Bundock, 2012). Given the robust literature base supporting the effectiveness of repeated reading, it is perhaps surprising that none of these reviews identified repeated reading as an evidence-based practice. These reviews have consistently found that too few studies on repeated reading meet criteria to be considered of methodologically high quality. Therefore the vast majority of studies on repeated reading have not been considered when determining the evidence-based status of repeated reading in these reviews. Clearly, the results of these reviews suggest caution when interpreting the research suggesting that repeated reading has positive effects. Simply stated, most of this research does not meet the rigorous standards for methodological quality required for evidence-based practices. However, not being identified as an evidence-based practice should not be interpreted as meaning repeated reading is ineffective. As Chard et al. (2009) noted, although their review concluded that repeated reading did not have enough high-quality, experimental research to consider the practice evidence based, the practice still has considerable theoretical and empirical support that should not be ignored. The findings of these evidence-based reviews suggest that more high-quality research be conducted on repeated reading to definitively verify the findings of the extant body of research indicating that repeated reading is an effective approach for improving reading fluency for students with and at-risk for learning and behavioral disabilities.

CONCLUSION

As in many professional fields, a marked research-to-practice gap exists in special education in which many instructional practices commonly used in the classroom are not supported by research as effective, and many practices shown by research to be highly effective are not regularly used with students (Cook & Odom, 2013). The consequence of the research-to-practice gap is that students with learning and behavioral disabilities do not receive the most effective instruction and therefore often fail to achieve their potentials. Bridging the research-to-practice gap will involve (a) identifying and implementing with fidelity highly effective instructional approaches and (b) avoiding practices shown by research not to reliably improve targeted outcomes. In this chapter we discussed two approaches that aim to increase reading fluency: repeated reading and colored filters. Based on reviews of these research bases, we recommend using repeated reading but avoiding colored filters to bridge the research-to-practice gap and improve the reading fluency of students with learning and behavioral disabilities.

REFERENCES

Alber-Morgan, S. R., Ramp, E. M., Anderson, L. L., & Martin, C. M. (2007). Effects of repeated readings, error correction, and performance feedback on the fluency and comprehension of middle school students with behavior problems. *The Journal of Special Education, 41*, 17–30. doi:10.1177/00224669070410010201

Albon, E., Adi, Y., & Hyde, C. (2008). The effectiveness and cost-effectiveness of coloured filters for reading disability: A systematic review. West Midlands Health Technology Assessment Collaboration, Department of Public Health and Epidemiology, University of Birmingham. Retrieved from http://www.birmingham.ac.uk/Documents/college-mds/haps/projects/WMHTAC/REPreports/2008/Colouredfiltersforreadingdisability FINALVERSION.pdf

Annie E. Casey Foundation. (2010). *Early warning! Why reading by the end of the third grade matters*. Baltimore, MD: Author. Retrieved from http://www.aecf.org/resources/early-warning-why-reading-by-the-end-of-third-grade-matters/

Ardoin, S. P., Williams, J. C., Klubnik, C., & McCall, M. (2009). Three versus six rereadings of practice passages. *Journal of Applied Behavior Analysis, 42*, 375–380. doi.10.1901/jaba.2009.42-375

CBS Los Angeles. (2014, October 20). Twins with severe headaches, stomach pains find a colorful cure. Retrieved from http://losangeles.cbslocal.com/2014/10/20/twins-with-severe-headaches-stomach-pains-find-a-colorful-cure-with-help-from-irlen-institute/

Chard, D. J., Ketterlin-Geller, L. R., Baker, S. K., Doabler, C., & Apichatabutra, C. (2009). Repeated reading interventions for students with learning disabilities: Status of the evidence. *Exceptional Children, 75*, 263–281.

Chard, D. J., Vaughn, S., & Tyler, B. (2002). A synthesis of research on effective interventions for building reading fluency with elementary students with learning disabilities. *Journal of Learning Disabilities*, *35*, 386–406. doi:10.1177/00222194020350050101

ChromaGen. (n.d.). *ChromaGen*. Retrieved from http://www.chromagen.us/

Cook, B. G., Buysse, V., Klingner, J. K., Landrum, T. J., McWilliam, R. A., Tankersley, M., & Test, D. W. (2015). CEC's standards for classifying the evidence base of practices in special education. *Remedial and Special Education*, *36*, 220–234. doi:10.1177/0741932514557271

Cook, B. G., & Odom, S. L. (2013). Evidence-based practices and implementation science in special education. *Exceptional Children*, *79*, 135–144.

Cook, C. R., Dart, E., Collins, T., Restori, A., Daikos, C., & Delport, J. (2012). Preliminary study of the confined, collateral, and combined effects of reading and behavioral interventions: Evidence for a transactional relationship. *Behavioral Disorders*, *38*, 38–56.

Crossbow Education. (n.d.). *Reading rulers*. Retrieved from http://www.crossboweducation.com/shop-now/visual-stress/reading-rulers

Daniel, S. S., Walsh, A. K., Goldston, D. B., Arnold, E. M., Reboussin, B. A., & Wood, F. B. (2006). Suicidality, school dropout, and reading problems among adolescents. *Journal of Learning Disabilities*, *39*, 507–514.

Dowhower, S. L. (1989). Repeated reading: Research into practice. *The Reading Teacher*, *42*, 502–507.

Escarpio, R., & Barbetta, P. M. (2015). Comparison of repeated and non-repeated readings on the reading performances of students with emotional and behavioral disorders. *Journal of Emotional and Behavioral Disorders*. doi:10.1177/1063426615574337

Evans, B. J., & Drasdo, N. (1991). Tinted lenses and related therapies for learning disabilities – A review. *Ophthalmic and Physiological Optics*, *11*, 206–217.

Evans, B. J. W., Wilkins, A. J., Brown, J., Busby, A., Wingfield, A., Jeanes, R., & Bald, J. (1996). A preliminary investigation into the aetiology of Meares–Irlen Syndrome. *Ophthalmic and Physiological Optics*, *16*, 286–296.

Fletcher, J. M., Lyon, G. R., Fuchs, L. S., & Barnes, M. A. (2007). *Learning disabilities: From identification to intervention*. New York, NY: Guilford.

Fuchs, L. S., Fuchs, D., & Maxwell, L. (1988). The validity of informal reading comprehension measures. *Remedial and Special Education*, *9*(2), 20–28. doi:10.1177/074193258800900206

Galuschka, K., Ise, E., Krick, K., & Schulte-Körne, G. (2014). Effectiveness of treatment approaches for children and adolescents with reading disabilities: A meta-analysis of randomized controlled trials. *PloS ONE*, *9*(2), e89900. doi:10.1371/journal.pone.0089900

Handler, S. M., & Fierson, W. M. (2011). Learning disabilities, dyslexia, and vision. *Pediatrics*, *127*(3), e818–e856.

Hasbrouck, J., & Tindal, G. A. (2006). Oral reading fluency norms: A valuable assessment tool for reading teachers. *The Reading Teacher*, *59*, 636–644.

Henderson, L. M., Tsogka, N., & Snowling, M. J. (2013). Questioning the benefits that coloured overlays can have for reading in students with and without dyslexia. *Journal of Research in Special Educational Needs*, *13*, 57–65. doi:10.1111/j.1471-3802.2012.01237.x

Hernandez, D. J. (2012). *Double jeopardy: How third-grade reading skills and poverty influence high school graduation*. Baltimore, MD: Annie E. Casey Foundation. Retrieved from http://gradelevelreading.net/wp-content/uploads/2012/01/Double-Jeopardy-Report-030812-for-web1.pdf

Hyatt, K. J., Stephenson, J., & Carter, M. (2009). A review of three controversial educational practices: Perceptual motor programs, sensory integration, and tinted lenses. *Education and Treatment of Children*, *32*, 313–342. doi:10.1353/etc.0.0054

Institute of Education Sciences. (2014). *WWC intervention report: Repeated reading*. Retrieved from http://ies.ed.gov/ncee/wwc/pdf/intervention_reports/wwc_repeatedreading_051314.pdf

Irlen, H. (1983). Successful treatment of learning difficulties. Paper presented at 91st annual convention of the American Psychological Association, Anaheim, CA.

Irlen, H., & Lass, M. J. (1989). Improving reading problems due to symptoms of scotopic sensitivity syndrome using Irlen lenses and overlays. *Education, 109,* 413–417.

Irlen Institute. (n.d.). *Irlen: Where the science of color transforms lives*. Retrieved from http://irlen.com/

Irlen Syndrome Foundation. (2015). *Irlen syndrome foundation*. Retrieved from http://www.irlensyndrome.org/

Irlen Visual Learning Center. (n.d.). *Initial screening/diagnostic testing info*. Retrieved from http://www.irlenvlcmd.com/screening-diagnostic/

Kavale, K. A., & Mostert, M. P. (2004). *The positive side of special education: Minimizing its fads, fancies, and follies*. Lanham, MD: Scarecrow Education.

Klauda, S. L., & Guthrie, J. T. (2008). Relationships of three components of reading fluency to reading comprehension. *Journal of Educational Psychology, 100,* 310–321. doi:10.1037/0022-0663.100.2.310

Kriss, I., & Evans, B. J. (2005). The relationship between dyslexia and Meares-Irlen syndrome. *Journal of Research in Reading, 28,* 350–364.

Kuhn, M. R., Schwanenflugel, P. J., & Meisinger, E. B. (2010). Aligning theory and assessment of reading fluency: Automaticity, prosody, and definitions of fluency. *Reading Research Quarterly, 45,* 230–251. doi:10.1598/RRQ.45.2.4

LaBerge, D., & Samuels, S. J. (1974). Toward a theory of automatic information processing in reading. *Cognitive Psychology, 6,* 293–323.

Lee, J., & Yoon, S. Y. (2015). The effects of repeated reading on reading fluency for students with reading disabilities: A meta-analysis. *Journal of Learning Disabilities.* doi:0022219415605194

Lesnick, J., Goerge, R., Smithgall, C., & Gwynne, J. (2010). Reading on grade level in third grade: How is it related to high school performance and college enrollment? Chapin Hall at the University of Chicago, Chicago, IL. Retrieved from http://literacyconnects.org/img/2013/03/Reading-on-Grade-Level-Chicago-Longitudinal-Study.pdf

Lyon, G. R., Shaywitz, S. E., & Shaywitz, B. A. (2003). A definition of dyslexia. *Annals of Dyslexia, 53*(1), 1–14. doi:10.1007/s11881-003-0001-9

Meyer, M. S., & Felton, R. H. (1999). Repeated reading to enhance fluency: Old approaches and new directions. *Annals of Dyslexia, 49,* 283–306.

Miles, S. B., & Stipek, D. (2006). Contemporaneous and longitudinal associations between social behavior and literacy achievement in a sample of low-income elementary school children. *Child Development, 77*(1), 103–117.

National Endowment for the Arts. (2007). To read or not to read: A question of national significance. Washington, DC: Author. Retrieved from https://www.arts.gov/sites/default/files/ToRead.pdf

National Institute of Child Health and Human Development. (2000). *Report of the national reading panel. Teaching children to read: An evidence-based assessment of the scientific research literature on reading and its implications for reading instruction.* NIH Publication No. 004769. U.S. Government Printing Office, Washington, DC.

Odom, S. L., Brantlinger, E., Gersten, R., Horner, R. H., Thompson, B., & Harris, K. R. (2005). Research in special education: Scientific methods and evidence-based practices. *Exceptional Children, 71,* 137–148. doi:10.1177/001440290507100201

O'Keeffe, B. V., Slocum, T. A., Burlingame, C., Snyder, K., & Bundock, K. (2012). Comparing results of systematic reviews: Parallel reviews of research on repeated reading. *Education and Treatment of Children, 35,* 333–366. doi:10.1353/etc.2012.0006

Pikulski, J. J., & Chard, D. J. (2005). Fluency: Bridge between decoding and reading comprehension. *The Reading Teacher*, 510–519.

Rashotte, C. A., & Torgesen, J. K. (1985). Repeated reading and reading fluency in learning
disabled children. *Reading Research Quarterly*, *20*, 180–188.

Rasinski, T. V. (2012). Why reading fluency should be hot! *The Reading Teacher*, *65*, 516–522.
doi:10.1002/TRTR.01077

Reid, R., Gonzalez, J. E., Nordness, P. D., Trout, A., & Epstein, M. H. (2004). A meta-
analysis of the academic status of students with emotional/behavioral disturbance.
Journal of Special Education, *38*, 130–143.

Samuels, S. J. (1979). The method of repeated reading. *The Reading Teacher*, *32*, 403–408.

Scott, T. M., & Shearer-Lingo, A. (2002). The effects of reading fluency instruction on the
academic and behavioral success of middle school students in a self-contained EBD
classroom. *Preventing School Failure*, *46*, 167–173.

Stanovich, K. E. (1986). Matthew effects in reading: Some consequences of individual differences in the acquisition of literacy. *Reading Research Quarterly*, *21*, 360–407.

Staubitz, J. E., Cartledge, G., Yurick, A. L., & Lo, Y. Y. (2005). Repeated reading for students
with emotional or behavioral disorders: Peer-and trainer-mediated instruction.
Behavioral Disorders, *31*, 51–64.

Strong, A. C., Wehby, J. H., Falk, K. B., & Lane, K. L. (2004). The impact of a structured
reading curriculum and repeated reading on the performance of junior high students
with emotional and behavioral disorders. *School Psychology Review*, *33*, 561–581.

Therrien, W. J. (2004). Fluency and comprehension gains as a result of repeated reading:
A meta-analysis. *Remedial and Special Education*, *25*, 252–261. doi:10.1177/
07419325040250040801

Therrien, W. J., & Kubina, R. M. (2006). Developing reading fluency with repeated reading.
Intervention in School and Clinic, *41*, 156–160.

Uccula, A., Enna, M., & Mulatti, C. (2014). Colors, colored overlays, and reading skills.
Frontiers in Psychology, *5*(833), doi:10.3389/fpsyg.2014.00833

Valleley, R. J., & Shriver, M. D. (2003). An examination of the effects of repeated readings
with secondary students. *Journal of Behavioral Education*, *12*, 55–76. doi:10.1023/
A:1022322422324

Wanzek, J., Al Otaiba, S., & Petscher, Y. (2014). Oral reading fluency development for children with emotional disturbance or learning disabilities. *Exceptional Children*, *80*,
187–204. doi:10.1177/001440291408000204

What Works Clearinghouse. (2014). *Repeated reading*. Retrieved from http://ies.ed.gov/ncee/
wwc/pdf/intervention_reports/wwc_repeatedreading_051314.pdf

Wilkins, A. (n.d.-a). *Colour in the treatment of visual stress*. Retrieved from http://www.essex.
ac.uk/psychology/overlays/index.htm

Wilkins, A. (n.d.-b). *Instructions for the use of intuitive overlays*. Retrieved from http://www.
essex.ac.uk/psychology/overlays/Overlay%20Instruction%20OC3.htm

Wilkins, A. J., & Evans, B. J. (2010). Visual stress, its treatment with spectral filters, and its
relationship to visually induced motion sickness. *Applied Ergonomics*, *41*, 509–515.
doi:10.1016/j.apergo.2009.01.011

Zimmerman, S. (2014). Looking at Irlen syndrome through a different lens. *Chicago Tribune*,
November 4. Retrieved from http://www.chicagotribune.com/lifestyles/health/sc-health-
1112-irlen-kids-reading-20141104-story.html

CHAPTER 3

DEVELOPING MATHEMATICAL PROBLEM SOLVING THROUGH STRATEGIC INSTRUCTION: MUCH MORE THAN A KEYWORD

Paul J. Riccomini, Jiwon Hwang and Stephanie Morano

ABSTRACT

While deficits for students with learning disabilities (LD) are prevalent in almost all aspects of mathematics, difficulty in the application and understanding of problem-solving tasks are much more challenging to remediate than computational and procedural skills. Given the complexities involved in authentic problem-solving activities emphasized in current mathematics standards and the inherent challenges presented to students with LD, the importance of using strategies and techniques guided by evidence-based practices is paramount. Yet, ineffective instructional strategies for problem solving are still widespread in both mathematics curricula and available teacher resources. In this chapter, we provide a description of a commonly used ineffective problem-solving strategy (i.e., the keyword strategy), an overview of the keyword research, and an explanation for its ineffectiveness. We conclude with a description of three evidenced-based

Instructional Practices with and without Empirical Validity
Advances in Learning and Behavioral Disabilities, Volume 29, 39–60
ISSN: 0735-004X/doi:10.1108/S0735-004X20160000029003

problem-solving approaches and practices that significantly improve the mathematical performance of students with LD.

Keywords: Mathematics; problem solving; keyword; schema-based; learning disabilities

Recent efforts to prepare all students for postsecondary educational opportunities and competitive careers have refocused educators once again on the importance of developing mathematical proficiency at advanced levels. No longer are basic levels of mathematical performance sufficient to guarantee access to postsecondary education and well-paying employment in our continually advancing and technologically rich society. The intensified focus of educators on the importance of mathematics has also highlighted the significant challenges teachers and students contend with in developing deeper levels of mathematical understanding.

Mathematical proficiency is generally described as encompassing five interconnected strands: (a) conceptual understanding, (b) procedural fluency, (c) strategic competence, (d) adaptive reasoning, and (e) productive disposition (National Research Council, 2001). Although each strand plays an important role in various aspects of mathematical proficiency, problem solving often requires the seamless integration of all strands in a strategic and organized approach. When individual strands are underdeveloped or lacking in depth, students' overall performance is negatively impacted, especially problem solving. This is uniquely evident when examining the overall mathematical performance of students with learning disabilities (LD).

The challenges that students with LD encounter during mathematics instruction are substantial, observed at young ages, persistent across time, and well documented (Duncan et al., 2007; Geary, 2004; Morgan, Farkas, & Qiong, 2009). Students with LD continue to significantly lag behind peers without disabilities in mathematics performance, although recent evidence suggests some improvement (National Center for Educational Statistics, 2013). The gap in performance reflects deep deficits or splinter subskills in student learning that are magnified as students progress through their mathematics education sequence. The learning gaps in mathematics for students with LD are evident in the areas of whole number and rational number computation, conceptual understanding, procedural execution, and reasoning and application of problem solving (Geary, 2011; Hunt & Vasquez, 2014; Jitendra & Star, 2011; Siegler et al., 2010). Such challenges in learning mathematics causes long-term barriers for individuals as they enter postsecondary education and begin to seek life-long careers (National Council of Teachers of Mathematics [NCTM], 2014; National Mathematics Advisory Panel [NMAP], 2008).

While deficits for students with LD are prevalent in almost all aspects of mathematics, difficulty in the application and understanding of problem solving should be a leading priority to improve students' capacity to apply and use mathematics in their daily lives. There are at least two main reasons for the emphasis on problem solving. First, problem solving encourages critical thinking and the use of mathematical principles in flexible and crea-tive ways that extend mathematics beyond straightforward computation. Second, problem solving is emphasized in all content areas because it is these high order thinking skills that will allow students to become successful in a world that rarely present solutions to problems in straightforward contexts.

Given the complexities involved in problem-solving tasks embedded in current mathematics standards, the importance of using evidenced-based stra-tegies and techniques is paramount. The purpose of this chapter is to provide information to guide educators in their efforts to improve the problem-solving expertise of students with LD. We hope to accomplish this goal by providing a description of a commonly used but ineffective problem-solving strategy (i.e., the keyword strategy), an overview of the research demonstrating its inef-fectiveness, and an explanation for its ineffectiveness. We conclude with a description of evidenced-based problem-solving techniques that significantly improve the mathematical problem-solving performance of students with LD.

AN INEFFECTIVE AND INCOMPLETE INSTRUCTIONAL PRACTICE: THE KEYWORD STRATEGY

One simple and common problem-solving strategy, the keyword strategy, is found in many basal mathematics programs. The keyword strategy teaches students to interpret keywords as cues for selecting operations to solve problems (Xin & Jitendra, 1999). For example, students are taught to perform subtraction when they encounter the word *difference* in a word problem, and to perform addition when they see the keywords *in all*. In the absence of formal instruction in the keyword strategy, some students will develop the strategy independently through noticing patterns between keywords and operations in simple word problems (Xin, Jitendra, & Deatline-Buchman, 2005). One experimental study that tested the effects of the keyword strategy (Walker & Poteet, 1990) was included in Xin and Jitendra's (1999) meta-analysis of problem-solving efficacy. Xin and Jitendra reported that the keyword strategy yielded a negative and moderately large effect size ($d = -0.42$), indicating that students' problem-solving performance actually deteriorated after instruction in the keyword strategy.

The apparent popularity of the strategy among math teachers is surprising given the lack of empirical support for its use. Despite the failure of the keyword strategy to produce outcomes that might qualify it as an evidence-based practice, a quick Google Image search yields a multitude of teacher created keyword strategy posters and printables (see Fig. 1). Many of these keyword strategy resources list a sample of keywords under operation headings. For example, *altogether* and *in all* are often listed under addition, *left* and *difference* are listed under subtraction, *times* is often listed under multiplication, and *between* is listed under division. Given the poor and in some cases negative impact on learning, it may be helpful to better understand why the keyword strategy is an ineffective and incomplete mathematical problem-solving instructional practice.

Why the Keyword Strategy Fails to Support Problem Solving

A key recommendation from the *Principles to Action: Ensuring Mathematical Success for All* (NCTM, 2014) is the importance of the purposeful use of

Math Keywords			
Addition **+**	Subtraction **—**	Multiplication **X**	Division **÷**
in all	fewer	times	share equally
plus	left	twice	half
more than	how many more	factor	equal groups
sum	difference	each	same
altogether	minus	product	divisor
	take away		dividend

Fig. 1. Example of a Typical Keyword Strategy Classroom Poster.

representations to facilitate problem-solving development. In addition, the results of numerous studies on the effects of strategy instruction on the problem-solving performance of students with and without disabilities suggest that performance improves significantly when students are taught to analyze a problem situation and create a representation of or model the problem structure (Jitendra, DiPipi, & Perron-Jones, 2002; Jitendra, Dupuis, Star, & Rodriguez, 2014; Jitendra & Hoff, 1996; Jitendra, Hoff, & Beck, 1999; van Garderen, 2007; Xin, 2008). In addition to the positive outcomes reported in individual intervention studies, a meta-analysis of problem-solving strategy efficacy reported a large average effect size ($d = 1.77$) for studies that taught students to analyze and represent problem situations (Xin & Jitendra, 1999). Where representation strategies emphasize problem structure, the keyword strategy focuses only on directly associating words or phrases with operations. Although effective, the deep structural analysis and representation of word problems is challenging. In effect, teachers and students may opt for a simpler, intuitively appealing strategy; hence, the continued popularity of the keyword technique.

Just as taking a few words out of context can create a misleading characterization of a speaker's message, taking keywords in a problem out of context or in isolation can create a misleading picture of the problem situation and send students down an inaccurate solution path. By focusing on keywords in isolation, students lose sight of the bigger picture. They also fail to develop any meaningful understanding of what is going on in a problem. Their primary concern becomes selecting an operation rather than making sense of the problem situation and context (Parmar, Cawley, & Frazita, 1996; Xin et al., 2005).

For example, notice how a student using the keyword strategy would be misled by the word *left* in the following problem. *On Halloween, Mark filled a big bag with candy while out trick-or-treating. When he got home, he gave 10 candies to his little sister. Mark has 73 candies left. How many candies did Mark get trick-or-treating?* According to the keyword strategy, *left* indicates that one must subtract, but this problem actually calls for addition. Consider a second example. *Julia's pumpkin patch has 10 rows of pumpkins. In each row, there are 11 pumpkins. How many pumpkins does Julia have altogether?* By focusing only on the keyword *altogether*, a student might mistakenly add the two numerals in the problem rather than perform the correct operation, multiplication. The underlying structure of the problem dictates the operation necessary to solve the problem, not the identified keyword.

Students' tendency to be misled by keywords is demonstrated in research dating back three decades. In a study where students were given problems including irrelevant keywords, results show that students almost always used the irrelevant keywords to select an inappropriate solution path (Carpenter, Hiebert, & Moser, 1981). This outcome highlights the danger of teaching a simple rule for solving complex problems. Students can easily learn and follow the rule, but come no closer to making sense of a problem and understanding the steps they must take to solve it. Another study used eye-tracking technology to track students' gaze and attention during problem solving. Results showed that students who spent the majority of their time focused on keywords chose inaccurate solution strategies significantly more often than students who spent most of their time focusing on variable names and words that signified relationships between variables (Hegarty, Mayer, & Monk, 1995).

The presence of misleading or irrelevant keywords in word problems poses an obvious difficulty for students who use the keyword strategy, but many word problems, like the following example, do not contain recognizable keywords at all. *Stacie and 15 friends are planning for a birthday party. They bought 3 quarts of juice. Will everyone get at least one glass of juice if each glass holds 10 ounces?* A student who relies solely on the keyword strategy will find no cues in a problem like this and would likely struggle to come up with a plan for solving. In contrast, the ability to analyze the problem situation and model the problem structure would help a student to solve this and other novel problems. As illustrated by these examples, the keyword strategy is inadequate for all but the simplest, most direct problems, which makes it insufficient in helping students understand and solve the now routine complex problem-solving tasks.

As students get older and problems get more complex, the keyword strategy will have less and less utility. An informal examination of word problems designed to align with the Common Core State Standards for math indicates that by fourth grade, knowledge of the keyword strategy alone would be insufficient for students to solve problems accurately (EngageNY, 2015). Even the most basic problems in various problem sets cannot be answered using the keyword strategy. Further, because the keyword strategy is so unreliable and does not require students to make sense of the problem structure, no amount of practice using the strategy will improve performance (Ben-Zeev & Star, 2001).

Students with disabilities are known to struggle with problem solving in general, and have particular trouble with problems that require multiple steps, use indirect language, and include extraneous information (Cawley, Parmar, Foley, Salmon, & Roy, 2001; Parmar et al., 1996). Teaching the keyword strategy for problem solving fails to help students negotiate any of these challenging word problem features. Rather than help students understand what is going on in a problem, the keyword strategy teaches a simple and fallible rule-based procedure. Although the simplicity of the keyword strategy is appealing, focusing on superficial cues and teaching simple rules will not improve problem-solving skill (Jitendra & Star, 2011).

EFFECTIVE PRACTICES FOR ENHANCING MATHEMATICAL PROBLEM SOLVING

In 2014, The National Council of Teachers of Mathematics once again in the *Principles and Actions: Ensuring Mathematical Success for All* reiterated that mathematical problem solving is a critical skill for students with and without disabilities. Current recommendations for problem-solving instruction emphasize the use of complex authentic problems situated in students' everyday lives (Kelly et al., 2013; Kilpatrick, 2001; Stacey, 2012). In educational settings, however, authentic problem solving is often equated with word problem solving because text-based problems are thought to simulate the real world. Given the documented ineffectiveness of the keyword strategy and emphasis on authentic, complex problem-solving tasks, it is imperative that educators use problem-solving instruction that is aligned with recommendations that has resulted in positive experimental outcomes.

Two Types of Knowledge for Problem Solving

The complexity of mathematical problem solving lies in the integration of cognitive processes. When given a problem, students are required to understand the language (e.g., reading ability) and factual information in the problem context, distinguish relevant information from irrelevant information, translate the problem into various representations, devise a solution plan, and execute procedures including calculations (Desoete, Roeyers, & De Clercq, 2003, Jitendra et al., 2007; Mayer, 1999). This integrated process requires students to interact with two types of knowledge, conceptual knowledge and procedural knowledge. Conceptual and procedural knowledge are both identified strands necessary for mathematical proficiency and points of emphasis in the Common Core State Standards Initiative (2015).

Conceptual knowledge refers to broad measures of understanding rather than procedural and/or computational steps. Conceptual knowledge requires connecting pieces of information to enhance understanding of underlying concepts and/or problem structures (Hiebert, 2013). Procedural knowledge is defined as the procedures, rules, or algorithms used to solve mathematical tasks in a predetermined linear sequence to complete a task (Mayer, 1987; Reif & Heller, 1982). Although conceptual and procedural knowledge may be emphasized differently depending on the targeted tasks and instructional design features, both knowledge types are interrelated and require instructional attention when teaching students to solve problems that involve multiple steps (Rittle-Johnson & Alibali, 1999; Star, 2005). The interconnected importance of procedural and conceptual knowledge is evident in problem solving because problem-solving tasks rarely only require one or the other.

Researchers do not yet agree regarding which knowledge type should precede the other; regardless, both conceptual and procedural knowledge must be adequately addressed for students with LD to become accomplished problem solvers. However, a large number of mathematics studies have heavily emphasized the teaching of procedural skills and deemphasized conceptual knowledge. As described earlier, the characteristics of a procedural, rule-based, problem-solving strategy such as the keyword strategy is insufficient to promote deep understanding, particularly in special education. Rather, the goal of procedural, rule-based instruction is often to achieve a correct answer rather than to develop understanding of underlying problem features and structures. Relying solely on procedural, rule-based instruction results in superficial learning as well as learner passivity. Clearly, students with LD require problem-solving instruction that explicitly merges conceptual and procedural knowledge in an organized manner to promote understanding of the underlying structures of word problems.

Emerging View of an Effective Instructional Approach

Researchers have suggested that some instructional strategies and/or problem-solving interventions associated with traditional approaches (e.g., rote practice) have serious limitations for generalization to different problems and can make students passive learners (Baroody & Hume, 1991; Bottge, 1999; Woodward & Montague, 2002). A different approach is necessary to compensate for the poor problem-solving skills characteristic of many students with LD. According to a recent review on mathematical problem solving (Hwang & Riccomini, 2015), there are two main categories of instructional approaches found among interventions for word problem solving: heuristic and semantic approaches. Regardless of the instructional approach, instructions are often guided by or combined with components of explicit instruction (e.g., modeling, guided practice, monitoring, corrective feedback, independent practice) (Archer & Hughes, 2011; Riccomini & Witzel, 2010). Explicit instruction is most widely used in special education settings across various subject domains (e.g., math, science, and reading), and has accumulated strong evidence of effectiveness (Archer & Hughes, 2011; NMAP, 2008). Explicit instruction is an essential foundation for the problem-solving instructional techniques described below.

Heuristic Instructional Approach

The heuristic approach relies on an information-processing and process-based framework, where procedural knowledge is prominent. In this approach, instruction is not merely focused on *what* to do, but instead teaches processes for *how* to do things (Goldman, 1989; Jitendra et al., 2002; Jitendra & Hoff, 1996). Procedural instruction targeting *"how* to do" is best delineated in Pólya's (1990) work on general heuristic approaches. In Pólya's work, four general steps (i.e., understand the problem, devise a plan, carry out the plan, and look back and reflect) provide guidance for students during problem-solving instruction and practice. The entire process of problem solving is divided into small phases to reduce cognitive load. Each small phase is explicitly taught and includes guided practice opportunities prior to independent practice.

The general heuristic model is the primary foundation of several problem-solving approaches with demonstrated effectiveness for students with LD. For example, Montague's "Solve It!" (Montague, Warger, & Morgan, 2000) and Maccini and colleagues' S-T-A-R strategies (Maccini & Hughes, 2000; Maccini & Ruhl, 2000) are both heuristic approaches with strong results. Generally, heuristic approaches include four to seven cognitive stages during the problem-solving progression (e.g., Read, Paraphrase, Visualize, Hypothesize, Estimate, Compute, and Check; Montague et al., 2000); comprehensive routines are taught through cognitive and corresponding meta-cognitive strategies (e.g., self-instruct, self-question, and self-monitoring) and other strategic prompts (e.g., cue cards, prompts cards, mnemonic devices, and structured work sheets). This structured strategic routine enhances understanding by internalizing the cognitive processes and strategies used during successful problem solving. These processes and strategies can also be applied successfully to more advanced problems. Therefore, a heuristic approach to instruction starts from a broader conceptual perspective and funnels student learning through a set of procedures that can be applied to a variety of mathematical problem-solving contexts. Because the instructional focus informs students *how* to go through a sequential problem-solving progression and *what* to do in each step, the effective use of heuristics incorporated with cognitive and/or meta-cognitive strategies enhances students' ability to compensate for working memory deficits and to tackle problems of different levels of complexity (Montague, 1992; Swanson, 2011; Swanson & Sachse-Lee, 2001; Trainin & Swanson, 2005; Zheng, Swanson, & Marcoulides, 2011). Evidence supports the heuristic approach to instruction, and suggests that heuristics provide efficient problem-solving guides for students who struggle in mathematics, especially those with LD (Montague, Enders, & Dietz, 2011; Montague et al., 2000). Therefore, this is an approach that teachers should use in their math classrooms.

Semantic Instructional Approach

Despite evidence highlighting the effectiveness of heuristic approaches grounded in the components of explicit instruction, researchers have pointed out that these structured, step-by-step approaches have limits and may require additional supports to be useful in solving more complex mathematical tasks (Griffin & Jitendra, 2009; Jitendra & Hoff, 1996; Jitendra & Star, 2011; Xin et al., 2005). Criticism focuses on the fact that heuristic approaches can result in superficial learning, and that focusing on procedural knowledge can lead students to inaccurately generalize problem-solving skills to problems with different problem structures (Jitendra, Star, Dupuis, & Rodriguez, 2013; Woodward & Montague, 2002). One possible means to enhance the effectiveness of heuristic approaches is to focus on conceptual understanding alongside the procedural and computational elements. Ultimately, a problem-solving approach that balances the features of conceptual and procedural knowledge will likely better facilitate a deeper understanding of problem solving and increase the ability of students with LD to meet the challenges of advanced mathematical tasks.

Reflecting a recent trend toward more balanced instruction, the semantic approach highlights the importance of building underlying conceptual ideas along with teaching problem structure. Rather than merely training procedures for problem solving, semantic instruction provides sufficient opportunities for students to explore the structure of a problem and organize mathematical knowledge before transitioning to problem solutions (Jitendra et al., 2009). The main focus in the semantic approach is the identification of the problem structure or schema (Jitendra et al., 2002). A *schema* is defined as a generalized description of two or more examples that individuals use to sort problems into groups requiring similar solution paths (Fuchs, Fuchs, Finelli, Courey, & Hamlett, 2004; Gick & Holyoak, 1983). Prior research supports the critical role of teaching schema in mathematical problem solving for the development of understanding the structural features of problems (Chen, 1999; Sweller, Chandler, Tierney, & Cooper, 1990). Schema-based instruction generally involves the use of schematic imagery (e.g., diagram) to map out information presented in a problem.

Schematic images, often referred to as *schema- or schematic-diagrams*, are instructional representations of mathematics problems and an essential characteristic of the semantic approach. Schema diagrams help students to map key information by depicting the spatial relations between objects in the problem (Hegarty & Kozhevnikov, 1999; Jitendra & Star, 2011; Jitendra, Star, Rodriguez, Lindell, & Someki, 2011). Using schematic-diagrams promotes understanding of the deep structure and semantic relations in a problem. Schematic images are distinguishable from pictorial representations that depict the visual appearance of the objects or persons described in a problem (i.e., the problem context). For example, if a word problem is presented in the context of using a basket to pick cherries, a pictorial representation might include a sketch of a basket of cherries. This pictorial representation may help the student understand the problem context, but will not help the student to understanding the underlying mathematical structure of the problem. In contrast, a schema diagram explicitly highlights mathematical structure.

Using schema diagrams enables learners to catalyze external and internal representations (i.e., mental image with semantic structure of the problem), which facilitates students' ability to generalize their learning to novel problems. Researchers have developed an extensive body of research supporting the use of schema diagrams, called *Schema-based Instruction (SBI)*, to help students with and without disabilities improve their problem-solving performance.

Enhanced SBI: Schema-Based Strategy Instruction
Early research on SBI focused entirely on the contribution of instruction focused on problems' semantic characteristics (i.e., the development of schema knowledge) to problem-solving performance. Over time, SBI has evolved to combine heuristics and strategy instruction as numerous studies have documented strong evidence that students with disabilities profit

from explicit, step-by-step instruction and strategy training in addition to instruction on semantic characteristics (Jitendra, Harwell et al., 2015). In this enhanced SBI, schema-based strategy instruction (SBSI), heuristics are specified for a set of problems (i.e., task-specific) as opposed to providing general problem-solving heuristics (e.g., read the problem, highlight keywords, solve the problem, check your work); and cognitive and/or meta-cognitive strategies are integrated in each step of the problem-solving process. The SBSI model suggests that multiple strategies should be used during problem solving, including those that prime schema training. In a recent review, Jitendra, Petersen-Brown et al. (2015) examined the evidence base of SBSI using the standards specified by Gersten et al. (2005), Horner et al. (2005), and the What Works Clearinghouse (2011) and concluded that SBSI is an evidence-based practice because multiple, high-quality studies have shown positive effects on problem solving in mathematics for students with LD.

General Structure of SBSI
SBSI is composed of four procedural steps (FOPS): (1) *F*ind the problem type (problem schema identification, schema knowledge), (2) *O*rganize the information in the problem using the schema-diagram (representation, elaboration knowledge), (3) *P*lan to solve the problem (strategic knowledge), and (4) *S*olution (execution knowledge) (Jitendra et al., 1998; Schwab, Tucci, & Jolivette, 2013). The FOPS heuristic is distinguishable from general heuristics in that it is linked to particular problem types (e.g., additive, multiplicative, compare, proportion). Students learn the FOPS problem-solving procedure through teacher-directed instruction that systemically incorporates explicit instruction components for each element. For example, a teacher can promote a four-step problem-solving strategy by modeling with thinking-aloud, or by using supplemental handouts (e.g., checklists, script). Instructional components of cognitive and meta-cognitive strategies (e.g., self-monitoring) are encouraged to facilitate the problem-solving process. Instructional time is allocated for students to learn the FOPS process before attempting to solve problems. After the problem types are learned and students master FOPS, instructional time is devoted to applying the FOPS strategy to solving problems.

Word Problem Type
Word problems are categorized based on problem structure and the underlying mathematical relationships in a problem (Jitendra *et al.* 2011; Marshall, 1995). In the domain of arithmetic word problems, problems are represented

by two main structures: additive (i.e., more or less) and multiplicative (i.e., multiple or part) structures. In the additive structure, the solution operation is either addition or subtraction, represented with *change, group*, and *compare* problem types. In the multiplicative structure, the solution operation can be either multiplication or division, represented with *restate* (i.e., multiplicative compare) and *vary* (e.g., ratio, proportion, and percent/ percent of change) problem types. Examples of problem types are presented in Tables 1 and 2. Students are taught how to classify word problems based on the underlying structure and receive guided and independent practice identifying underlying structures and classifying the problem types. This is done through teacher-directed explicit instruction that includes corrective feedback and re-teaching when necessary. This word problem type instruction is done prior to students solving problems.

Implementing SBSI

Students first learn the types and features of the problem schema to identify the appropriate schema for a given problem. Then, a teacher introduces and teaches the four-step strategy (FOPS) to mastery. Students receive a checklist containing the four steps with descriptions and self-instructions to use during the initial stages of learning. For each step, the teacher incorporates components of explicit instruction (e.g., modeling, prompting, think-aloud) in teaching problem-solving steps based on students' instructional needs. Students with LD require explicit and systematic instruction of the FOPS strategy as well as ample opportunities for guided practice. Specifically, SBSI encourages teachers to *model* the use of the strategy by *thinking-aloud* and stating *self-instructions* for each step. Consider the following example from Jitendra and Star (2011, p.16).

> **Problem.** Joe used exactly 2 cans of icing to cover 24 cupcakes. How many cupcakes can she ice with 3 cans of icing?

In *Step 1* (Find the problem type), the teacher models reading, retelling, and examining the problem information to identify the problem type (e.g., *vary: proportion*) using self-questioning (e.g., Is there a proportional statement that tells about proportional relationship between two quantities?). In *Step 2* (Organize the information in the problem using the schema-diagram), the teacher explains how to organize information in the schema diagram. Self-questioning is used to identify critical pieces of information, for example, "What does this problem compare?" (*cans* of icing and cupcakes; unit is can) and "Does the problem describe a specific ratio between cans of icing and cupcakes?" (yes, both the statement and question in the problem

Table 1.   Additive Word Problem Type.

Problem Type	Example
Change	
Ending quantity unknown	Jenna had 3 candies. Then Tyler gave her 5 more candies. How many candies does Jenna have now?
Change quantity unknown	Jenna had 3 candies. Then Tyler gave her some more candies. Now Jenna has 8 candies. How many candies did Tyler give her?
Beginning quantity unknown	[a]Jenna had some candies. Then Tyler gave her 5 more candies. Now Jenna has 8 candies. How many candies did Jenna have in the beginning?

Schema diagram and example

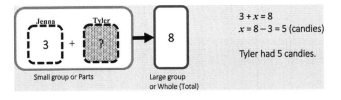

$x + 5 = 8$
$x = 8 - 5 = 3$ (candies)

Jenna had 3 candies in the beginning.

Group	
Whole quantity unknown	Jenna has 3 candies. Tyler has 5 candies. How many candies do they have?
Part quantity unknown	[a]Jenna and Tyler have 8 candies altogether. Jenna has 3 candies. How many candies does Tyler have?

Schema diagram and example

$3 + x = 8$
$x = 8 - 3 = 5$ (candies)

Tyler had 5 candies.

Compare	
Difference quantity unknown	Jenna has 8 candies. Tyler has 5 candies. How many more candies does Jenna have than Tyler?
Compared quantity unknown	[a]Jenna has 3 candies. Tyler has 5 more candies than Jane. How many candies does Tyler have?
Referent quantity unknown	Jenna has 8 candies. She has 5 more than Tyler. How many candies does Tyler have?

Table 1.   (*Continued*)

Compare

Schema diagram and example
Type 1

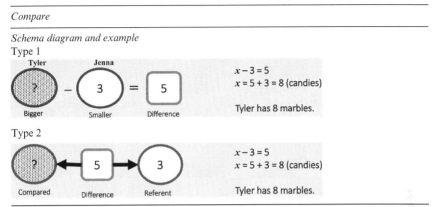

Type 2

Problem examples are adopted from Jitendra and Hoff (1996), schema diagrams are adapted from Griffin and Jitendra (2009).
[a]Indicates it is used for an example.

describe the number of cans of icing and cupcakes) (Jitendra & Star, 2011, p. 16). After the quantities are filled in on the diagram, the teacher will proceed to *Step 3* (Plan to solve the problem) and translate or interpret the information on the diagram into a mathematical equation. This step involves exploring a particular solution strategy to plan for the easiest way to solve the problem. In our example, students may consider the use of cross-multiplication, equivalent fractions, or a unit rate strategy. If they decide to apply the unit rate strategy, the teacher models using self-questioning by asking, "2 multiplied by what number equals 24?" Then the teacher asks students what the multiplier, 12, means (the unit rate of cupcakes per can of icing), and demonstrates how this can be applied to the other ratio to get an unknown value x. Lastly, in *Step 4* (Solution execution), students solve the problem based on the solution strategy planned in Step 3 to get an answer ($3 \times 12 = x$).

The SBSI instructional progression systematically scaffolds students through the problem-solving process in an organized and structured manner that enhances understanding and promotes accurate solutions. It is this systematic and explicit progression that provides the instructional scaffolding necessary to support students with LD in developing problem-solving expertise. Additionally, SBSI purposefully and directly connects the five identified strands (i.e., conceptual understanding, procedural fluency, strategic competence, adaptive reasoning, and productive disposition) essential

Table 2. Multiplicative Word Problem Type.

Problem Type	Description and Problem Example
Multiplicative compare	David earned $12 from shoveling snow over the weekend. He earned 1/3 as much as his friend Paul did. How much did Paul earn from shoveling snow?

Schema diagram and example

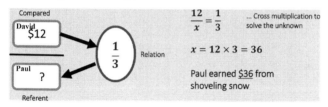

Ratio	Last weekend, John helped his father clean the garage. For every 3 hours of work, he took a 2-hour break. If he worked for 6 hours (not including breaks), how many hours did he spend taking breaks?

Schema-diagram and example

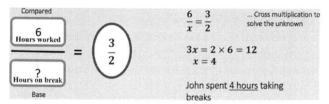

Percent: Part-whole comparison	On a chapter test, Sarah got a grade of 80%. The test had a total of 35 possible points. How many points did Sarah earn on the test?

Schema diagram and example

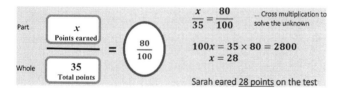

Table 2. (*Continued*)

Percent of change   Alex's parents increased his weekly allowance by 10% from last year. If he was getting $20 a week last year, how much will he get per week this year?

Schema diagram and example

Step 1

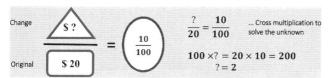

Step 2

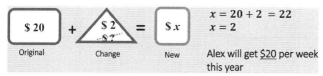

Proportion   Andy used exactly 2 cans of icing to cover 24 cupcakes. How many cupcakes can he ice with 3 cans of icing?

Schema diagram and example

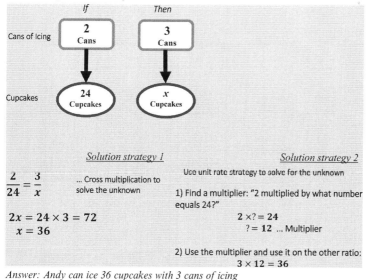

Answer: Andy can ice 36 cupcakes with 3 cans of icing

Note: Problem examples are adopted from (1) Jitendra et al. (2013); (2) Jitendra and Star (2011).

for the development of overall mathematical proficiency. Educators should consider making the SBSI approach a common element of their mathematical problem-solving instruction for students with LD.

CONCLUSION

Mathematical problem solving requires the simultaneous and intricate blending of a number of subskills in an organized and structured approach to facilitate both understanding and solution accuracy. Students with LD often lack the critical subskills, are unorganized in their approach to problem solving, and demonstrate poor understanding. It is well documented that when teachers employ evidenced-based practices such as those described in this chapter, significant and meaningful improvement in mathematical problem solving is possible for students with LD. Just like mathematics is much more than the answer, effective problem-solving instruction for students with LD is unquestionably much more than a keyword.

REFERENCES

Archer, A. L., & Hughes, C. A. (2011). *Explicit instruction: Effective and efficient teaching.* New York, NY: Guilford.

Baroody, A. J., & Hume, J. (1991). Meaningful mathematics instruction: The case of fractions. *Remedial and Special Education, 12*(3), 54–68.

Ben-Zeev, T., & Star, J. R. (2001). Spurious correlations in mathematical thinking. Cognition *and Instruction, 19*, 253–275.

Bottge, B. A. (1999). Effects of contextualized math instruction on problem solving of average and below-average achieving students. *The Journal of Special Education, 33*, 81–92.

Carpenter, T. P., Hiebert, J., & Moser, J. M. (1981). Problem structure and first-grade children's initial solution processes for simple addition and subtraction problems. *Journal for Research in Mathematics Education, 12*, 27–39.

Cawley, J., Parmar, R., Foley, T. E., Salmon, S., & Roy, S. (2001). Arithmetic performance of students: Implications for standards and programming. *Exceptional Children, 67*, 311–328.

Chen, Z. (1999). Schema induction in children's analogical problem solving. Journal of *Educational Psychology, 91*, 703–715.

Common Core State Standards Initiative. (2015). *Common core state standards for mathematics.* Retrieved from http://www.corestandards.org/assets/CCSSI_Math%20Standards.pdf

Desoete, A., Roeyers, H., & De Clercq, A. (2003). Can offline metacognition enhance mathematical problem solving? *Journal of Educational Psychology, 95*(1), 188–200.

Duncan, G. J., Dowsett, C. J., Claessens, A., Magnuson, K., Hutson, A. C., Klebanov, P., ... Japel, C. (2007). School readiness and later achievement. *Developmental Psychology, 43*, 1428–1446.

EngageNY. (2015). *Grade 4 mathematics curriculum map.* Retrieved from https://www.enga-geny.org/resource/grade-4-mathematics

Fuchs, L. S., Fuchs, D., Finelli, R., Courey, S. J., & Hamlett, C. L. (2004). Expanding schema-based transfer instruction to help third graders solve real-life mathematical problems. *American Educational Research Journal, 41*, 419–445.

Geary, D. C. (2004). Mathematics and learning disabilities. *Journal of Learning Disabilities, 37*(1), 4–15.

Geary, D. C. (2011). Cognitive predictors of individual differences in achievement growth mathematics: A five year longitudinal study. *Developmental Psychology, 47*, 1539–1552.

Gersten, R., Fuchs, L. S., Compton, D., Coyne, M., Greenwood, C., & Innocenti, M. S. (2005). Quality indicators for group experimental and quasi-experimental research in special education. *Exceptional Children, 71*, 149–164.

Gick, M. L., & Holyoak, K. J. (1983). Schema induction and analogical transfer. *Cognitive psychology, 15*(1), 1–38.

Goldman, S. R. (1989). Strategy instruction in mathematics. *Learning Disability Quarterly, 12*(1), 43–55.

Griffin, C. C., & Jitendra, A. K. (2009). Word problem-solving instruction in inclusive third-grade mathematics classrooms. *Journal of Educational Research, 102*(3), 187–202.

Hegarty, M., & Kozhevnikov, M. (1999). Types of visual–spatial representations and mathematical problem solving. *Journal of Educational Psychology, 91*, 684–689.

Hegarty, M., Mayer, R. E., & Monk, C. A. (1995). Comprehension of arithmetic word problems: A comparison of successful and unsuccessful problem solvers. *Journal of Educational Psychology, 87*, 18–31.

Hiebert, J. (Ed.) (2013). *Conceptual and procedural knowledge: The case of mathematics.* New York, NY: Routledge.

Horner, R. H., Carr, E. G., Halle, J., McGee, G., Odom, S., & Wolery, M. (2005). The use of single-subject research to identify evidence-based practice in special education. *Exceptional Children, 71*, 165–179.

Hunt, J. H., & Vasquez III, E. (2014). Effects of ratio strategies intervention on knowledge of ratio equivalence for students with learning disability. *Journal of Special Education, 48*, 180–190.

Hwang, J., & Riccomini, P. J. (2015). *Enhancing mathematical literacy for secondary students with learning disabilities or at-risk: A literature review.* Manuscript submitted for publication.

Jitendra, A., DiPipi, C. M., & Perron-Jones, N. (2002). An exploratory study of schema-based word-problem-solving instruction for middle school students with learning disabilities: An emphasis on conceptual and procedural understanding. *Journal of Special Education, 36*, 22–38.

Jitendra, A. K., Dupuis, D. N., Star, J. R., & Rodriguez, M. C. (2014). The effects of schema-based instruction on the proportional thinking of students with mathematics difficulties with and without reading difficulties. *Journal of Learning Disabilities, 50*, 12–19.

Jitendra, A. K., Griffin, C. C., Haria, P., Leh, J., Adams, A., & Kaduvettoor, A. (2007). A comparison of single and multiple strategy instruction on third-grade students' mathematical problem solving. *Journal of Educational Psychology, 99*(1), 115–127.

Jitendra, A. K., Griffin, C. C., McGoey, K., Gardill, M. C., Bhat, P., & Riley, T. (1998). Effects of mathematical word problem solving by students at risk or with mild disabilities. *Journal of Educational Research, 91*, 345–355.

Jitendra, A. K., Harwell, M. R., Dupuis, D. N., Karl, S. R., Lein, A. E., Simonson, G., & Slater, S. C. (2015). Effects of a research-based intervention to improve seventh-grade students' proportional problem solving: A cluster randomized trial. *Journal of Educational Psychology, 107*, 1019–1034.

Jitendra, A. K., & Hoff, K. (1996). The effects of schema-based instruction on the mathematical word-problem-solving performance of students with learning disabilities. *Journal of Learning Disabilities, 29*, 422–431.

Jitendra, A. K., Hoff, K., & Beck, M. M. (1999). Teaching middle school students with learning disabilities to solve word problems using a schema-based approach. *Remedial and Special Education, 20*, 50–64.

Jitendra, A. K., Petersen-Brown, S., Lein, A. E., Zaslofsky, A. F., Kunkel, A. K., Jung, P. G., & Egan, A. M. (2015). Teaching mathematical word problem solving: the quality of evidence for strategy instruction priming the problem structure. *Journal of learning disabilities, 48*(1), 51–72.

Jitendra, A. K., & Star, J. R. (2011). Meeting the needs of students with learning disabilities in inclusive mathematics classrooms: The role of schema-based instruction on mathematical problem-solving. *Theory into Practice, 50*(1), 12–19.

Jitendra, A. K., Star, J. R., Dupuis, D. N., & Rodriguez, M. C. (2013). Effectiveness of schema-based instruction for improving seventh-grade students' proportional reasoning: A randomized experiment. *Journal of Research on Educational Effectiveness, 6*, 114–136.

Jitendra, A. K., Star, J. R., Rodriguez, M., Lindell, M., & Someki, F. (2011). Improving students' proportional thinking using schema-based instruction. *Learning and Instruction, 21*, 731–745.

Jitendra, A. K., Star, J. R., Starosta, K., Leh, J. M., Sood, S., Caskie, G., … Mack, T. R. (2009). Improving seventh grade students' learning of ratio and proportion: The role of schema-based instruction. *Contemporary Educational Psychology, 34*, 250–264.

Kelly, D., Xie, H., Nord, C. W., Jenkins, F., Chan, J. Y., & Kastberg, D. (2013). Performance of U.S. 15- year-old students in mathematics, science, and reading literacy in an international context: First look at PISA 2012. NCES Publication No. 2014-024. U.S Department of Education, National Center for Education Statistics. Retrieved from http://nces.ed.gov/pubs2014/2014024rev.pdf

Kilpatrick, J. (2001). Understanding mathematical literacy: The contribution of research. *Educational Studies in Mathematics, 47*(1), 101–116.

Maccini, P., & Hughes, C. A. (2000). Effects of a problem-solving strategy on the introductory algebra performance of secondary students with learning disabilities. *Learning Disabilities Research & Practice, 15*(1), 10–21.

Maccini, P., & Ruhl, K. L. (2000). Effects of a graduated instructional sequence on the algebraic subtraction of integers by secondary students with learning disabilities. *Education & Treatment of Children, 23*, 465–489.

Marshall, S. P. (1995). *Schemas in problem solving*. New York, NY: Cambridge University Press.

Mayer, R. E. (1987). Learnable aspects of problem solving: Some examples. In D. E. Berger, K. Pezdek, & W. Banks (Eds.), *Applications of cognitive psychology: Problem solving, education, and computing* (pp. 109–122). Hillsdale, NJ: Erlbaum.

Mayer, R. E. (1999). *The promise of educational psychology, Vol. 1: Learning in the content areas.* Upper Saddle River, NJ: Merrill Prentice Hall.

Montague, M. (1992). The effects of cognitive and metacognitive strategy instruction on the mathematical problem solving of middle school students with learning disabilities. *Journal of Learning Disabilities, 25,* 230–248.

Montague, M., Enders, C., & Dietz, S. (2011). Effects of cognitive strategy instruction on math problem solving of middle school students with learning disabilities. *Learning Disability Quarterly, 34,* 262–272.

Montague, M., Warger, C., & Morgan, T. H. (2000). Solve it! Strategy instruction to improve mathematical problem solving. *Learning Disabilities Research & Practice, 15,* 110–116.

Morgan, P. L., Farkas, G., & Qiong, W. (2009). Five-year growth trajectories of kindergarten children with learning difficulties in mathematics. *Journal of Learning Disabilities, 42,* 306–321.

National Center for Educational Statistics. (2013). The nation's report card: A first look: 2013 mathematics and reading. NCES 2014–2015. Institute of Education Sciences, U.S. Department of Education, Washington, DC. Retrieved from htpp://nationsreportcard. gov. Accessed on November 1, 2015.

National Council of Teachers of Mathematics. (2014). *Principles to actions: Ensuring mathematical success for all.* Reston, VA: Author.

National Mathematics Advisory Panel. (2008). *Foundations for success: The final report of the national mathematics advisory panel.* U.S. Department of Education, Washington, DC.

National Research Council. (2001). Adding it up: Helping children learn mathematics. In J. Kilpatrick, J. Swafford, & B. Findell (Eds.), *Mathematics learning study committee, center for education, division of behavioral and social sciences, and education* (pp. 5–14). Washington, DC: National Academies Press.

Parmar, R. S., Cawley, J. F., & Frazita, R. R. (1996). Word problem-solving by students with and without mild disabilities. *Exceptional Children, 62,* 415–429.

Pólya, G. (1990). *How to solve it.* London, UK: Penguin. (Original work published in 1945).

Reif, F., & Heller, J. I. (1982). Knowledge structure and problem solving in physics. *Educational Psychologist, 17*(2), 102–127.

Riccomini, P. J., & Witzel, B. S. (2010). *Response to intervention in math.* Thousand Oaks, CA: Corwin Press.

Rittle-Johnson, B., & Alibali, M. W. (1999). Conceptual and procedural knowledge of mathematics: Does one lead to the other? *Journal of Educational Psychology, 91*(1), 175–189.

Schwab, J. R., Tucci, S., & Jolivette, K. (2013). Integrating schema-based instruction and response cards for students with learning disabilities and challenging behaviors. *Beyond Behavior, 22,* 24–30.

Siegler, R., Carpenter, T., Fennell, F., Geary, D., Lewis, J., Okamoto, Y., ... Wray, J. (2010). Developing effective fractions instruction for kindergarten through 8th grade: A practice guide. NCEE #2010-4039. National Center for Education Evaluation and Regional Assistance, Institute of Education Sciences, U.S. Department of Education, Washington, DC.

Stacey, K. (2012). The international assessment of mathematical literacy: PISA 2012 framework and items. Paper presented at the 12th International Congress on Mathematical Education, July 2012, Seoul, Korea.

Star, J. R. (2005). Reconceptualizing procedural knowledge. *Journal for Research in Mathematics Education, 36,* 404–411.

Swanson, H. L. (2011). Working memory, attention, and mathematical problem solving: A longitudinal study of elementary school children. *Journal of Educational Psychology*, *103*, 821–837.

Swanson, H. L., & Sachse-Lee, C. (2001). Mathematical problem solving and working memory in children with learning disabilities: Both executive and phonological processes are important. *Journal of Experimental Child Psychology*, *79*, 294–321.

Sweller, J., Chandler, P., Tierney, P., & Cooper, M. (1990). Cognitive load as a factor in the structuring of technical material. *Journal of Experimental Psychology: General*, *119*(2), 176–192.

Trainin, G., & Swanson, H. L. (2005). Cognition, metacognition, and achievement of college students with learning disabilities. *Learning Disability Quarterly*, *28*, 261–272.

van Garderen, D. (2007). Teaching students with LD to use diagrams to solve mathematical word problems. *Journal of Learning Disabilities*, *40*, 540–553.

Walker, D. W., & Poteet, J. A. (1990). A Comparison of two methods of teaching mathematics story problem-solving with learning disabled students. *National Forum of Special Education Journal*, *1*, 44–51.

What Works Clearinghouse. (2011). *WWC procedures and version 2.1 standards handbook*. Washington, DC: Author. Retrieved from http://ies.ed.gov/ncee/wwc/documentsum.aspx?sid = 19

Woodward, J., & Montague, M. (2002). Meeting the challenge of mathematics reform for students with LD. *Journal of Special Education*, *36*, 89–101.

Xin, Y. P. (2008). The effect of schema-based instruction in solving mathematics word problems: An emphasis on prealgebraic conceptualization of multiplicative relations. *Journal for Research in Mathematics Education*, *39*, 526–551.

Xin, Y. P., & Jitendra, A. K. (1999). The effects of instruction in solving mathematical word problems for students with learning problems: A meta-analysis. *Journal of Special Education*, *32*, 207–225.

Xin, Y. P., Jitendra, A. K., & Deatline-Buchman, A. (2005). Effects of mathematical word problem-solving instruction on middle school students with learning problems. *Journal of Special Education*, *39*, 181–192.

Zheng, X., Swanson, H. L., & Marcoulides, G. A. (2011). Working memory components as predictors of children's mathematical word problem solving. *Journal of Experimental Child Psychology*, *110*, 481–498.

CHAPTER 4

EFFECTIVE AND INEFFECTIVE WRITING PRACTICES FOR STUDENTS WITH DISABILITIES

Amy Gillespie Rouse and Alyson A. Collins

ABSTRACT

Struggling writers and students with disabilities tend to have difficulties with multiple aspects of the writing process. Therefore, in this chapter, we describe Self-Regulated Strategy Development (SRSD; Harris, Graham, Mason, & Friedlander, 2008). SRSD is a writing intervention with extensive research demonstrating its effectiveness for improving the writing quality of struggling writers and students with disabilities when implemented by both teachers and researchers in a variety of educational settings. We also describe an ineffective writing practice, stand-alone grammar instruction. Although this type of grammar instruction is explicit, it is removed from an authentic writing context, and decades of research have demonstrated its negative effects on students' writing quality. We close the chapter with recommendations for future research on SRSD as well as general suggestions for teachers who provide writing instruction to struggling writers and students with disabilities.

Keywords: Students with disabilities; SRSD; grammar; writing; strategy instruction

Instructional Practices with and without Empirical Validity
Advances in Learning and Behavioral Disabilities, Volume 29, 61–84
ISSN: 0735-004X/doi:10.1108/S0735-004X20160000029004

Writing is a 21st century skill. It permeates our society and daily lives (e.g., email, text messaging, social media) and is necessary for success in our nation's classrooms and work force (The National Commission on Writing, 2003, 2004, 2006). In K-12 classrooms, teachers often use writing to assess students' learning across subject areas (e.g., essays in History, summaries of what was read in English/Language Arts, lab reports in Science; Graham, 2006). At the postsecondary level, writing skills are typically assessed for college admissions and used as a measure of learning in most college coursework. Additionally, employers evaluate writing skills for hiring and promotion decisions (The National Commission on Writing, 2004, 2006).

Yet, both teachers and students report spending little time on writing in the classroom, with teachers assigning few written tasks that involve multiple paragraphs and few that require students to analyze or interpret information (Cutler & Graham, 2008; Lenhart, Arafeh, Smith, & Macgill, 2008). Moreover, less than half of primary-grade teachers who completed a national survey reported receiving adequate college preparation and training to teach writing (Cutler & Graham, 2008), and less than one-fourth of secondary teachers reported adequate training to teach writing (Kiuhara, Graham, & Hawken, 2009).

With inadequate teacher preparation and little instructional time spent on writing, it may not be surprising that the majority of students in grades 4, 8, and 12 in the United States do not demonstrate *proficient*, or grade-level, writing skills (National Center for Education Statistics, 2012; Persky, Daane, & Jin, 2003). In the most recent assessment years, only 28% of fourth-graders (Persky et al., 2003) and 27% each of eighth and twelfth graders (National Center for Education Statistics, 2012) met or exceeded grade-level writing expectations on the National Assessment of Education Progress (NAEP) writing assessment. Furthermore, because NAEP writing scores have not significantly changed since 1998 (National Center for Education Statistics, 2012; Persky et al., 2003), it appears current writing instruction is not adequate for producing students who can create thoughtful, engaging, and coherent written compositions (The National Commission on Writing, 2003).

For certain subgroups of students, the need for better writing instruction is more pressing. Compared to their nondisabled peers, only 7% of fourth-grade students with disabilities and 5% each of eighth and twelfth grade students with disabilities performed at or above grade-level expectations on the most recent NAEP writing assessments (National Center for Education Statistics, 2012; Persky et al., 2003). These results are particularly disconcerting given what we know about the writing struggles many students with disabilities face.

Much of the research examining effective writing instruction for students with disabilities has focused on students with learning disabilities (LD), so more is known about the typical developmental trajectory and writing performance of this group of students (De La Paz, 2007). However, research also shows that the writing difficulties experienced by students with LD are often similar to those of struggling writers and students with other disabilities (i.e., students with emotional and behavioral disorders [EBD], speech/language difficulties, attention deficit/hyperactivity disorders; De La Paz, 2007; Graham & Harris, 2005a; Little et al., 2010). Therefore, next we examine common writing difficulties across all of these groups of students.

Students with disabilities tend to have difficulties learning and mastering writing skills when compared to their peers without disabilities (De La Paz, 2007; Graham & Harris, 2005a). They often produce writing that is shorter, less coherent, and less sophisticated than that of their nondisabled peers. Furthermore, students with disabilities frequently have difficulties with self-regulation, which impede their ability to manage the multiple cognitive processes involved in skilled writing (Englert, Zhao, Dunsmore, Collings, & Wolbers, 2007; Harris, Graham, & Mason, 2003). Often, students with disabilities struggle with more basic writing skills, such as handwriting and spelling. With increased focus on these lower-level writing skills, students with disabilities have less cognitive space to devote to the higher-level writing processes needed to generate meaningful writing content targeted for their topic and audience (Baker, Gersten, & Graham, 2003). Students with disabilities also tend to spend less time planning for, revising, and editing their writing compared to their peers without disabilities (Graham & Harris, 2012). This may be because they often have less knowledge about what the writing process entails; thus, they use a simplified version of the steps needed to produce high-quality texts (Graham, Schwartz, & MacArthur, 1993; Saddler & Graham, 2007). Lastly, students with disabilities often lack motivation to write and fail to persist when writing tasks become difficult (Harris et al., 2003).

To address the writing challenges frequently experienced by students with disabilities (and those at-risk for disabilities), we feel it is important to highlight an effective practice carefully designed to meet the multifaceted writing needs of these students that has high-quality research support. Self-Regulated Strategy Development, or SRSD, developed by Karen Harris, Steve Graham, and their colleagues (Harris, 1982; Harris, Graham, Mason, & Friedlander, 2008), is a widely researched writing intervention, is effective for struggling writers and students with a wide range of disabilities (Ennis & Jolivette, 2012; Gillespie & Graham, 2014; Graham, Harris, & McKeown, 2013), and meets standards for an evidence-based practice (Baker, Chard, Ketterlin-Geller, Apichatabutra, & Doabler, 2009). We contrast SRSD with stand-alone grammar instruction, a writing practice shown to have negative effects on students' writing quality (Graham & Perin, 2007a, 2007b), explaining why this type of instruction is likely ineffective and providing a research-supported alternative for grammar instruction. We conclude the chapter with directions for future research on SRSD as well as general recommendations for providing effective writing instruction to students with disabilities.

SRSD: AN EVIDENCE-BASED WRITING PRACTICE

Developed in the early 1980s, Harris and colleagues (Harris, 1982; Harris & Graham, 1992) originally designed SRSD to address the cognitive, behavioral, and affective difficulties students with LD experience in writing. Since then, SRSD has been tested with a variety of student populations, and its positive effects are well documented for struggling writers (Graham & Perin, 2007b; Rogers & Graham, 2008), students with LD (Cook & Bennett, 2014; Gillespie & Graham, 2014), and students with EBD (Ennis & Jolivette, 2012; Graham et al., 2013). As previously noted, students with disabilities encounter a number of obstacles when writing as consequence of inadequate self-regulation strategies, weaknesses in critical writing skills, lack of knowledge about writing and what the writing process entails, and less motivation to write (Graham, 2006). The SRSD framework consists of six instructional stages designed to directly and explicitly address these writing difficulties (Harris, 1982; Harris et al., 2003). The six instructional stages were constructed on sound theoretical models, which is one reason SRSD is highly effective.

Theoretical Basis and Rationale

At the core, SRSD relies on theories that depict the multiple cognitive, behavioral, and affective processes that make the act of writing so complex (Graham & Harris, 2012; Harris et al., 2003). Although models of the writing process have become increasingly sophisticated over the years, they have consistently recognized the contribution of cognitive processes, knowledge, task environment, and more recently motivation (Graham, 2006). Seminal models of writing depict writing as a problem-solving activity during which the writer coordinates a number of mental processes to meet writing goals (Bereiter & Scardamalia, 1987; Flower & Hayes, 1981). To produce a composition, a writer draws upon knowledge of the content (i.e., topic) and the process of writing from long-term memory, while simultaneously receiving input from the environment and from the text he or she is producing. The writer must also self-monitor critical writing processes, including planning, translating or transcribing ideas, and reviewing what has been written (Flower & Hayes, 1981). In Hayes' revised model of writing (1996), motivation and affect also exert influence, with writing goals, predispositions towards writing, and feelings or attitudes about writing impacting the writer throughout the process.

SRSD draws on these theoretical models as it focuses on modifying cognitive behaviors and providing strategy instruction to address important components of the writing process (Graham & Harris, 2009, 2012). Specifically, SRSD provides students with explicit instruction in strategies that support basic writing processes such as planning, composing, and revising (Harris et al., 2008). As students move through the six instructional stages of SRSD, they learn to engage in more complex writing processes (e.g., planning for writing, self-regulation of strategy use) and to independently use specific writing strategies. By directly teaching students effective and efficient writing strategies, SRSD facilitates improvement in writing performance (Graham et al., 2013) and also increases confidence and motivation for writing (Mason, Meadan, Hedin, & Cramer, 2012).

In addition to its strong theoretical base, more than three decades of research offer evidence that SRSD improves writing quality as well as enhances students' motivation and self-efficacy for writing (Graham & Harris, 2012; Harris et al., 2008). Below, we present a detailed description of the SRSD instructional framework along with an overview of the substantial research base demonstrating its effectiveness.

SRSD Instructional Framework

Numerous writing strategies can be taught within the SRSD instructional framework, ranging from genre-specific (e.g., strategies for story writing, strategies for writing a persuasive essay) to more skills-based (e.g., strategies for including more vocabulary words in writing, strategies for revising).

Regardless of the writing genre or writing skill taught, all SRSD lessons are organized around six basic stages described in detail below (Harris et al., 2008).

Stage 1: Develop Background Knowledge
In Stage 1, students develop the background knowledge and skills needed to learn the writing strategy. Teachers explicitly define and discuss key vocabulary words related to the writing genre and strategy. To prepare students for learning the writing strategy, teachers read examples of texts in the writing genre, identifying characteristics unique to the genre. At this early stage, teachers also introduce self-instructions, with an emphasis on how self-talk contributes to the writing process.

Stage 2: Discuss It
In Stage 2, students evaluate the significance and benefits of the writing and self-regulation strategies. Together, teachers and students identify contexts and situations in which the writing strategy could be applied. During these conversations, teachers explicitly discuss how to use the strategy when writing. In addition, students learn to examine and graph current writing performance as a precursor to setting future learning goals.

Stage 3: Model It
In Stage 3, teachers explicitly model how to use the writing strategy, complete the composing process, and use self-instructions. During this stage, teachers use think-alouds, or demonstrations of the thought processes required for successful strategy use. Teachers simultaneously model self-regulation strategies during the think-alouds. Students also learn how to set attainable goals and how to self-assess progress towards those goals. Benefits of using the writing strategy, self-regulation strategies, self-statements, and goal setting remain a consistent focus of discussions throughout this stage.

Stage 4: Memorize It
In Stage 4, students memorize the associated mnemonic and steps of the writing strategy. This stage typically spans across the other SRSD stages, often occurring during the early stages. During each SRSD lesson, students spend time memorizing the mnemonic and strategy steps, which can be accomplished through a number of activities. For example, students may practice memorizing the strategy with cue cards, teachers may quiz students, or students may quiz each other.

Stage 5: Support It

In Stage 5, teachers scaffold and support students' use of the writing strategy, self-instructions, and other self-regulation procedures during the composing process. In this stage, teachers and students often engage in collaborative writing activities, while teachers gradually fade scaffolds to encourage student independence in the writing process. Teachers also begin discussing generalization and maintenance to facilitate transfer and long-term strategy use.

Stage 6: Independent Performance

In Stage 6, teachers provide students with opportunities to independently practice applying the writing strategy, self-instructions, and other self-regulation procedures during the composing process. Students evaluate strategy effectiveness, goals met, and improvements in writing performance. Lessons also promote generalization and maintenance to ensure transfer and long-term strategy use.

Implementing SRSD

Table 1 provides an example of how an instructor might proceed through the six stages of SRSD to teach students to use the POW + TIDE strategy (Mason, Reid, & Hagaman, 2012) for composing informative texts. For further information on specific SRSD strategies, we recommend the following books (full citations are in the reference list at the end of the chapter): *Writing Better: Effective Strategies for Teaching Students with Learning Difficulties* (Graham & Harris, 2005b), *Making the Writing Process Work: Strategies for Composition and Self Regulation* (Harris & Graham, 1996), *Powerful Writing Strategies for All Students* (Harris et al., 2008), and *Building Comprehension in Adolescents: Powerful Strategies for Improving Reading and Writing in Content Areas* (Mason et al., 2012). Interested readers can also consult www.thinkSRSD.com for SRSD lesson plans as well as videos of students and teachers using SRSD in their classrooms.

Embedded in the six stages of SRSD is explicit instruction in four types of self-regulation: (a) goal setting, (b) self-instructions, (c) self-monitoring, and (d) self-reinforcement (Harris et al., 2008). For goal setting, students learn to identify areas for personal writing growth and to set specific goals that are attainable in both difficulty and proximity. Like goal setting, self-instructions are explicitly modeled throughout the SRSD lessons to encourage students to develop an internal dialogue (self-talk) to help them actively engage in critical writing processes. During lessons, teachers model and encourage the use of positive self-statements (e.g., I can do this, I like

Table 1.   SRSD Example with POW + TIDE for Informative Writing
(Mason et al., 2012).

SRSD Stage	Examples of Teaching Activities
Stage 1: Develop Background Knowledge	• Review mnemonics (POW: *P*ick my idea, *O*rganize my notes, *W*rite and say more; TIDE: *T*opic sentence, at least three *I*mportant *D*etails, *E*nding). • Tell students they will use TIDE to complete the *O* step in POW. • Read aloud examples of the informative genre, pointing out genre-specific characteristics and what makes a good informative response.
Stage 2: Discuss It	• Discuss when to use the POW + TIDE strategy. • Students read (or listen to) an example of informative writing, identifying each part of TIDE in the writing. • Students examine their own informative writing and graph how many parts of TIDE they included. • Discuss learning goals (i.e., to include all parts of TIDE the next time they write an informative response).

Stage 3: Model It	• Model the POW + TIDE strategy by using a graphic organizer to make notes for each step of the strategy.
	• Model how to transfer notes from the graphic organizer to complete sentences and paragraphs in a written response.
	• Think aloud while modeling how to:
	  ○ Address the writing prompt (*P* of POW)
	  ○ Make notes to plan for writing (*O* of POW, all steps of TIDE)
	  ○ Use self-statements (e.g., I'm almost done, I like this idea)
	  ○ Write the informative response (*W* of POW)
	• Ask students to identify self-statements the instructor used.
	• Students write their own self-statements (i.e., things to say to themselves to get started with a writing task, motivate themselves, evaluate their writing, and reinforce themselves when finished).

Stage 4: Memorize It	• Practice memorizing POW + TIDE with cue cards. • Give quick quizzes to assess memorization. • Review mnemonics and strategies to aid memorization as needed. *Note.* This stage can occur throughout other stages as well.
Stage 5: Support It	• Guide students through the POW + TIDE steps (e.g., I remember that I start with P, pick the idea I am going to write about), allowing them to share ideas with their classmates. • Students may collaborate or write about the same ideas, but each student should write notes and an informative response on their own. • Have students graph the number of parts of TIDE included in their responses. • Begin discussing other settings where using POW + TIDE might be appropriate.
Stage 6: Independent Performance	• Provide opportunities for students to use POW + TIDE independently. • Remind students to apply POW + TIDE in other classes and other situations, when appropriate.

what I've written here, I'm almost done) to highlight writing growth and progress towards achievement goals. Intertwined with goal setting and self-instructions are strategies for facilitating self-monitoring of writing behaviors and documenting, or self-recording, if certain behaviors occurred. Instruction in self-monitoring may focus on teaching students to (a) understand writing prompts and what they require, (b) pre-plan before composing, (c) self-evaluate writing performance and strategy use, and (d) use coping statements and self-encouragement dialogue. Students are taught how to self-assess personal writing performance and to graph their progress in using writing strategies. Additionally, SRSD promotes continuous self-reinforcement during the writing process to teach students how to select and apply reinforcement strategies for goals that have been met (Harris et al., 2008).

One final premise of SRSD that differentiates it from other types of writing strategy instruction is that it is criterion-based and the six stages are designed to be recursive and flexible (Harris et al., 2008). Because they are not linear or rigid in progression, SRSD lessons often span across multiple stages and at any given time students may be in different stages from their classmates. Booster sessions, or repeated lessons, can be interwoven into the lesson sequence to ensure students master key writing strategies. This aspect of SRSD allows teachers to monitor students' writing progress and gives them the autonomy to pace their progression through the six stages based on student response to instruction. Moreover, the criterion-based, systematic instruction of SRSD ensures all students successfully master key writing strategies that support the development of good writing behaviors and critical writing skills (Harris et al., 2008).

Research and the Effectiveness of SRSD

As previously noted, SRSD is supported by more than 30 years of research (Graham & Harris, 2012; Harris et al., 2008). As the number of existing studies has exponentially increased, a number of meta-analyses have aggregated the effects of SRSD across studies (Gillespie & Graham, 2014; Graham et al., 2013; Rogers & Graham, 2008). The statistics we report from these meta-analyses include effect sizes (ESs) and percentage of nonoverlapping data points (PND). ESs are aggregates of the individual study effects from true-experiments, quasi-experiments, and, in some cases, studies where students served as their own controls (Gillespie & Graham, 2014; Graham et al., 2013; Graham & Perin, 2007a, 2007b). The overall (i.e., average weighted) ESs we report account for study sample sizes, under the assumption that the effects from studies with larger samples should receive more weight in overall calculations. ESs provide an estimate, in standard deviation units, of how much better the students who received SRSD instruction performed than a control or comparison group (Borenstein, Hedges, Higgins, & Rothstein, 2009). For single-subject studies, we report average PND. PND for an individual single-subject study is the percentage of data points during the SRSD treatment phase (and sometimes generalization or maintenance phases) that did not overlap with data points from the baseline phase, when students were not receiving SRSD instruction (Scruggs, Mastropieri, & Casto, 1987). PNDs from individual studies were averaged across all relevant SRSD studies to calculate the average PNDs we discuss in this chapter.

Although reviewing the entire body of SRSD research is beyond the scope of this chapter, we summarize the results and key findings from the most recent and comprehensive meta-analysis of SRSD research (Graham et al., 2013) to describe the types of students, instructors, and educational contexts for which SRSD has been shown to be most effective. In addition, we include results from meta-analyses examining SRSD with specific student populations, such as students who are struggling writers and students with LD.

Diverse Groups of Learners
Over the years, researchers have examined the effectiveness of SRSD with diverse student populations, including groups of students with disabilities. Across six studies, Graham et al. (2013) found a large statistically significant effect (ES = 2.37) of SRSD on the writing quality of students with LD in grades 4 to high school. In single-subject design studies, Graham and colleagues reported average PND at posttest for writing quality was 90 (across six studies) and average PND for inclusion of genre elements was 95 (across 11 studies) for students with LD in grades 2 to college who received SRSD instruction. In most of these studies, students maintained gains in writing quality and elements after the SRSD treatment (average PND for writing quality = 79 at maintenance; average PND for genre elements = 86 at maintenance). In a later meta-analysis, Gillespie and Graham (2014) found strategy instruction (a key component in SRSD) had a large, statistically significant effect (ES = 1.09) on the writing quality of students with LD in grades 4−10 (across 15 studies). More specifically, they reported that studies implementing SRSD produced statistically larger effects (ES = 1.33; seven studies) on the writing quality of students with

LD than studies implementing other types of strategy instruction (ES = 0.76; eight studies; Gillespie & Graham, 2014).

Parallel lines of research have also investigated the effects of SRSD with students with EBD or those at-risk for EBD. Graham et al. (2013) found SRSD to be highly effective for improving writing quality (ES = 1.97; four studies) and inclusion of genre elements (average PND = 81; eight studies) for students with EBD in grades 2–10. Particularly important for students with EBD, SRSD was successfully used as a secondary intervention within the context of a Positive Behavior Support (PBS) program. In this context, second-grade students with internalizing and externalizing behaviors as well as generally antisocial behaviors all benefited from SRSD instruction, demonstrating improvements in writing quality and inclusion of genre elements (Lane et al., 2008; Little et al., 2010).

On a broader scale, evidence for the effectiveness of SRSD goes beyond studies focused on implementation with students with LD or EBD. For more generally identified struggling writers (i.e., writers who performed below the 25th percentile on a standardized writing test), Graham et al. (2013) found large, statistically significant effects of SRSD on writing quality and inclusion of genre elements (ESs = 1.73 and 1.36, respectively) for students in grades 2–10. Rogers and Graham (2008) also reported an average PND of 96 for the writing quality of struggling writers in grades 2–8 who received SRSD instruction; the gains made in writing quality were maintained after treatment (average PND = 90 at maintenance).

In addition, researchers have investigated the efficacy of SRSD when implemented with a full range of students in the general education classroom, where many students with disabilities receive at least some, if not all, of their writing instruction (Forness, Kim, & Walker, 2012; Pastor & Reuben, 2008). For all students (grades 2–8), Graham et al. (2013) reported ESs of 1.51 and 2.93 (for writing quality and elements, respectively) when SRSD instruction was provided in the general education classroom.

Finally, researchers have compared the effectiveness of SRSD across different ages of students (i.e., elementary vs. secondary). Across the extant literature, SRSD has been shown to be an effective writing intervention at all grade levels. For elementary students, Graham et al. (2013) reported large effects of SRSD on writing quality (ES = 1.40, average PND = 85) and inclusion of genre elements (ES = 2.41, average PND = 96). For secondary students, effects of SRSD on writing quality (ES = 2.18, average PND = 88) and elements (ES = 1.86, average PND = 89) were also large (Graham et al., 2013). For both true- and quasi-experimental studies as well as single-subject design studies, Graham et al. found no statistically significant differences when comparing the two age groups (elementary vs. secondary). Thus, SRSD was not more effective for one age group over the other.

Different Educational Environments and Instructors
The majority of the empirical research on SRSD involves students receiving instruction in small groups or one-on-one settings (Ennis & Jolivette, 2012; Gillespie & Graham, 2014), contexts most commonly referred to in Response to Intervention (RTI) models as Tier 2 and Tier 3. A few recent studies, however, have also shown that SRSD produced positive writing outcomes when implemented in general education classrooms as Tier 1 instruction with students in grades 2 and 3 (Harris, Lane, Driscoll et al., 2012; Harris, Lane, Graham et al., 2012). These studies found students who received Tier 1 SRSD instruction made greater writing gains when composing story and opinion essays than students in control classrooms. The effectiveness of SRSD across Tiers 1, 2, and 3 demonstrates the versatility of its instructional framework and the capabilities for adaptions in different educational environments.

Critical to the practicality of SRSD in school contexts, researchers have also investigated differences in the effectiveness of SRSD when implemented by researchers versus teachers. Graham et al. (2013) reported large effects on the writing quality of students in grades 2 to high school when researchers delivered SRSD instruction (ES = 2.17) as well as when teachers delivered SRSD instruction (ES = 1.52). Graham and colleagues found similarly large ESs for inclusion of genre elements (ES = 1.86: SRSD delivered by researchers; ES = 2.55: SRSD delivered by teachers). Interestingly, there were no statistically significant differences for students' writing quality based on who delivered the SRSD instruction, but Graham et al. found statistically larger ESs for inclusion of genre elements when *teachers* provided SRSD instruction.

Social Validity
Another consideration important for implementation is that studies have repeatedly demonstrated the social validity of SRSD (Baker et al., 2009; Ennis & Jolivette, 2012; Harris, Lane, Driscoll et al., 2012; Harris, Lane, Graham et al., 2012). Teachers have commented on the improvements in writing and attitudes of students who received SRSD instruction (Harris, Graham, & Adkins, 2015; Harris, Lane, Graham et al., 2012). In many studies, SRSD exceeded both teachers' and students' expectations (Harris, Lane, Graham et al., 2012), and each indicated that they would recommend

SRSD to others (Kiuhara, O'Neill, Hawken, & Graham, 2012). Studies also showed students viewed SRSD positively and identified it as a means for helping them organize their ideas and become better writers (MacArthur & Philippakos, 2010; Mason, Snyder, Sukhram, & Kedem, 2006). Furthermore, SRSD has bolstered students' self-efficacy and confidence in their writing skills (Kiuhara et al., 2012; MacArthur & Philippakos, 2010).

Collectively, the preceding findings underscore the effectiveness of SRSD in improving writing quality and inclusion of genre elements for diverse populations of learners when implemented by different instructors in a variety of educational contexts. Additionally, social validity data indicate practicality and feasibility of SRSD practices and procedures. Thus, we contend that SRSD is an instructional intervention that should be in the toolbox of all teachers, particularly those who instruct struggling writers and students with disabilities. In contrast, stand-alone grammar instruction, which we describe next, is a practice that has proven ineffective for improving the writing quality of struggling writers and students with disabilities. We describe this type of grammar instruction, present research demonstrating its negative effects on students' writing quality, and offer alternatives for providing grammar instruction in meaningful writing contexts.

STAND-ALONE GRAMMAR INSTRUCTION: AN INEFFECTIVE WRITING PRACTICE

Stand-alone, or *traditional*, grammar instruction has been defined in multiple ways (Smith, Cheville, & Hillocks, 2006), but in the educational context it typically refers to explicit teaching of parts of speech (e.g., noun, verb), parts of sentences (e.g., subject, predicate), and rules for writing mechanics (e.g., capitalization, punctuation) and usage. Often, teachers provide such instruction through worksheets or workbook activities, sentence diagraming exercises, and lessons in defining components of the English language (Graham & Perin, 2007b; Saddler & Graham, 2007), all of which take place out of the context of authentic writing.

Theoretical Basis and Rationale

Given what researchers have theorized about the writing process (discussed earlier in the chapter), grammar instruction seems to make sense. When translating ideas for writing into written (or typed) text, students must understand multiple aspects of written English, including grammar, to make appropriate word- and sentence-level (i.e., syntax) choices to convey their meaning (Flower & Hayes, 1981; Saddler, 2007). If a student is preoccupied with remembering appropriate grammar (e.g., Is this the correct verb tense? Do I use the article *a* or *an* before this word? Do the words make sense in this order?), then he or she has less room in working memory to attend to other important writing activities, such as generating and organizing text, conveying meaning to the audience, reviewing and revising what has been written, and monitoring writing goals (Saddler & Graham, 2005; Scardamalia & Bereiter, 1986).

Similarly, grammar instruction makes sense given what we know about the difficulties many students with disabilities experience with writing. Research shows that compared to their peers, struggling writers and students with disabilities produce writing that is shorter, is less syntactically complex, and contains more grammatical errors (De La Paz, 2007; Saddler & Graham, 2005). These grammatical errors can influence how teachers (or other raters) score and interpret the written texts of these students (Graham, Harris, & Hebert, 2011). Thus, teaching struggling writers and students with disabilities to use correct grammar should improve their overall writing quality, because it would free up working memory space to focus on higher-level writing processes and because it would remove errors from writing that could impact meaning and judgment of overall writing quality.

However, despite the need to understand and apply appropriate grammar in their writing, stand-alone grammar instruction is not supported by research as an effective practice for students with disabilities. We, as well as others (Andrews et al., 2006; Hillocks, 1984; Smith et al., 2006), believe that the critical feature of traditional, or stand-alone, grammar instruction that likely renders it ineffective is that it is decontextualized and provided outside of authentic writing tasks.

Research on Stand-Alone Grammar Instruction

Decades of research indicate that teaching grammar rules and routines out of the context of actual writing, as with stand-alone grammar instruction, does not positively impact students' writing quality (Andrews et al., 2006; Graham & Perin, 2007a, 2007b). In fact, some argue that stand-alone grammar instruction can have a negative impact on students' writing skills and is a waste of valuable instructional time (Hillocks, 1984; Perera, 1984).

Additionally, in their influential chapter synthesizing research and theory on written composition, Scardamalia and Bereiter (1986) critiqued the use of writing activities or exercises that removed the authenticity (i.e., an audience for whom one is writing) and intent (i.e., to communicate thoughts and ideas to that audience) of actual writing, instead offering sentence combining (discussed later in this section of the chapter) as a plausible alternative.

Likely a result of years of research on its ineffectiveness (Andrews et al., 2006; Graham & Perin, 2007a, 2007b), research on stand-alone grammar instruction for students with disabilities is scarce. In their meta-analysis, Graham and Perin (2007a, 2007b) found 11 studies of traditional, or stand-alone, grammar instruction. Overall, explicit teaching of parts of speech and sentence structure had a small but statistically significant *negative* effect (ES = −0.32) on the writing quality of students in grades 4–11. Of the studies Graham and Perin reviewed, only two involved students who were struggling writers (Saddler & Graham, 2005) or students with disabilities (i.e., students with LD, a student with other health impairments [OHI], and a student with a hearing impairment; Anderson, 1997). In these two studies, students in grade 4 (Saddler & Graham, 2005) and grade 5 (Anderson, 1997) who received stand-alone grammar instruction performed worse on measures of writing quality than peers who received sentence-combining instruction (Saddler & Graham, 2005; ES = −0.42) or peers who received writing strategy instruction (Anderson, 1997; ES = −1.40).

In contrast, several single-subject design studies reported positive impacts of grammar instruction for struggling writers (Hermann, Semb, & Hopkins, 1976) and students with LD (Campbell, Brady, & Linehan, 1991; Dowis, 1991; Dowis & Schloss, 1992) and intellectual disabilities (ID; Campbell et al., 1991). However, researchers in these studies did not measure students' writing quality after receiving grammar instruction, as with the grammar studies Graham and Perin (2007a, 2007b) reviewed. Instead, students took assessments measuring their ability to apply the specific grammar rules they had learned during intervention; that is, students learned grammar skills via traditional, decontextualized methods and were asked to demonstrate their learning on multiple choice and fill-in-the-blank exercises that were also removed from an authentic writing context.

Hermann et al. (1976) found positive effects on grammar knowledge posttests for struggling writers in grade 6 who learned rules for using capitalization, conjunctions, and subject-verb agreement (PND = 88). Similarly, in Dowis and Schloss (1992), grade 6 students with LD who learned grammar rules for adverbial phrases and possessives had a PND of

88 on grammar knowledge assessments at posttest. In Dowis (1991), students with LD in grades 5 and 6 who learned rules for using adjectives, forming possessives, and using proper capitalization had a PND of 75 on a grammar probes at posttest. Lastly, in Campbell et al. (1991) two students with LD and one student with ID (all age 9) who received instruction from a peer on using correct capitalization demonstrated a PND of 79 on grammar posttests. In two of the studies (Campbell et al., 1991; Dowis, 1991) students maintained gains in grammar knowledge after treatment and in one study (Dowis & Schloss, 1992) students did not maintain gains in grammar knowledge; Hermann et al. did not assess maintenance effects.

From our review of the existing literature, it is evident that stand-alone grammar instruction is an ineffective practice that fails to facilitate acquisition of critical writing skills needed to become a proficient writer. Although stand-alone grammar instruction may lead to improvement in discrete grammar skills, as evidenced in several single-subject design studies (Campbell et al., 1991; Dowis, 1991; Dowis & Schloss, 1992; Hermann et al., 1976), instruction in this writing area rarely transfers to application in the writing process and has been shown to negatively impact students' writing quality (Graham & Perin, 2007a, 2007b).

An Alternative to Stand-Alone Grammar Instruction: Sentence Combining

Because there are many years of research showing the ineffectiveness of stand-alone grammar instruction for students in general (Andrews et al., 2006; Hillocks, 1984) and a small literature indicating this type of grammar instruction has negative impacts on the writing quality of struggling writers and students with disabilities (Graham & Perin, 2007a, 2007b), it is important to consider research-based alternatives. As discussed earlier, students with disabilities tend to make frequent grammatical errors in their writing and a focus on correct grammar could deter them from focusing on the content and meaning of their written compositions (De La Paz, 2007; Graham et al., 2011; Saddler & Graham, 2005). Therefore, we offer a brief description of sentence combining, a research-supported practice for teaching students about syntactical choices as well as grammatical rules within an authentic writing context. Although much of the research on sentence combining has focused on the general student population (i.e., students with a full range of writing skills), researchers have shown positive effects of sentence-combining interventions for struggling writers (Saddler & Graham, 2005) and students with LD (Saddler, Asaro, & Behforooz, 2008; Saddler, Behforooz, & Asaro, 2008).

Sentence combining has more than 40 years of research demonstrating, with only a few exceptions, its positive effects on students' syntactical maturity (Andrews et al., 2006; Saddler, 2007) and gains in syntactical maturity lead to higher quality writing (Saddler & Graham, 2005). In fact, in five studies of sentence combining with students in grades 4–11, Graham and Perin (2007a, 2007b) found students who received sentence-combining instruction demonstrated higher quality writing than students who received traditional grammar instruction (ES = 0.50). For struggling and lower-performing writers, the ES was 0.46 (Saddler & Graham, 2005). In addition, Saddler and colleagues (Saddler, Asaro et al., 2008; Saddler, Behforooz et al., 2008) demonstrated positive effects of sentence combining on the writing quality of struggling writers and students with LD in grade 4 (PND for writing quality = 88 and 100 for each study, respectively).

With sentence combining, students learn about different syntactical choices as they practice combining simple phrases into more complex ones (Saddler & Graham, 2005). They are not taught discrete rules or routines for syntax, as with stand-alone grammar instruction. Rather, students are instructed to consider a variety of alternatives when combining (or decombining run-on) sentences, with a focus on the meaning, content, and clarity of their writing (Saddler, 2007). During sentence-combining activities, teachers can also focus on specific grammar skills, such as teaching students to use (a) proper punctuation, (b) conjunctions and compound sentences, (c) adjectives and adverbs, (d) compound subjects and predicates, (e) possessive nouns, (f) adverbial clauses, (g) relative clauses, and (h) appositives (Saddler, 2007, 2013). Saddler (2007, 2013) recommended teachers find material for conducting short (10–15 minutes) sentence-combining sessions from students' own writing or from literature students are familiar with, thus, creating an authentic context for syntax and grammar practice. For a more thorough description of sentence combining, see two chapters (Saddler, 2007, 2013) on this topic.

CONCLUSIONS

We wrote this chapter to provide a description of SRSD, a writing practice with years of research supporting its effectiveness with struggling writers and students with disabilities. We countered this effective practice with a commonly used but ineffective writing practice: stand-alone, or traditional, grammar instruction. The robustness of SRSD (i.e., with a variety of learners, delivered by teachers and researchers in a variety of settings) makes it an indispensable instructional tool for teachers of students who struggle with writing, are at-risk for future writing difficulties, or who have disabilities that impact their writing performance. In contrast, the overwhelming evidence that stand-alone grammar instruction does not have positive impacts on students' writing quality makes it a practice we suggest teachers avoid implementing with their students. Teachers should instead use research-supported alternatives for instruction in syntax and grammar skills, such as sentence combining.

Directions for Future Research

Despite the substantial body of research supporting the effectiveness of SRSD, there is still more work needed to extend the empirical evidence and expand the existing research to other populations of learners. Although there is some evidence that SRSD instruction leads to improvements in writing quality, length, and inclusion of genre elements for students who are English language learners (ELLs; Akincilar, 2010; Korducki, 2001), fewer studies have examined the magnitude of SRSD effects with ELLs compared to other student groups. Similarly, while SRSD is effective in improving writing outcomes across all age groups (Graham et al., 2013), the research on elementary-aged students is more abundant than the research examining secondary learners and beyond (Ennis & Jolivette, 2012). Future research involving high school and college students with varying disabilities would allow for a more thorough evaluation of SRSD and potential adaptations needed for older students. Furthermore, while there is considerable research supporting the effectiveness of SRSD for students with LD and EBD, less is known about SRSD's effects on the writing of students with multiple disabilities, students who are ELLs and have disabilities, or students with ID. Future research should also examine the effects of SRSD with these types of students.

In addition to expanding SRSD research across different populations of learners, more studies are also needed to determine the best methods for disseminating SRSD practices for widespread implementation in classrooms and schools. Recently, researchers have begun examining practice-based professional development to train teachers how to implement SRSD effectively and with high fidelity (Harris et al., 2015; Harris, Lane, Driscoll et al., 2012; Harris, Lane, Graham et al., 2012). Practice-based professional development allows teachers to understand SRSD and its components before implementing it with students; teachers also receive ongoing feedback and support as they implement SRSD in their classrooms (see Harris, Lane, Graham et al., 2012 for a more detailed description of this model). Future studies should continue to examine the conditions and factors that make practice-based professional development in SRSD effective (Graham et al., 2013). It is possible video modeling or webcam coaching may be effective extensions of the established practice-based professional development models, but more research is needed to investigate the extent to which these interventions are effective.

Finally, researchers and teachers have primarily applied the SRSD framework in the writing domain, and our review only focuses on the research conducted in writing. In some studies, researchers examined if the SRSD framework is effective when generalized to other academic domains, such as reading or mathematics (Case, Harris, & Graham, 1992; Mason, 2004). However, the SRSD literature extending beyond writing is scarce. The consistently large effects found for SRSD in writing suggest it may be a viable intervention framework to adapt for other domains. Therefore, future studies should explore if the SRSD intervention framework is equally as effective for improving student outcomes in other key academic areas, such as reading comprehension or mathematics problem solving (Graham et al., 2013).

Final Remarks

Although we provided substantial evidence of the effectiveness of SRSD in this chapter, we remind teachers that SRSD by itself does not constitute a writing curriculum. We hope teachers will seek out resources to implement SRSD combined with other effective writing interventions that best meet their students' instructional needs, with the knowledge that currently there is no research supporting a perfect mix of writing practices (Graham & Perin, 2007b). An effective combination of writing practices and instruction will likely change from year to year, as teachers encounter students with different writing needs. Furthermore, effective writing instruction is responsive to students' growth and progress, likely changing throughout the school year as their writing skills develop. We suggest teachers closely monitor the effectiveness of the research-based writing instruction they choose to use in their classrooms, monitoring not only students' writing performance after receiving such instruction but also students' engagement and motivation for writing.

One aspect of writing instruction that we do know works with struggling writers and students with disabilities is explicitness (De La Paz, 2007; Gillespie & Graham, 2014). A second component of effective writing instruction is authenticity (Graham & Perin, 2007b). Therefore, in sum, we remind teachers that writing instruction is best delivered explicitly within authentic and meaningful contexts for writing, just as in the effective writing practices (i.e., SRSD and sentence combining) we discussed in this chapter.

REFERENCES

Akincilar, V. (2010). *The effect of "PLEASE" strategy training through the self-regulated strategy development (SRSD) model on fifth grade EFL students' descriptive writing: Strategy training on planning*. Master's thesis. Retrieved from https://etd.lib.metu.edu.tr/upload/3/12611947/index.pdf

Anderson, A. A. (1997). *The effects of sociocognitive writing strategy instruction on the writing achievement and self-efficacy of students with disabilities and typical achievement in an urban elementary school*. Unpublished doctoral dissertation. University of Houston, Houston, TX.

Andrews, R., Torgerson, C., Beverton, S., Freeman, A., Locke, T., Low, G., Robinson, A., & Zhu, D. (2006). The effects of grammar teaching on writing development. *British Educational Research Journal, 32*(1), 39−55.

Baker, S., Chard, D., Ketterlin-Geller, L., Apichatabutra, C., & Doabler, C. (2009). Teaching writing to at-risk students: The quality of evidence for self-regulated strategy development. *Exceptional Children, 75*, 303−318.

Baker, S., Gersten, R., & Graham, S. (2003). Teaching expressive writing to students with learning disabilities: Research-based applications and examples. *Journal of Learning Disabilities, 36*, 109−123. doi:10.1177/002221940303600204

Bereiter, C., & Scardamalia, M. (1987). *The psychology of written composition*. Hillsdale, NJ: Lawrence Erlbaum.

Borenstein, M., Hedges, L. V., Higgins, J. P. T., & Rothstein, H. R. (2009). *Introduction to meta analysis*. Chichester: Wiley. doi:10.1002/9780470743386

Campbell, B. J., Brady, M. P., & Linehan, S. (1991). Effects of peer-mediated instruction on the acquisition and generalization of written capitalization skills. *Journal of Learning Disabilities, 24*(1), 6−14.

Case, L. P., Harris, K. R., & Graham, S. (1992). Improving the mathematical problem-solving skills of students with learning disabilities: Self-regulated strategy development. *The Journal of Special Education, 26*, 1−19. doi:10.1177/002246699202600101

Cook, K. B., & Bennett, K. E. (2014). Writing interventions for high school students with disabilities: A review of single-case design studies. *Remedial and Special Education, 35*, 344−355.

Cutler, L., & Graham, S. (2008). Primary grade writing instruction: A national survey. *Journal of Educational Psychology*, *100*, 907−919. doi:10.1037/a0012656

De La Paz, S. (2007). Best practices in teaching writing to students with special needs. In S. Graham, C. A. MacArthur, & J. Fitzgerald (Eds.), *Best practices in writing instruction* (pp. 308−328). New York, NY: The Guilford Press.

Dowis, C. L. (1991). *The effects of mini-lesson instruction on the writings of students with learning disabilities within the writing process using whole group instruction.* Unpublished doctoral dissertation. University of Missouri, Columbia, MS.

Dowis, C. L., & Schloss, P. (1992). The impact of mini-lessons on writing skills. *Remedial and Special Education*, *13*(5), 34−42.

Englert, C. S., Zhao, Y., Dunsmore, K., Collings, N. Y., & Wolbers, K. (2007). Scaffolding the writing of students with disabilities through procedural facilitation: Using an internet-based technology to improve performance. *Learning Disability Quarterly*, *30*(1), 9−29.

Ennis, R. P., & Jolivette, K. (2012). Existing research and future directions for self-regulated strategy development with students with and at risk for emotional and behavioral disorders. *The Journal of Special Education*, *48*, 32−45. doi:10.1177/0022466912454682

Flower, L., & Hayes, J. R. (1981). A cognitive process theory of writing. College Composition *and Communication*, *32*, 365−387.

Forness, S. R., Kim, J., & Walker, H. M. (2012). Prevalence of students with EBD: Impact on general education. *Beyond Behavior*, *21*(2), 3−10.

Gillespie, A., & Graham, S. (2014). A meta-analysis of writing interventions for students with learning disabilities. *Exceptional Children*, *80*, 454−473. doi:10.1177/0014402914527238

Graham, S. (2006). Writing. In E. Anderman, P. H. Winne, P. A. Alexander, & L. Corno (Eds.), *Handbook of educational psychology* (2nd ed., pp. 457−478). New York, NY: Routledge.

Graham, S., & Harris, K. R. (2005a). Improving the writing performance of young struggling writers: Theoretical and programmatic research from the center on accelerating student learning. *Journal of Special Education*, *39*(1), 19−33. doi:10.1177/00224669050390010301

Graham, S., & Harris, K. R. (2005b). Writing better: Effective strategies for teaching students *with learning difficulties.* Baltimore, MD: Paul H. Brookes.

Graham, S., & Harris, K. R. (2009). Almost 30 years of writing research: Making sense of it all with The Wrath of Khan. *Learning Disabilities Research & Practice*, *24*, 58−68. doi:10.1111/j.1540-5826.2009.01277

Graham, S., & Harris, K. R. (2012). The role of strategies, knowledge, will, and skills in a 30 year program of research (with homage to Hayes, Fayol, and Boscolo). In V. Berninger (Ed.), *Past, present, and future contributions of cognitive writing research to cognitive psychology* (pp. 177−196). London: Psychology Press.

Graham, S., Harris, K. R., & Hebert, M. (2011). It is more than just the message: Presentation effects in scoring writing. *Focus on Exceptional Children*, *44*(4), 1−12.

Graham, S., Harris, K. R., & McKeown, D. (2013). The writing of students with learning disabilities, meta-analysis of self-regulated strategy development writing intervention studies, and future directions: Redux. In H. L. Swanson, K. R. Harris, & S. Graham (Eds.), *Handbook of learning disabilities* (2nd ed., pp. 405−428). New York, NY: The Guilford Press.

Graham, S., & Perin, D. (2007a). A meta-analysis of writing instruction for adolescent students. *Journal of Educational Psychology*, *99*, 445–476. doi:10.1037/0022-0663.99.3.445

Graham, S., & Perin, D. (2007b). Writing next: Effective strategies to improve writing of adolescents in middle and high schools. A Report to the Carnegie Corporation of New York. Alliance for Excellent Education, Washington, DC.

Graham, S., Schwartz, S. S., & MacArthur, C. A. (1993). Knowledge of writing and the composing process, attitude toward writing, and self-efficacy for students with and without learning disabilities. *Journal of Learning Disabilities*, *26*, 237–249.

Harris, K. R. (1982). Cognitive-behavior modification: Application with exceptional students. *Focus on Exceptional Children*, *15*, 1–16.

Harris, K. R., & Graham, S. (1992). Self-regulated strategy development: A part of the writing process. In M. Pressley, K. R. Harris, & J. T. Guthrie (Eds.), *Promoting academic competence and literacy in school* (pp. 277–309). New York, NY: Academic Press.

Harris, K. R., & Graham, S. (1996). Making the writing process work: Strategies for *composition and self-regulation*. Cambridge, MA: Brookline Books.

Harris, K. R., Graham, S., & Adkins, M. (2015). Practice-based professional development and self-regulated strategy development for Tier 2, at-risk writers in second grade. *Contemporary Educational Psychology*, *40*, 5–16. doi:10.1016/j.cedpsych.2014.02.003

Harris, K. R., Graham, S., & Mason, L. H. (2003). Self-regulated strategy development in the classroom: Part of a balanced approach to writing instruction for students with disabilities. *Focus on Exceptional Children*, *35*, 1–16.

Harris, K. R., Graham, S., Mason, L. H., & Friedlander, B. (2008). Powerful writing strategies *for all students*. Baltimore, MD: Paul H. Brookes.

Harris, K. R., Lane, K. L., Driscoll, S. A., Graham, S., Wilson, K., Sandmel, K., … Schatschneider, C. (2012). Tier 1, teacher-implemented self-regulated strategy development for students with and without behavioral challenges. *The Elementary School Journal*, *113*, 160–191. doi:10.1086/667403

Harris, K. R., Lane, K. L., Graham, S., Driscoll, S. A., Sandmel, K., Brindle, M., & Schatschneider, C. (2012). Practice-based professional development for self-regulated strategies development in writing: A randomized controlled study. *Journal of Teacher Education*, *63*, 103–119. doi:10.1177/0022487111429005

Hayes, J. R. (1996). A new framework for understanding cognition and affect in writing. In C. M. Levy & S. Ransdell (Eds.), *The science of writing: Theories, methods, individual differences, and applications* (pp. 1–27). Mahwah, NJ: Erlbaum.

Hermann, J. A., Semb, S., & Hopkins, B. L. (1976). Effects of formal "grammar" and "direct method" training on the number of errors in compositions written by sixth-graders. *Revista Mexicana de Analisis de la Conducta*, *2*(1), 68–84.

Hillocks, G. (1984). What works in teaching composition: A meta-analysis of experimental treatment studies. *American Journal of Education*, *93*, 133–170.

Kiuhara, S., Graham, S., & Hawken, L. (2009). Teaching writing to high school students: A national survey. *Journal of Educational Psychology*, *101*, 136–160. doi:10.1037/a0013097

Kiuhara, S. A., O'Neill, R. E., Hawken, L. S., & Graham, S. (2012). The effectiveness of teaching 10th-grade students STOP, AIMS, and DARE for planning and drafting persuasive text. *Exceptional Children*, *78*, 335–355. doi:10.1177/001440291207800305

Korducki, R. A. (2001). *An instructional program integrating strategies for composition and self-regulation: Effects on the English and Spanish language writing skills of bilingual*

Latino students with learning difficulties. Unpublished doctoral dissertation. University of Wisconsin, Milwaukee, WI.

Lane, K. L., Harris, K. R., Graham, S., Weisenbach, J. L., Brindle, M., & Morphy, P. (2008). The effects of self-regulated strategy development on the writing performance of second-grade students with behavioral and writing difficulties. *The Journal of Special Education, 41*, 234–253. doi:10.1177/0022466907310370

Lenhart, A., Arafeh, S., Smith, A., & Macgill, A. R. (2008). *Writing, technology and teens*. Retrieved from Pew Internet and American Life Project website: http://www.pewinternet.org/2008/04/24/writing-technology-and-teens/

Little, M. A., Lane, K. L., Harris, K. R., Graham, S., Story, M., & Sandmel, K. (2010). Self regulated strategies development for persuasive writing in tandem with schoolwide positive behavioral support: Effects for second-grade students with behavioral and writing difficulties. *Behavioral Disorders, 35*, 157–179.

MacArthur, C. A., & Philippakos, Z. (2010). Instruction in a strategy for compare-contrast writing. *Exceptional Children, 76*, 438–456.

Mason, L. H. (2004). Explicit self-regulated strategy development versus reciprocal questioning: Effects on expository reading comprehension among struggling readers. *Journal of Educational Psychology, 96*, 283–296. doi:10.1037/0022-0663.96.2.283

Mason, L. H., Meadan, H., Hedin, L. R., & Cramer, A. M. (2012). Avoiding the struggle: Instruction that supports students' motivation in reading and writing about content material. *Reading & Writing Quarterly, 28*, 70–96. doi:10.1080/10573569.2012.632734

Mason, L. H., Reid, R., & Hagaman, J. L. (2012). *Building comprehension in adolescents: Powerful strategies for improving reading and writing in content areas*. Baltimore, MD: Paul H. Brookes.

Mason, L. H., Snyder, K. H., Sukhram, D. P., & Kedem, Y. (2006). TWA + PLANS strategies for expository reading and writing: Effects for nine fourth-grade students. *Exceptional Children, 73*, 69–89.

National Center for Education Statistics. (2012). *The nation's report card: Writing 2011*. NCES 2012-470. Institute of Education Sciences, U.S. Department of Education, Washington, DC.

Pastor, P. N., & Reuben, C. A. (2008). Diagnosed attention deficit hyperactivity disorder and learning disability: United States, 2004–2006. *National Center for Health Statistics, 10*(237), 1–22.

Perera, K. (1984). *Children's writing and reading: Analysing classroom language*. London: Blackwell Publishers.

Persky, H. R., Daane, M. C., & Jin, Y. (2003). The nation's report card: Writing 2002. NCES 2003-529. National Center for Education Statistics, Institute of Education Sciences, U.S. Department of Education, Washington, DC.

Rogers, L., & Graham, S. (2008). A meta-analysis of single subject design writing intervention research. *Journal of Educational Psychology, 100*, 879–906. doi:10.1037/0022-0663.100.4.879

Saddler, B. (2007). Improving sentence construction skills through sentence-combining practice. In S. Graham, C. A. MacArthur, & J. Fitzgerald (Eds.), *Best practices in writing instruction* (pp. 163–178). New York, NY: The Guilford Press.

Saddler, B. (2013). Best practices in sentence construction skills. In S. Graham, C. A. MacArthur, & J. Fitzgerald (Eds.), *Best practices in writing instruction* (2nd ed., pp. 238–256). New York, NY: The Guilford Press.

Saddler, B., Asaro, K., & Behforooz, B. (2008). The effects of peer-assisted sentence-combining practice on four young writers with learning disabilities. *Learning Disabilities: A Contemporary Journal, 6*(1), 17–31.

Saddler, B., Behforooz, B., & Asaro, K. (2008). The effects of sentence-combining instruction on the writing of fourth-grade students with writing difficulties. *Journal of Special Education, 42*(2), 79–90. doi:10.1177/0022466907310371

Saddler, B., & Graham, S. (2005). The effects of peer-assisted sentence-combining instruction on the writing performance of more and less skilled writers. *Journal of Educational Psychology, 97*(1), 43–54.

Saddler, B., & Graham, S. (2007). The relationship between writing knowledge and writing performance among more and less skilled writers. *Reading & Writing Quarterly, 23*, 231–247. doi:10.1080/10573560701277575

Scardamalia, M., & Bereiter, C. (1986). Written composition. In M. Wittrock (Ed.), *Handbook of research on teaching* (3rd ed., pp. 778–803). New York, NY: MacMillan.

Scruggs, T. E., Mastropieri, M. A., & Casto, G. (1987). The quantitative synthesis of single subject research methodology and validation. *Remedial and Special Education, 8*, 24–33.

Smith, M. W., Cheville, J., & Hillocks, G. (2006). I guess I'd better watch my English: Grammars and the teaching of the English language arts. In C. A. MacArthur, S. Graham, & J. Fitzgerald (Eds.), *Handbook of writing research* (pp. 263–274). New York, NY: The Guilford Press.

The National Commission on Writing. (2003). *The neglected "R": The need for a writing revolution*. Retrieved from The College Board website: http://www.collegeboard.com/prod_downloads/writingcom/neglectedr.pdf

The National Commission on Writing. (2004). *Writing: A ticket to work or a ticket out*. A survey of business leaders. Retrieved from The College Board website: http://www.collegeboard.com/prod_downloads/writingcom/writing-ticket-to-work.pdf

The National Commission on Writing. (2006). *Writing and school reform*. Retrieved from The College Board website: http://www.collegeboard.com/prod_downloads/writingcom/writing-school-reform-natl-comm-writing.pdf

CHAPTER 5

PICTURE EXCHANGE COMMUNICATION SYSTEM AND FACILITATED COMMUNICATION: CONTRASTING AN EVIDENCE-BASED PRACTICE WITH A DISCREDITED METHOD

Jason C. Travers, Matt Tincani, Julie L. Thompson and Richard L. Simpson

ABSTRACT

Learners with autism require specialized education and supports to ensure acquisition and mastery of various communication skills. This is particularly true for individuals whose disability significantly impacts their language development. Without functional communication, these individuals often engage in severe behavior, have reduced self-determination, and experience diminished quality of life. Accordingly, researchers in special education and related fields have sought ways to improve the communication skills of learners with autism who need specialized language and communication interventions. Although the Picture Exchange Communication

Instructional Practices with and without Empirical Validity
Advances in Learning and Behavioral Disabilities, Volume 29, 85–110
Copyright © 2016 by Emerald Group Publishing Limited
All rights of reproduction in any form reserved
ISSN: 0735-004X/doi:10.1108/S0735-004X20160000029005

System (PECS) is well-established in the empirical literature and has helped countless individuals learn to communicate, the method known as facilitated communication (FC; which also is being called "supported typing" and "rapid prompting method") has become increasingly popular in recent years. Few methods in special education have been as thoroughly discredited as FC and perhaps none are as dangerous. This chapter contrasts the thoroughly debunked FC and its pseudoscientific characteristics with those underpinning PECS. A brief historical account of each method is provided along with key scientific and pseudoscientific features that distinguish science from pseudoscience. Ultimately, our intent is to further clarify how FC is not an augmentative or alternative communication method and why PECS is.

Keywords: Autism; augmentative and alternative communication; facilitated communication; pseudoscience

Whether spoken, written, or through bodily expression (e.g., facial expression, gestures, dance, art), communication is a core feature of humankind unrivaled in diversity of form and function. Communication, or what Skinner (1957) called verbal behavior, is vital to human development, collaboration, and technological advancement. Indeed, communication, in all its forms throughout history, is the edifice on which all knowledge has been conserved and transmitted. Thus, learning to communicate arguably is a human right inherently conferred to every individual, regardless of circumstance or difference, including disability (Light & McNaughton, 2014). Given this presupposition, special education and related professions (e.g., speech and language pathology, behavior analysis) have dedicated human, financial, and intellectual capital to support acquisition and use of communication skills in learners with disabilities who do not develop speech (Beukelman & Mirenda, 2013; Ganz, Earles-Vollrath et al., 2012; McNaughton & Light, 2013).

Contemporary special education was born out of civil, social, and human rights activism during the 1960s and 1970s. Such advocacy was motivated by moral argumentation and patronage for the rights of people with disabilities (National Council on Disability, 2002). Activism led to federal laws, like the Individuals With Disabilities Education Act, 20 U.S.C.

§ 1400 (2004), and related policies that protect children with disabilities and their families from the whims of the majority (Kauffman, Anastasiou, Badar, Travers, & Wiley, in press). Special education has recently shifted emphasis to an empirical paradigm that calls for and depends on science for identifying effective practices. The shift aims to maximize the positive impact of education on children with disabilities and their families (Council for Exceptional Children, 2014). Of particular relevance is the impact of interventions aimed at supporting the communication skills of children and youth with autism spectrum disorders (ASD).

ASD affects language and social-communication skills development. The manifestation of these deficits varies considerably from minor difficulty initiating and maintaining conversation to severe impairments in verbal and nonverbal communication (American Psychiatric Association [APA], 2013). Among individuals with more severe forms of ASD, verbal communication skills typically are very limited. When learners with severe forms of ASD do learn to communicate, they often use single words, fragmented sentences or phrases, and poor syntax (e.g., pronoun reversal) and have general difficulties with other abstract concepts of language (Ogletree, 2008).

Because communication is human right, central to quality of life, and necessary for self-determination, maximizing communication skills should be a top priority of ASD intervention teams. Multiple methods have been identified for supporting communication, including speech, gestures, sign language, voice output devices, and picture exchange (Beukelman & Mirenda, 2013). A large body of evidence supports a few methods, some methods are emerging, and yet others have failed to demonstrate any benefit (Wong et al., 2015). Attaining best possible outcomes of youth with ASD depends on access to evidence-based communication interventions rather than methods founded on appeals to emotion, anecdote, or deeply held personal beliefs (Travers & Ayers, 2015; Travers, Tincani, & Lang, 2014).

Identifying scientifically valid and efficacious communication interventions for individuals with disabilities is no small charge. Indeed, the painstaking and deliberate process of scientific investigation has given rise to intervention strategies and methods that now are more likely than ever before to support acquisition and use of communication skills by learners with ASD. Yet there remains a sense of frustration about how to effectively and efficiently provide communicative interventions and supports for individuals with ASD who have very severe language and communication impairments (Maljaars, Noens, Jansen, Scholte, & VanBerckelaer-Onnes,

2011). Communication interventions and supports for these learners may have limited beneficial effects despite consistent applications over prolonged periods of time. Oftentimes, difficulty in the acquisition and use of socially appropriate communication (e.g., speech, symbol exchange, speech generating devices) is accompanied by behavior that serves a communicative purpose (Carr & Durand, 1985). It is not uncommon for a person with severe communication impairments to engage in self-injurious behavior, stereotyped behavior (e.g., body rocking, hand flapping, repetitive vocalizations), property destruction, and aggression in order to communicate (Durand & Carr, 1991). Such situations may result in a sense of desperation and seeking of an immediate, effective solution to the person's communication needs, but also is ideal for the proliferation of bogus therapies (Travers, Ayers, Simpson, & Crutchfield, 2016; Vyse, 2016).

Facilitated communication (FC) is a prototypical bogus method and has unparalleled endurance (Heinzen, Lilinefeld, & Nolan, 2015; Lilienfeld, Marshall, Todd, & Shane, 2014). The method involves a facilitator moving a person's body, usually by holding their hand, wrist, elbow, or shoulder, in order to make them type letters on a keyboard. Believers attribute the writing to the person with ASD, but studies revealed facilitators were actually subconsciously authoring the messages (Shane, 1994a, 1994b). Subsequent to being exposed as a spurious method in the 1990s (Wheeler, Jacobson, Paglieri, & Schwartz, 1993), FC has experienced renewed popularity in recent years. The resurgence has nothing to do with newly available evidence supporting the method – there is none. Instead, the returned popularity appears to be based on strategic rebranding as supported typing, assisted typing, facilitated typing, and typed communication, among other things (Travers et al., 2014). Rapid prompting method is a relatively newer variant of FC (Tostanoski, Lang, Raulston, Carnett, & Davis, 2014), but has a qualitatively different façade because it entails the facilitator moving a letter board or tablet computer toward the user's finger rather than moving the hand of the user toward a keyboard (Todd, 2016). Although thoroughly refuted, FC is dangerous to the extent that it can ruin lives (Boynton, 2012; Todd, 2012) and has been construed a human rights violation (Chan & Nankervis, 2014). Despite this, FC has been embraced by a vocal contingent of proponents who continue to erroneously pronounce FC as a form of augmentative and alternative communication (AAC) (Autism National Committee, 2008; Institute on Communication and Inclusion [ICI], n.d.-a; Stubblefield, 2011; TASH, 2000, 2014).

Travers et al. (2014) briefly contrasted FC with AAC in order to demonstrate some of the distinguishing features between synthetic and authentic

AAC. The aim of this chapter is to further distinguish between an evidence-based method of AAC and the empirically discredited pseudoscientific method known as FC. Accordingly, we have chosen to contrast FC with the picture exchange communication system (PECS; Bondy & Frost, 1994) because FC is perhaps the most discredited method in the history of developmental disabilities (Todd, 2016) and PECS is perhaps the most validated method for teaching communication skills to learners with ASD (Wong et al., 2014, 2015). We begin with a brief description of science in order to contextualize the contrasting differences between PECS and FC. A brief history of both FC and PECS is provided along with the evidence associated with each method. We also illustrate the differences between the meticulous empirical process undergirding PECS and the claims of sudden and dramatic breakthroughs associated with FC. We contrast concepts of science associated with PECS and the pseudoscience of FC to aid recognition of the hallmarks of each.

SCIENCE, FACILITATED COMMUNICATION, AND PICTURE EXCHANGE COMMUNICATION SYSTEM

The Oxford dictionary defines science as "the intellectual and practical activity encompassing the systematic study of the structure and behavior of the physical and natural world through observation and experiment." Science therefore can be considered a set of behaviors for better understanding the order, uniformity, and lawfulness of our surroundings. Science also depends on an attitudinal orientation toward facts over opinion, logical consistency over fallacious reasoning, evidence over authority, and the acceptance of experimental observations even when in conflict with personal desires (Skinner, 1953). These scientific concepts, attitudes, and behaviors are foundational to an evidence-based special education.

Although science is the best approach ever devised to develop an understanding of our surroundings, it is an imperfect process applied by fallible people; even the most highly skilled scientists can be mistaken. Accordingly, several mechanisms are in place to ensure maximum validity and reliability of observations, including experimental controls (e.g., randomization, double-blind tests), rigorous peer review, and reliance on independent replication as the means of verification (Travers, Cook, Therrien, & Coyne, 2016). These and other controls generally result in a gradual accumulation of facts that are organized and interpreted to form a broad explanation (i.e., a theory). Facts and theories develop in tandem and are refined with the accumulation of reliable observations of a phenomenon. Eventually, the discovery of facts and the theories used to explain them give rise to practical applications. For example, early discoveries about electricity eventually led to the development of the light bulb, radio, television, computer, Internet, and mobile communications technology. In turn, these inventions have further spurred scientific discovery and innovation. Similarly, PECS was derived from research that informed a sound scientific theory, verbal behavior (Skinner, 1957), and advanced systematically based on empirical findings. Conversely, FC was disseminated immediately upon discovery, without sound empirical research or theoretical grounding, and remains an entirely disproven pseudoscience.

Science and Pseudoscience

Pseudoscience differs from science, but it can be difficult to distinguish between the two. Nonetheless, professionals can identify the hallmarks of pseudoscience when examining claims of intervention efficacy. Whereas science depends on withholding belief in a claim until sufficient evidence is available to inform a decision, pseudoscience depends on adopting a belief and seeking evidence that conforms to that belief, usually by cherry picking favorable evidence. The dissimilarity between scientific and pseudoscientific dispositions toward new evidence also is striking. Scientists change their beliefs in accordance with the evidence; they recognize that all claims to knowledge are tentative and new evidence may better explain observed phenomena. Conversely, pseudoscientists are dogmatic when presented with evidence contrary to their beliefs; for them, no amount or kind of evidence will change their minds.

Scientists depend on precise terminology and instruments conducive to measurement, understanding, and independent verification. This technical precision is also necessary for the criticism of ideas. Scientists seek out harsh criticism of their ideas as a means of rooting out those that are flawed, an acknowledgment there are far more flawed ideas than accurate ones. One of the highest favors a scientist can perform is to provide criticism of their peer's work (e.g., peer review). When differences of opinion occur, scientists engage in reasoned debate and logically consistent argument to establish whether acceptance of a claim is warranted. This collegial approach to science is absent in pseudoscience. Pseudoscientists view criticism of their work as unfair collusion against them; peer review is better defeated or avoided rather than a method for vetting the merit of ideas and experiments. That is, pseudoscientists claim mainstream scientists conspire to suppress their ideas and treat peers as adversaries rather than colleagues.

Pseudoscientists depend on convoluted explanations and jargon that appears technical and scientific, but is actually inconsistent with authentic technical application. Similarly, pseudoscientists apply logically fallacious arguments (e.g., ad hominem, straw man, shifting the burden of proof, moving the goalposts). This is perhaps because individuals who advance indefensible beliefs view critics as adversaries instead of colleagues; they prefer to work in isolation rather than in concert with the scientific mainstream, often while claiming special knowledge suppressed by the status quo. Schmaltz and Lilienfeld (2014) identified other salient features of pseudoscience including (1) reliance on anecdotes and testimonials (e.g., qualitative case reports) as evidence for intervention efficacy, (2) extraordinary claims without evidence that also conflict with what is well-established and generally accepted, (3) claims that cannot be measured or scientifically tested (e.g., non-measurable "emotional support" is a critical feature of FC), and (4) absence of self-correction over time in accordance with new evidence. The history of FC is replete with these and other features of pseudoscience.

History and Implementation of Facilitated Communication

From the outset FC has been defined and described by key proponents in various and often inconsistent ways (Shane, 1994a, 1994b). FC involves providing a person with communication impairments physical and emotional support to point to or type letters. The facilitator holds the hand, wrist, or arm of the FC user in order to facilitate pointing to or typing letters and alleges to produce words and sentences that reflect those of the FC user. The facilitator is expected to steady the hand of the FC user while also delivering various verbal cues (e.g., "look here, keep going") and providing emotional support (Biklen, 1993). FC users have been alleged to produce immediate results (i.e., within minutes).

According the Syracuse ICI, training in FC requires a facilitator to attain competencies related to (a) history of FC, (b) neuromotor concepts, (c) physical support, (d) behavioral supports, (e) communicative supports, (f) emotional support, (g) monitoring and feedback, (h) documentation, and (i) fostering independence (Facilitated Communication Institute, 2000; Institute on Communication and Inclusion [ICI], n.d-a.). For example, facilitators are told to ensure the FC user looks at the keyboard, presumably because FC users were often observed to point at letters without looking at them, which renders the communications meaningless (Palfreman, 1993, 1994). Facilitators are also advised to ensure proper positioning of the FC user and device, change their physical support (e.g., from holding the hand/finger to wrist, forearm, elbow, upper arm, shoulder, and back), ignore speech of the FC user, and seek clarification of unclear messages, among other things. Although several competencies are listed, training is informal, confined primarily to workshops for FC users, parents, laypeople, and professionals in as little as two hours.

Facilitated communication burst onto the special education scene in the early 1990s and spread fervently throughout the United States. The method originated in Australia with Rosemary Crossley during the 1970s and involved 12 students who primarily had physical disabilities (e.g., cerebral palsy) accompanied by some degree of intellectual disability (Jacobson, Mulick, & Schwartz, 1995). One of Crossley's first students was 13-year-old Anne McDonald, a girl with cerebral palsy who had been institutionalized since birth and had not received even one day of education (as was unfortunately common at the time). McDonald appeared to demonstrate various forms of advanced academic knowledge and skills (e.g., algebra, psychology) after only two months of using FC (Palfreman, 1994). During this time, McDonald alleged via FC that a nurse attempted to suffocate her with a pillow, foreshadowing the danger associated with FC (Green, 1994; Palfreman, 1994). McDonald was moved from the institution to live with Crossley after a highly politicized decision. Ironically, the decision lent undue legitimacy to FC while serving as a lightning rod for deinstitutionalization in Australia (Palfreman, 1994).

Crossley opened a communication center in 1986 that soon after was visited by Syracuse University professor Douglas Biklen (Biklen, 1990). Without first pursuing careful studies to establish the validity of FC and the procedures for reliable application of the technique, Biklen quickly engaged in broad dissemination of FC via publication of qualitative reports and commentaries in peer reviewed journals (Biklen, 1990; Biklen & Duchan, 1994; Schubert & Biklen, 1993). Popular books (Biklen, 1993) as well as television appearances, newspaper and magazine interviews, and newsletters (Jacobson et al., 1995; Palfreman, 2012) touted the fantastic power and utility of FC. Countless people with severe ASD and other developmental disabilities were provided FC, and a number were alleged to have responded with miraculous results. Although it was (and remains) unpopular to question the authenticity of FC and the presumed communicative and intellectual ability of FC users, many researchers were skeptical of the extraordinary claims and initiated validation studies of FC.

Subsequent to initial unfounded and unverified reports, Wheeler et al. (1993) studied FC by asking 12 FC users with ASD and their nine facilitators to label or describe pictures. Wheeler et al. sometimes showed a FC user and their facilitator identical pictures (e.g., both shown a picture of a ball), but occasionally showed them different pictures. Their aim was to use these message passing tests to determine whether the FC user or facilitator was authoring responses. Wheeler et al. found that when pictures were the same, the answer was always correct; but when pictures were different, the label for the item shown to the facilitator (and not the user) was typed. They concluded facilitators were authoring messages during FC. Several other independent studies used similar message passing tests and found evidence of facilitator control (Bligh & Kupperman, 1993; Cabay, 1994; Eberlin, McConnachie, Ibel, & Volpe, 1993; Klewe, 1993; Moore, Donovan, & Hudson, 1993; Moore, Donovan, Hudson, Dykstra, & Lawrence, 1993; Regal, Rooney, & Wandas, 1994; Shane & Kearns, 1994; Simpson & Myles, 1995; Szempruch & Jacobson, 1993; Vasquez, 1994). Dozens of studies have revealed FC is invalid (Mostert, 2001, 2010; Simpson & Myles, 1995).

In response to the studies indicating facilitators unwittingly authored the messages, FC proponents began publishing qualitative reports that did not test the validity of FC, but instead were intended to explain its purported efficacy. Qualitative research differs from quantitative research in that the latter aims to answer questions about what is and isn't true (according to what can be verified through repeated, objective, and controlled observation) while the former aims to describe in detail the features of a phenomenon or observation. Collectively, over 100 qualitative (i.e., anecdotal) and so-called case study and anecdotal research reports comprise almost the entirety of research supportive of FC (Cardinal & Falvey, 2014). But qualitative reports cannot attest to the authenticity of FC. Mostert (2001, 2010) conducted comprehensive reviews of the experimental studies of FC, including the few experimental studies by FC proponents that reported participants passed messages. Mostert's reviews showed (a) all soundly designed studies failed to find any evidence that FC produced authentic communication and (b) all studies reporting FC users passed messages were so deeply flawed that results were rendered uninterpretable. Nonetheless, FC advocates continue to dishonestly promote FC using bald assertions, strategic rebranding, and other manipulative marketing tactics (Travers et al., 2014).

History and Implementation of the Picture Exchange
Communication System

PECS was developed by Andy Bondy, Lori Frost, and colleagues at the Delaware Autism Program, Delaware's statewide public school program for children with ASD, beginning in the late 1980s (Bondy, 2012). Following its initial development, PECS was subsequently disseminated through two versions of the *Picture Exchange Communication System Training Manual*, a detailed and comprehensive manual that precisely describes the teaching procedures for the six phases of the PECS protocol (Frost & Bondy, 1994, 2001). The term Picture Exchange Communication *System* [italics added] emphasized a systematic teaching protocol that begins with relatively simple responses (e.g., reaching for and exchanging a symbol with a training partner to obtain a desired item) and advances to more complex communication (e.g., discriminating between symbols, responding to questions, commenting). A detailed description of the PECS protocol is beyond the scope of this chapter and readers are referred to the Picture Exchange Communication System Training Manual (Frost & Bondy, 2001) for specifics of the training procedure and to Pyramid Educational Consultants (www.pecs.com) for resources on PECS implementation. However, a brief description of the six phases of PECS is useful for contrasting it with FC.

First, a preference assessment is conducted to determine highly preferred items the student will request. This helps to ensure that the student is sufficiently motivated to communicate prior to training. Phase I teaches the student how to communicate by using two trainers, one positioned behind the student to provide physical prompting, and the other positioned in front of the student to act as the communicative partner. Using a system of most-to-least prompts, the student learns to exchange a picture for a highly preferred item with the communicative partner. In Phase II, which teaches distance and persistence, the student learns to remove a picture symbol from a communication board, get the communicative partner's attention, and to exchange the picture symbol at a distance. At this time, the second trainer positioned behind the student is faded from teaching. In Phase III, picture discrimination, the student is taught to request the appropriate picture symbol from an array. Initially, the student learns to discriminate between just two picture symbols, but the protocol includes procedures for building the student's vocabulary to discriminate between multiple symbols, and contains correspondence checks to ensure the student is exchanging the correct symbol. In Phase IV, the student is taught sentence structure by using a multiword sentence strip (i.e., "I want _____."). In Phase V, the student learns to communicate in response to others' questions (i.e., "What do you want?"). Finally, in Phase VI, the student is taught to comment on the environment by answering the questions "What do you see?" "What do you have?" "What do you hear?" and "What is it?"

Trainings and consultations on how to implement PECS are currently conducted by Bondy and Frost's company, Pyramid Educational Consultants, in more than 60 countries in North America, Central and South America, Europe, and Asia (Pyramid Educational Consultants, 2014). Although the number of individual PECS users is not formally tracked, PECS is regarded as one of the most popular communication intervention strategies for individuals with ASD. Stahmer, Collings, and Palinkas (2005) reported that 95% of children with ASD served in California early intervention programs received PECS, making it the most popular intervention strategy.

PECS was developed in accordance with sound scientific theories, namely behavior analysis and verbal behavior (Skinner, 1953, 1957). Skinner explained how all communication, spoken or not, was a form of "verbal behavior" (i.e., verbal operants). A core difference between verbal behavior theory and linguistics theory is the latter tends to focus largely on the structure of language (syntax, semantics, phonology, morphology, etc.), while the former focuses on the functional aspects of communication (e.g., requesting, commenting, responding). PECS is derived from Skinner's (1957) analysis of verbal behavior and emphasizes functional communication. Early reports of PECS's efficacy were based on clinical and anecdotal reports (Bondy & Frost, 1993). These early accounts, which reported promising results, motivated researchers to more systematically evaluate PECS. In the late 1990s and early 2000s, research studies began to emerge demonstrating the positive effects of the PECS protocol on functional communication (Schwartz, Garfinkle, & Bauer, 1998) and collateral behaviors such as speech (Charlop-Christy, Carpenter, Le, LeBlanc, & Kellet, 2002). As a result of these studies and subsequent experimental work, PECS now is among the most researched interventions for learners with ASD, with solid evidence of efficacy for improving functional communication of children and adults with moderate to severe communication difficulties (Ganz, Davis, Lund, Goodwyn, & Simpson, 2012; Tincani & Devis, 2011; Wong et al., 2015).

Unlike other popular intervention strategies for children with ASD (Lovaas, 1987), PECS was not developed in a university-based clinic or by academic researchers, but by practitioners working in a public school setting (Bondy, 2012). Its developers describe PECS as an applied behavior analysis (ABA) intervention influenced by Skinner's (1957) analysis of verbal behavior, utilizing many teaching procedures commonly used in the practice of ABA (Cooper, Heron, & Heward, 2007) and supported with substantial empirical evidence (Bondy, 2012; Bondy & Frost, 1994, 2001; Bondy, Tincani, & Frost, 2004). Although PECS was not developed as part of a research project to advance the empirical base of communication interventions, the earliest reports featured quantitative outcome data (Bondy & Frost, 1994) and the system itself requires objective data to evaluate intervention efficacy and user benefit (Frost & Bondy, 2001). Early outcome reports by its developers were positive, but were tempered with the caveat that some users did not respond as favorably as others (Bondy & Frost, 1994). PECS's popularity, combined with a sound conceptual foundation and spirit of empiricism in which the system was developed, was perhaps best reflected by the researchers' willingness to evaluate via peer review the system to confirm (or disconfirm) early reports of desirable effects. Subsequent scientific investigations of PECS confirmed both its efficacy and social validity (cf., Ganz et al., 2012).

CONTRASTING FACILITATED COMMUNICATION AND THE PICTURE EXCHANGE COMMUNICATION

A 1999 National Academies of Sciences report called for significant improvements in the field of education as a research discipline (National Research Council, Committee on a Feasibility Study for a Strategic Education Research Program, 1999). The report focused on the weak record of research within education, noting:

> One striking fact is that the complex world of education — unlike defense, health care, or industrial production — does not rest on a strong research base. In no other field are personal experience and ideology so frequently relied on to make policy choices, and in no other field is the research base so inadequate and little used. (p. 1)

The emergence and continued use of FC is a prototypical illustration of this denunciation. In contrast, PECS is an example exemplary illustration of a method that was developed and validated via science. Here we use the divergent paths of FC and PECS to discuss the inherent problems of pseudoscience in education and the desire for an education profession linked to the concepts, attitudes, and behaviors associated with science.

The Pseudoscience of Facilitated Communication

Examination of claims made by FC proponents reveals their dependence on pseudoscience (see Table 1 for a summary of pseudoscientific elements of FC, in comparison to scientific tenets of PECS). First and perhaps most obvious, Biklen and other FC proponents quickly accepted claims that FC was legitimate and began disseminating the method without ever conducting studies of (a) the validity of the method or (b) the procedures necessary for ensuring its reliable use. If studies had resulted in evidence that FC was valid, then the next responsible step would have been to carefully investigate what procedures were necessary to appropriately and ethically apply the method (i.e., identify crucial elements for training professionals to use the method). Instead, beliefs were formulated without evidence, and subsequent steps were taken to confirm and maintain those beliefs. The result was an exclusive reliance on testimonials and anecdotes disguised as

Table 1. Salient Differences between the Picture Exchange Communication System (PECS) and Facilitated Communication (FC).

	Picture Exchange Communication System	Facilitated Communication
Origin	Developed in late 1980s by Andy Bondy, Lori Frost, and colleagues at the Delaware Autism Program	Developed in the 1970s–1980s by Rosemary Crossley in Australia and brought to the United States in early 1990s by Douglas Biklen
Conceptual foundation	Behavior analysis, applied behavior analysis, verbal behavior, very well established	Supernatural, divine, praxis, not established
Quality of empirical support for conceptual foundation	Strong	Poor
Teaching protocol	Systematic and replicable	Non-systematic and non-replicable
Use of data	Data used to document formative outcomes and intervention effectiveness	Data not used to document formative outcomes and data collection is said to hinder user communication
Initial supporting evidence	Anecdotal and quantitative	Anecdotal
Subsequent evidence and quality of evidence	Quantitative and experimental; strong	Anecdotal and non-experimental; weak
Disconfirming evidence	Weak and scarce	Strong and prevalent

"qualitative research" and poorly conducted empirical research (Mostert, 2001, 2010) that could not attest to intervention efficacy (Myles & Simpson, 1994; Simpson & Myles, 1995; Singer, Horner, Dunlap, & Wang, 2014).

When confronted with evidence that the method did not appear valid, FC proponents engaged in a variety of fallacious explanations that included blaming facilitators for bad form, suggesting an untestable element (e.g., "emotional support") was integral to FC, and appealing to faith (i.e., FC works only when used by believers; Biklen & Cardinal, 1997; Crossley, 1997; Palfreman, 1993). Perhaps the most obvious indication of intellectual dishonesty was the distasteful and erroneous personal attacks on skeptics of FC who were accused of hate speech for relying on evidence to inform conclusions about the method (Stubblefield, 2011). When a mountain of unequivocal evidence showed FC did not work, believers refused to accept the evidence or engage in reasoned debate. In contrast to scientists who have been clear and steadfast about what is needed to consider FC a potentially useful tool, even if only "for some people" (e.g., demonstration of a simple message passing test), believers actively avoid validation tests. Furthermore, they cannot explain what would be necessary to convince them FC is ineffective. Instead, FC believers insist without evidence that FC is a form of AAC despite only having anecdotes and testimonials of fellow believers and FC users themselves (Biklen & Burke, 2006; Rubin et al., 2001). Dogmatic adherence to beliefs in spite of evidence and fallacious appeals to authority are indicators of pseudoscience.

FC proponents have asserted for decades without any credible evidence that ASD primarily affects motor skills and not language development, literacy learning, or general intelligence (Biklen, 1990; Kliewer, Biklen, & Petersen, 2015). However, these assertions fly in the face of everything known about ASD. ASD in fact is not a motor disorder, but is a pervasive disorder that affects language and communication skills (American Psychiatric Association [APA], 2013). The acquisition of rudimentary communication skills among those with more severe impairments requires intensive and prolonged intervention in highly specialized environments, usually over several years if not decades during the lifetime of the individual (Keen, 2005; Paul, 2008). Some people with severe forms of ASD demonstrate hyperlexia (i.e., a precocious ability to decode text in the absence of formal reading instruction), but this phenomenon is accompanied by severe difficulties with reading comprehension (Grigorenko et al., 2002; Grigorenko, Klin, & Volkmar, 2003; Nation & Norbury, 2005). Rare cases of hyperlexia notwithstanding, learning to read and understand printed text typically requires multiple years of systematic and explicit instruction, even when students have less severe disabilities that affect language and literacy development like dyslexia (Rupley, Blair, & Nichols, 2009).

However, FC users with severe ASD who never received systematic and explicit literacy instruction appeared to demonstrate instantaneous written communication. Neophyte FC users, whose facilitators were undoubtedly literate, purportedly produced advanced, abstract, and grammatically correct written language, including poetry and deeply moving, insightful narratives about liberation from trapped bodies. It is likely no coincidence that stories of liberation came from FC users whose literate facilitators had been told their children/clients/students would be unlocked from a prison of silence (Palfreman, 1993). Nonetheless, FC proponents have never provided objective and scientifically valid evidence that (a) the defining characteristics of ASD are wrong, (b) literacy instruction is unnecessary to use written language to express thoughts, or (c) a radically different paradigm for serving the communication needs of persons with ASD was warranted.

Various theoretical explanations have been provided for FC, ranging from Haskew and Donnellan's (1993) description of supernatural autistic telepathy to divine inspiration from a deity as suggested by Bilu and Goodman (1997). FC proponents have continued to suggest people with ASD have difficulty making their bodies move in ways that correspond with mental intention. In haste to explain (rather than test) his belief in FC, Biklen (1990) suggested the notion that "praxis" (i.e., difficulty moving the body in accordance with mental intentions) was a potentially useful theory to explain his observations of FC. In other words, Biklen claimed people with ASD did not necessarily have cognitive impairment or language deficits. Instead, he suggested ASD inhibited movement and that the language and cognitive abilities of people with ASD were generally intact. This notion spawned a popular but unfounded belief that people with ASD simply need to be "unlocked" from a trapped mind (Biklen, 1993), a belief that remains prominent. Despite a quarter of a century, there remains no credible empirical evidence for the praxis theory of FC. Notwithstanding this fact, FC proponents continue to advance this idea using simple and unsupported assertions (Stubblefield, 2011) and pseudoscientific reasoning (Donnellan, Hill, & Leary, 2010). Perhaps the coup de grâce is an argument offered in identical articles published in two journals by Donnellan et al. (2010, 2013). Appealing to neuroscience, but without neuroscience expertise, facts, or evidence, Donnellan et al. argued for the praxis theory of FC with a *Facebook quote* allegedly authored by an individual with ASD:

> I think the fluidity of access to various places in my brain is dependent upon neurological movement between places. I'm no scientist, but have always been able to "see" this inside of me. Sometimes my speaking is hindered, other times my thinking, and sometimes my physical movement. The hardest is when thinking is not working smoothly. When that happens, I have to line up one thought at a time, like train cars. I like it much better when my thoughts do not have to be methodically lined up, but are more fluid with colors coming in and out and swirling into unique and beautiful patterns. (para 9)

The Science of Picture Exchange Communication System

In 2014, the National Professional Development Center on Autism Spectrum Disorders at the Frank Porter Graham Child Development Institute identified PECS as an evidence-based practice (Wong et al., 2014). Unlike FC, which had no evidence supporting it when Biklen (1990) began promoting it, over 20 years of careful and independently replicated empirical research had accumulated before claims about the beneficial effects of PECS were widely accepted by ASD researchers. Though arguably a slow progression, especially when compared with instantaneous results accompanied by pseudoscience, the steady advancement of scientific investigation has resulted in better interventions today than were previously available. In contrast, retention of FC has denied children with ASD access to effective interventions like PECS. Furthermore, it could be argued that the extensive human, intellectual, and financial resources dedicated to initial examination and the continued refutation necessary to counter peddlers of this farce has slowed the progression toward more effective interventions. This fact demonstrates why the meticulous progress of science is the best way to ensure students with disabilities have access to interventions that are most likely to confer benefit.

Science entails accounting for a collection of observed facts into a broad explanation called a theory. As mentioned previously, PECS was derived, in part, from Skinner's (1957) analysis of verbal behavior, which was based on extensive basic laboratory research (Firster & Skinner, 1957) and conceptually sound principles of behavior (Skinner, 1953). The procedures of PECS as a structured implementation system were derived from empirically supported teaching practices validated by hundreds of ABA research studies (Cooper et al., 2007). In contrast, FC was not based in a sound, empirically supported theory or recognized system of evidence; the "theory" underlying FC (e.g., praxis) runs counter to accepted research on the origins and etiology of ASD, intellectual disability, and other developmental disabilities.

Although PECS is a highly structured system that requires skilled practitioners, FC is merely a collection of nebulous support techniques (Biklen, 1992). The precise description of teaching procedures found in the PECS protocol enabled researchers to replicate and confirm early reports of positive effects, and to investigate ways to improve the system to enhance positive outcomes (Tincani, Crozier, & Alazeta, 2006). In contrast, the collection of ill-defined support techniques that comprise FC thwarts systematic attempts to empirically evaluate the system or to improve it in any manner. This intentional tactic by FC acolytes eludes scrutiny and prevents independent attempts to empirically evaluate the approach (Lilienfeld et al., 2014).

Why Facilitated Communication Is Not Augmentative and Alternative Communication

Travers et al. (2014) explained how several university faculty, organizations, and self-proclaimed FC "master trainers" erroneously assert that FC is a form of AAC, including the ICI at Syracuse University (ICI, n.d.-a), University of Northern Iowa (n.d.), TASH (2000, 2014), and Autism National Committee (2008), to name a few. AAC involves using various forms of communication-enhancing methods other than self-generated speech. AAC tools allow individuals to express their thoughts, ideas, interests, and needs through use of aided devices (e.g., communication books, speech generating devices) and unaided systems (e.g., manual sign language, gestures) (American Speech and Hearing Association [ASHA], n.d.).

Speech and language professionals who provide AAC to individuals with disabilities are expected to receive graduate level training in several areas. The ASHA Scope of Practice and related AAC Knowledge and Skills for Service Delivery (2002) code provides a thorough, detailed outline of the knowledge, skills, roles, and proficiencies associated with the delivery of therapeutic interventions that incorporate AAC for learners with disabilities. Importantly, these documents emphasize the obligation to rely on evidence-based practices rooted in behavior analysis (and verbal behavior), including incidental teaching, environmental arrangement, time delay procedures, and manding (i.e., requesting, American Speech-Language-Hearing Association [ASHA], 2002). In other words, a systematic and explicit model of professional development for AAC is available and is based on a comprehensive body of evidence from multiple theoretical paradigms as well as contributions from the foremost scholars in the field. These documents do not endorse, condone, or even mention FC. Furthermore, the American Speech-Language-Hearing Association [ASHA] (1994) has long had a position statement explicitly warning against the use of FC because it has never been demonstrated to be scientifically valid.

FC is without a systematic and explicit set of knowledge, skills, roles, and proficiencies derived from empirical research. Accordingly, legitimate professional organizations such as ASHA offer no guidelines or instructional or ethical codes for using FC. Instead, the ICI (formerly the Facilitated Communication Institute) at Syracuse University provides several guiding documents. These documents come with a warning that simply reading them is insufficient for ensuring adequate practice; users must also attend a minimum two-hour training before starting FC. One might suspect that the ICI (2014) training standards serve as supplemental material and information to other professional standards. Inspection of the credentials of the FC master trainers and the people they provide training to reveals this is not the case. Master trainers have various backgrounds and include individuals who do not appear to have a college degree. Importantly, there is no certification or accrediting body associated with FC training and master trainers appear to be an exclusive group that confers the status upon themselves using subjective criteria. The Institute on Communication and Inclusion [ICI] (n.d.-b) at Syracuse University indicates:

> Master trainers are individuals who have been working with FC users for many years, have attended FC trainings ranging from introductory workshops to advanced Training of Trainers, and became skilled and experienced to provide consultations and advising to families and individuals with autism.

Learners with ASD have a proclivity toward attending to specific and rather nuanced details in their environment (Lovaas & Schreibman, 1971; Rieth, Stahmer, Suhrheinrich, & Schreibman, 2015). Teacher educators, speech and language pathology experts, and behavior analysts who focus on the education and treatment of children with ASD often spend considerable time demonstrating how teacher behavior can serve as subtle cues to the learner, which may have the effect of preventing meaningful learning. For example, a teacher or therapist may instruct a child with ASD to "Point to the ball" while also looking at the ball, orienting their body toward the ball, placing the ball closer to the child than a different stimulus (e.g., toy car), or giving an array of various cues. Learners with ASD often pick up on such cues rather than attending to important information (e.g., the stated label of the object) and, accordingly, point to the ball without ever learning the name of the object. This is true for number of skills; the child may learn to touch, point to, or give a long list of objects, letters, words, and etcetera without ever actually learning the intended skill.

Similarly, the seemingly benign placement of the instructor's feet, hands, tone and volume of voice, or any non-tactile cue can serve to signal a particular response from the learner. As any successful poker player can attest, physical touch is not prerequisite for recognizing and responding to subtle cues (aka "tells"). The technical term for this phenomenon is "stimulus control" and has been used by magicians and exploited by charlatans for hundreds of years (Heinzen et al., 2015; Todd, 2016). When FC proponents claim that a FC user is able to independently type, they are saying the individual may sometimes type without physical touch. However, cues need not come from physical touch in order to produce simple responses like striking a keyboard. Whereas PECS depends on very explicit use and withdrawal of physical prompts and persistent testing (e.g., correspondence checks) for independent communication irrespective of environments, FC promotes indefinite dependence on the presence of a specific communication-support person or people. Proponents attempt to portray facilitators as advocates for and emotional supporters of the FC user. Importantly, no FC user, including those proclaimed to now be independent typists, have ever demonstrated the ability to type in the absence of their facilitators.

Stimulus control explains how FC users come to produce the messages (i.e., touching letters on a keyboard), but the content of the messages originate with the facilitator (Wheeler et al., 1993). A reason why some people find FC (as well as rapid prompting method) so compelling is that the messages generated have the appearance of being authentic. This is the result of a phenomenon known as the ideomotor effect (Knuf, Aschersleben, & Prinz, 2001; McDougal, 1905; Stock & Stock, 2004), and its role in FC is well documented (Burgess et al., 1998; Green, 1994; Kezuka, 1997; Lilienfeld, 2005; Wegner, Fuller, & Sparrow, 2003). The ideomotor effect has been used to explain a variety of observations, including so-called supernatural phenomena (e.g., table tipping, automatic writing, Ouija board, water dowsing/divining, and so forth). As explained by Wegner et al. (2003), the ideomotor process involves subconscious motor movements that are primed by a variety of environmental stimuli:

> Facilitators in FC may be influenced by just such uncontrolled intelligence, the production of intelligent actions that occurs without conscious intention, or even in opposition to such intention. The typical facilitator doubtless has at hand information about the client's activities and circumstances, after all, and is also likely to have expectations for

what the client wants, or what might arouse the client's interest or emotions. Such knowledge could prime the facilitator to influence the actions that the facilitator and client make together at the keyboard, percolating subtly into the choices of letters and words even while the facilitator may be attempting to counteract such influences. The facilitator is thus intrinsically primed by his or her own prior knowledge. The facilitator's knowledge can inform his or her judgments even when he or she is attempting to respond in a way that does not depend on this knowledge. (p. 7)

CONCLUSION

FC and its variants (e.g., rapid prompting method) are synthetic and not genuine AAC methods. When FC is viewed in light of the overwhelming evidence of facilitator authorship, and when the purportedly positive evidence of FC is situated in the context of stimulus control and a manipulative ideomotor effect, it becomes clear how even highly educated individuals come to mistakenly believe the method is authentic. It can reasonably be concluded that FC has never and probably cannot ever produce independent, authentic communication. Accordingly, FC users become mere puppets in their own lives, subjected to the whims of their facilitators and at the cost of subverted opportunities to learn genuine self-expression. We think it is logical and prudent to advise professionals as well as parents and families to abstain from believing in and using FC. In contrast to FC, PECS is supported by a substantial body of research, is accepted as an evidence-based practice, and has well-established roots in applied behavior analysis and verbal behavior. PECS is scientifically proven method for bringing about meaningful and socially valid improvement of communication skills that yield that, in turn, enhance quality of life and self-determination for individuals with ASD.

REFERENCES

American Psychiatric Association. (2013). Diagnostic and statistical manual of mental disorders. Washington, DC: Author.
American Speech-Language-Hearing Association. (1994). Facilitated communication. Rockville, MD: Author.
American Speech-Language-Hearing Association. (2002). Augmentative and alternative communication: Knowledge and skills for service delivery. Rockville, MD: Author.
American Speech-Language-Hearing Association. (n.d.). Augmentative and alternative communication. Retrieved from http://www.asha.org/public/speech/disorders/AAC/

Autism National Committee. (2008). Autism national committee policy and principles regarding facilitated communication. Forrest Knolls, CA: Author.

Beukelman, D. R., & Mirenda, P. (2013). *Augmentative and alternative communication* (4th ed.). Baltimore, MD: Brookes Publishing.

Biklen, D. (1990). Communication unbound: Autism and praxis. *Harvard Educational Review*, *60*, 291–314.

Biklen, D. (1992). Typing to talk: Facilitated communication. *American Journal of Speech and Language Pathology*, *1*, 15–17, 21–22.

Biklen, D. (1993). *Communication unbound: How facilitated communication is challenging Traditional views of autism and ability/disability*. New York, NY: Teachers College Press.

Biklen, D., & Burke, J. (2006). Presuming competence. *Equity & Excellence in Education*, *39*, 166–175.

Biklen, D., & Duchan, J. F. (1994). "I am intelligent": The social construction of mental retardation. *Journal of the Association for Persons with Severe Handicaps*, *19*, 173–184.

Biklen, D. E., & Cardinal, D. N. (1997). *Contested words, contested science: Unraveling the facilitated communication controversy*. New York, NY: Teachers College Press.

Bilu, Y., & Goodman, Y. C. (1997). What does the soul say? Metaphysical uses of facilitated communication in the Jewish Ultraorthodox community. *Ethos*, *25*, 375–407.

Bligh, S., & Kupperman, P. (1993). Evaluation procedure for determining the source of the communication in facilitated communication accepted in a court case. *Journal of Autism and Developmental Disorders*, *23*, 553–557.

Bondy, A., & Frost, L. (1994). The picture exchange communication system. *Focus on Autistic Behavior*, *9*, 1–19.

Bondy, A., & Frost, L. (2001). The picture exchange communication system. *Behavior Modification*, *25*, 725–744.

Bondy, A. S. (2012). The unusual suspects: Myths and misconceptions associated with PECS. *The Psychological Record*, *62*, 789–816.

Bondy, A. S., & Frost, L. A. (1993). Mands across the water: A report on the application of the picture-exchange communication system in Peru. *The Behavior Analyst*, *16*, 123–128.

Bondy, A., Tincani, M., & Frost, L. (2004). Multiply controlled verbal operants: An analysis and extension to the picture exchange communication system. *The Behavior Analyst*, *27*, 247–261.

Boynton, J. (2012). Facilitated communication—What harm it can do: Confessions of a former facilitator. *Evidence-Based Communication Assessment and Intervention*, *6*, 3–13.

Burgess, C. A., Kirsch, I., Shane, H., Niederauer, K. L., Graham, S. M., & Bacon, A. (1998). Facilitated communication as an ideomotor response. *Psychological Science*, *9*, 71–74.

Cabay, M. (1994). A controlled evaluation of facilitated communication with four autistic children. *Journal of Autism and Developmental Disorders*, *24*, 517–527.

Cardinal, D. N., & Falvey, M. A. (2014). The maturing of facilitated communication as a means toward independent communication. *Research and Practice for Persons with Severe Disabilities*, *39*, 189–194.

Carr, E. G., & Durand, V. M. (1985). Reducing behavior problems through functional communication training. *Journal of Applied Behavior Analysis*, *18*, 111–126.

Chan, J., & Nankervis, K. (2014). Stolen voices: Facilitated communication is an abuse of human rights. *Evidence-Based Communication Assessment and Intervention*, *8*, 151–156.

Charlop-Christy, M. H., Carpenter, M., Le, L., LeBlanc, L. A., & Kellet, K. (2002). Using the picture exchange communication system (PECS) with children with autism: Assessment of PECS acquisition, speech, social-communicative behavior, and problem behavior. *Journal of Applied Behavior Analysis, 35,* 213–231.

Cooper, J. O., Heron, T. E., & Heward, W. L. (2007). *Applied behavior analysis* (2nd ed.). Upper Saddle River, NJ: Pearson.

Council for Exceptional Children. (2014). Council for exceptional children standards for evidence-based practice in special education. Washington, DC: Author.

Crossley, R. (1997). Postscript: Taking the test—A facilitator's view. In D. Biklen & D. N. Cardinal (Eds.), *Contested words, contested science* (pp. 209–219). New York, NY: Teachers College Press.

Donnellan, A., Hill, D., & Leary, M. (2010). Rethinking autism: Implications of sensory and movement differences. *Disability Studies Quarterly, 30*(1).

Donnellan, A. M., Hill, D. A., & Leary, M. R. (2013). Rethinking autism: Implications of sensory and movement differences for understanding and support. *Frontiers in Integrative Neuroscience, 6,* 124. doi:10.3389/fnint.2012.00124

Durand, V., & Carr, E. (1991). Functional communication training to reduce challenging behavior: Maintenance and application in new settings. *Journal of Applied Behavior Analysis, 24,* 251–264.

Eberlin, M., McConnachie, G., Ibel, S., & Volpe, L. (1993). Facilitated communication: A failure to replicate the phenomenon. *Journal of Autism and Developmental Disorders, 23,* 507–530.

Ferster, C. B., & Skinner, B. F. (1957). *Schedules of reinforcement.* New York, NY: Appleton-Century-Crofts.

Frost, L. A., & Bondy, A. S. (1994). *The picture exchange communication system training manual.* Cherry Hill, NJ: Pyramid Educational Consultants.

Frost, L. A., & Bondy, A. S. (2001). *The picture exchange communication system training manual* (2nd ed.). Cherry Hill, NJ: Pyramid Educational Consultants.

Ganz, J. B., Davis, J. L., Lund, E. M., Goodwyn, F. D., & Simpson, R. L. (2012). Meta-analysis of PECS with individuals with ASD: Investigation of targeted versus non-targeted outcomes, participant characteristics, and implementation phase. *Research in Developmental Disabilities, 33,* 406–418.

Ganz, J. B., Earles-Vollrath, T. L., Heath, A. K., Parker, R. I., Rispoli, M. J., & Duran, J. B. (2012). A meta-analysis of single case research studies on aided augmentative and alternative communication systems with individuals with autism spectrum disorders. *Journal of Autism and Developmental Disorders, 42,* 60–74.

Green, G. (1994). Facilitated communication: Mental miracle or sleight of hand. Behavior and *Social, 4,* 69–85.

Grigorenko, E. L., Klin, A., Pauls, D., Senft, R., Hooper, C., & Volkmar, F. (2002). A descriptive study of hyperlexia in a clinically referred sample of children with developmental delays. *Journal of Autism and Developmental Disorders, 32,* 3–12.

Grigorenko, E. L., Klin, A., & Volkmar, F. (2003). Hyperlexia: Disability or superability? *Journal of Child Psychology and Psychiatry, 44,* 1079–1091.

Haskew, P., & Donnellan, M. (1993). *Emotional maturity and well-being: Psychological lessons of facilitated communication.* Madison, WI: DRI Press.

Heinzen, T. E., Lilinefeld, S. O., & Nolan, S. A. (2015). *The horse that won't go away: Clever Hans, facilitated communication, and the need for clear thinking.* New York, NY: Worth Publishers.

Individuals With Disabilities Education Act, 20 U.S.C. § 1400. (2004).

Institute for Communication and Inclusion. (n.d.-a). What is supported typing? Retrieved from http://soe.syr.edu/centers_institutes/institute_communication_inclusion/what_is_supported_typing/default.aspx.

Institute for Communication and Inclusion. (n.d.-b). Master trainers. Retrieved from http://soe.syr.edu/centers_institutes/institute_communication_inclusion/about_the_ici/Master_Trainers.aspx

Institute on Communication and Inclusion. (2014, May 14). Section II: Fundamental principles and best practices. Retrieved from http://soe.syr.edu/media/documents/2010/6/Section_II_Fundamental_principles_and_best_practices.pdf

Jacobson, J., Mulick, J., & Schwartz, A. (1995). A history of facilitated communication: Science, pseudoscience, and antiscience. *American Psychologist, 50,* 750–765.

Kauffman, J., Anastasiou, D., Badar, J., Travers, J. C., & Wiley, A. (in press). Inclusive education moving forward. In J. P. Bakken, F. E. Obiakor, & A. Rotatori (Eds.). *Advances in special education: General and special education in an age of change.* Bingley, UK: Emerald Group Publishing Limited.

Keen, D. (2005). The use of non-verbal repair strategies by children with autism. *Research in Developmental Disabilities, 26,* 243–254.

Kezuka, E. (1997). The role of touch in facilitated communication. *Journal of Autism and Developmental Disorders, 27,* 571–593.

Klewe, L. (1993). An empirical evaluation of spelling boards as a means of communication for the multihandicapped. *Journal of Autism and Developmental Disorders, 23,* 559–566.

Kliewer, C., Biklen, D., & Petersen, A. (2015). At the end of intellectual disability. *Harvard Educational Review, 85,* 1–28.

Knuf, L., Aschersleben, G., & Prinz, W. (2001). An analysis of ideomotor action. *Journal of Experimental Psychology: General, 130,* 779–798.

Light, J., & McNaughton, D. (2014). Communicative competence for individuals who require augmentative and alternative communication: A new definition for a new era of communication? *Augmentative and Alternative Communication, 30,* 1–18.

Lilienfeld, S. O. (2005). Scientifically unsupported and supported interventions for childhood psychopathology: A summary. *Pediatrics, 115,* 761–764.

Lilienfeld, S. O., Marshall, J., Todd, J. T., & Shane, H. C. (2014). The persistence of fad interventions in the face of negative scientific evidence: Facilitated communication for autism as a case example. *Evidence-Based Communication Assessment and Intervention, 8,* 62–101.

Lovaas, O. I. (1987). Behavioral treatment and normal educational and intellectual functioning in young autistic children. *Journal of Consulting and Clinical Psychology, 5,* 3–9.

Lovaas, O. I., & Schreibman, L. (1971). Stimulus overselectivity of autistic children in a two stimulus situation. *Behaviour Research and Therapy, 9,* 305–310.

Maljaars, J., Noens, I., Jansen, R., Scholte, E., & VanBerckelaer-Onnes, I. (2011). Intentional communication in nonverbal and verbal low-functioning children with autism. *Journal of Communication Disorders, 44,* 601–614.

McDougal, W. (1905). *Physiological psychology.* London: JM Dent.

McNaughton, D., & Light, J. (2013). The iPad and mobile technology revolution: Benefits and challenges for individuals who require augmentative and alternative communication. *Augmentative and Alternative Communication, 29*, 107–116.

Moore, S., Donovan, B., & Hudson, A. (1993). Facilitator-suggested conversational evaluation of facilitated communication. *Journal of Autism and Developmental Disorders, 23*, 541–551.

Moore, S., Donovan, B., Hudson, A., Dykstra, J., & Lawrence, J. (1993). Evaluation of facilitated communication: Eight case studies. *Journal of Autism and Developmental Disorders, 23*, 531–539.

Mostert, M. P. (2001). Facilitated communication since 1995: A review of published studies. *Journal of Autism and Developmental Disorders, 31*, 287–313.

Mostert, M. P. (2010). Facilitated communication and its legitimacy—Twenty-first century developments. *Exceptionality, 18*, 31–41.

Myles, B. S., & Simpson, R. L. (1994). Facilitated communication with children diagnosed as autistic in public school settings. *Psychology in the Schools, 31*, 208–220.

Nation, K., & Norbury, C. F. (2005). Why reading comprehension fails: Insights from developmental disorders. *Topics in Language Disorders, 25*, 21–32.

National Council on Disability. (2002). An international convention on the human rights of people with disabilities. Washington, DC: Author.

National Research Council, Committee on a Feasibility Study for a Strategic Education Research Program. (1999). *Improving student learning: A strategic plan for education research and its utilization.* Washington, DC: National Academy Press.

Ogletree, B. (2008). The communicative context of autism. In R. Simpson & B. S. Myles (Eds.), *Educating children and youth with autism* (pp. 223–266). Austin, TX: Pro-Ed.

Palfreman, J. (Producer). (1993, October 19). Frontline: Prisoners of silence. Boston, MA: WGBH Public Television.

Palfreman, J. (1994). The Australian origins of facilitated communication. In H. C. Shane (Ed.). *Facilitated communication: The clinical and social phenomenon.* San Diego, CA: Singular Publishing Group.

Palfreman, J. (2012). The dark legacy of FC. *Evidence-Based Communication Assessment and Intervention, 6*, 14–17.

Paul, R. (2008). Interventions to improve communication. *Child and Adolescent Psychiatric Clinics of North America, 17*, 835–856.

Pyramid Educational Consultants. (2014). *Countries served by pyramid educational consultants as of June 2014.* Newark, DE: Author.

Regal, R. A., Rooney, J. R., & Wandas, T. (1994). Facilitated communication: An experimental evaluation. *Journal of Autism and Developmental Disorders, 24*, 345–355.

Rieth, S. R., Stahmer, A. C., Suhrheinrich, J., & Schreibman, L. (2015). Examination of the prevalence of stimulus overselectivity in children with ASD. *Journal of Applied Behavior Analysis, 48*, 71–84.

Rubin, S., Biklen, D., Kasa-Hendrickson, C., Kluth, P., Cardinal, D. N., & Broderick, A. (2001). Independence, participation, and the meaning of intellectual ability. *Disability & Society, 16*, 415–429.

Rupley, W. H., Blair, T. R., & Nichols, W. D. (2009). Effective reading instruction for struggling readers: The role of direct/explicit teaching. *Reading & Writing Quarterly, 25*, 125–138.

Schmaltz, R., & Lilienfeld, S. O. (2014). Hauntings, homeopathy, and the Hopkinsville Goblins: Using pseudoscience to teach scientific thinking. *Frontiers in Psychology, 5,* 336.

Schubert, A., & Biklen, D. (1993). Issues of influence: Some concerns and suggestions. *Facilitated Communication Digest, 1*(3), 11–12.

Schwartz, I. S., Garfinkle, A. N., & Bauer, J. (1998). The picture exchange communication system communicative outcomes for young children with disabilities. *Topics in Early Childhood Special Education, 18,* 144–159.

Shane, H. C. (1994a). Facilitated communication: Factual, fictional, or factitious? In H. C. Shane (Ed.). *Facilitated communication: The clinical and social phenomenon.* San Diego, CA: Singular Publishing Group.

Shane, H. C. (1994b). *Facilitated communication: The clinical and social phenomenon.* San Diego, CA: Singular Publishing Group.

Shane, H. C., & Kearns, K. (1994). An examination of the role of the facilitator in "facilitated communication". *American Journal of Speech-Language Pathology, 3,* 48–54.

Simpson, R. L., & Myles, B. S. (1995). Effectiveness of facilitated communication with children and youth with autism. *The Journal of Special Education, 28,* 424–439.

Singer, G. H., Horner, R. H., Dunlap, G., & Wang, M. (2014). Standards of proof, TASH, facilitated communication, and the science-based practices movement. *Research and Practice for Persons with Severe Disabilities, 39,* 178–188.

Skinner, B. F. (1953). *Science and human behavior.* New York, NY: Macmillan.

Skinner, B. F. (1957). *Verbal behavior.* New York, NY: Appleton-Century-Crofts.

Stahmer, A., Collings, N., & Palinkas, L. (2005). Early intervention practices for children with autism: Descriptions from community providers. *Focus on Autism and Other Developmental Disabilities, 20,* 66–79.

Stock, A., & Stock, C. (2004). A short history of ideo-motor action. *Psychological Research, 68,* 176–188.

Stubblefield, A. (2011). Sound and fury: When opposition to facilitated communication functions as hate speech. *Disability Studies Quarterly, 31*(4).

Szempruch, J., & Jacobson, J. W. (1993). Evaluating the facilitated communications of people with developmental disabilities. *Research in Developmental Disabilities, 14,* 253–264.

TASH. (2000). TASH resolution on augmentative and alternative communication and the right to communicate. Retrieved from https://tash.org/about/resolutions/tash-resolution-https://tash.org/about/resolutions/tash-resolution-right-communicate/

TASH. (2014, May 1). About facilitated communication. Retrieved from https://archive. is/QbkeI

Tincani, M., Crozier, S., & Alazeta, L. (2006). The picture exchange communication system: Effects on manding and speech development for school-aged children with autism. *Education & Training in Autism and Developmental Disabilities, 41,* 177–184.

Tincani, M., & Devis, K. (2011). Quantitative synthesis and component analysis of single-participant studies on the picture exchange communication system. *Remedial and Special Education, 32,* 458–470.

Todd, J. (2016). Old horses in new stables: Rapid prompting, facilitated communication, science, ethics, and the history of magic. In R. M. Foxx & J. A. Mulick (Eds.), *Controversial therapies for autism and intellectual disabilities* (2nd ed.). New York, NY: Routledge.

Todd, J. T. (2012). The moral obligation to be empirical: Comments on Boynton's "facilitated communication—What harm it can do: Confessions of a former facilitator." *Evidence-Based Communication Assessment and Intervention, 6*, 36−57.

Tostanoski, A., Lang, R., Raulston, T., Carnett, A., & Davis, T. (2014). Voices from the past: Comparing the rapid prompting method and facilitated communication. *Developmental Neurorehabilitation, 17*, 219−223.

Travers, J. C., & Ayers, K. (2015). A critique of presuming competence of learners with autism or other developmental disabilities. *Education and Training in Autism and Developmental Disabilities, 50*, 371−387.

Travers, J. C., Ayers, K., Simpson, R. L., & Crutchfield, S. (2016). Fad, pseudoscientific, and controversial interventions. In R. Lang, T. Hancock, & N. Singh (Eds.). *Early intervention for young children with autism spectrum disorder*. New York, NY: Springer.

Travers, J. C., Cook, B., Therrien, W., & Coyne, M. (2016). Replication research and special education. *Remedial and Special Education*. doi:10.1177/0741932516648462

Travers, J. C., Tincani, M., & Lang, R. (2014). Facilitated communication denies people with disabilities their voice. *Research and Practice in Severe Disabilities, 39*, 195−202.

University of Northern Iowa College of Education. (n.d.). 2014 Midwest Summer Institute: Communication and inclusion for all. Retrieved from http://www.vpaf.uni.edu/events/inclusion/. Accessed on July 7, 2014.

Vasquez, C. (1994). A multi-task controlled evaluation of facilitated communication. *Journal of Autism and Developmental Disorders, 24*, 369−379.

Vyse, S. (2016). Where do fads come from? In R. M. Foxx & J. A. Mulick (Eds.). *Controversial therapies for autism and intellectual disabilities* (2nd ed.). New York, NY: Routledge.

Wegner, D. M., Fuller, V. A., & Sparrow, B. (2003). Clever hands: Uncontrolled intelligence in facilitated communication. *Journal of Personality and Social Psychology, 85*, 5−19.

Wheeler, D., Jacobson, J., Paglieri, R., & Schwartz, A. (1993). An experimental assessment of facilitated communication. *Mental Retardation, 31*, 49−60.

Wong, C., Odom, S., Hume, K., Cox, A., Fettig, A., Kucharczyk, S., … Schulz, T. (2015). Evidence-based practices for children, youth, and young adults with autism spectrum disorder: A comprehensive review. *Journal of Autism and Developmental Disorders, 45*, 1951−1966.

Wong, C., Odom, S. L., Hume, K., Cox, A. W., Fettig, A., Kucharczyk, S., & Schultz, T. R. (2014). Evidence-based practices for children, youth, and young adults with autism spectrum disorder. University of North Carolina, Frank Porter Graham Child Development Institute, Autism Evidence Based Practice Review Group, Chapel Hill, NC.

CHAPTER 6

MOVEMENT AS BEHAVIORAL MODERATOR: WHAT DOES THE RESEARCH SAY?

Amy E. Ruhaak and Bryan G. Cook

ABSTRACT

Disruptive student behavior contributes to poor student outcomes, loss of classroom instructional time, and teacher burnout. Physical movement is an intervention that has been used to target and ameliorate disruptive student behavior for students with learning and behavioral disabilities. A review of two movement-based interventions — Brain Gym® and antecedent bouts of exercise — reveals different levels of research support. Brain Gym®, a commercial movement-based curriculum, is not supported by extant empirical research. Alternatively, a growing body of research empirically supports antecedent bouts of exercise as an effective behavioral intervention. This chapter provides a description and review of research for each intervention. Implications for instructional practice and recommendations are provided.

Keywords: Brain Gym; antecedent bouts of exercise; student behavior

Instructional Practices with and without Empirical Validity
Advances in Learning and Behavioral Disabilities, Volume 29, 111–134
Copyright © 2016 by Emerald Group Publishing Limited
All rights of reproduction in any form reserved
ISSN: 0735-004X/doi:10.1108/S0735-004X20160000029008

Disruptive student behaviors have the potential to create chaos in the classroom and derail even the most carefully planned lessons. Externalizing behaviors, such as "destructive and aggressive behavior, defiance, temper tantrums, impulsive, and hyperactive behaviors" (Henricsson & Rydell, 2004, p. 112), are particularly disruptive. Although internalizing behaviors (e.g., depression, anxiety, shyness) can cause stress in the classroom, externalizing behaviors are the most disruptive to classroom instruction and challenging for teachers to address. Indeed, chronic disruptive behavior has many deleterious effects in the classroom. In order for learning to occur, teachers need to establish an orderly and positive environment; disruptive student behavior impedes learning and diminishes instructional time for all students (Bru, 2009; Emmer & Stough, 2001). In addition, disruptive behavior increases teacher burnout and attrition rate (McCarthy, Lambert, O'Donnell, & Melendres, 2009). And, as to be expected, disruptive behavior can have devastating consequences for the students who exhibit the behavior.

Students who are disruptive face marked challenges both in the classroom and in the community. Their behaviors defy commonly accepted social norms and frustrate teachers, peers, and parents and contribute to poor lifetime outcomes. For instance, many students with emotional and behavioral disorders (EBD) experience an increased involvement with the juvenile justice system, a higher dropout rate, and lower academic achievement compared to their peers (Bradley, Doolittle, & Bartolotta, 2008). Students who exhibit disruptive behavior experience less instructional exposure, diminished opportunities to respond, and diluted academic expectations (Sutherland & Oswald, 2005). As adults, this population experiences impaired family relationships and high unemployment rates (Bradley, et al., 2008; Wagner & Davis, 2006).

Due to the pernicious effects of disruptive behaviors, it is critical that teachers select effective interventions to target these behaviors. In this chapter, we describe two different interventions for addressing disruptive behaviors: Brain Gym® and antecedent bouts of exercise. Both of these interventions use physical movement to decrease the frequency of disruptive behaviors in the classroom. Additionally, both interventions attempt to "set the stage" for appropriate behavior − they are antecedent interventions − to prime students for the learning environment. However, these interventions call for different types and intensity of physical expression. Brain Gym® incorporates the use of non-strenuous movements; antecedent bouts of exercise include cardiovascular and moderate to rigorous motor activities. As described in the following sections, though it has been frequently used for decades Brain Gym® has limited support in the research literature, whereas a body of research supports antecedent bouts of exercise as an effective intervention for reducing disruptive behaviors.

BRAIN GYM®

Brain Gym® is a movement-based learning program sold by Brain Gym International (BGI) and is a registered trademark of the Educational Kinesiology Foundation. Originally developed in the 1970s by Paul and Gail Dennison, Brain Gym® is currently available in over 80 countries and has been translated into more than 40 different languages. General information about the basic components of Brain Gym®, Brain Gym® workshops, instructor training, and licensed practitioners is available on the official Brain Gym® website (www.braingym.org). The most recent iteration of the Brain Gym® program is outlined in *Brain Gym®: The Teacher's Edition* (Dennison & Dennison, 2010).

Brain Gym® consists of a detailed set of 26 simple physical movements that purportedly improve outcomes in a number of areas. Specific to disruptive classroom behaviors, Brain Gym® claims to improve students' abilities in the following areas: (a) concentration and focus, (b) relationships, (c) self-responsibility, (d) organization skills, and (e) attitude (BGI, 2015). Brain Gym® does not provide students with explicit, operationalized instruction in any of these areas, nor does it offer opportunities to assess student growth related to these domains. Instead, the movements are to be used as primers to learning. Theoretically, the movements are meant to activate the brain in order to create the mind/body balance requisite for ameliorating disruptive behaviors and improving other outcomes.

As detailed on the official Brain Gym® website, the program is not meant to replace classroom curricula or explicit interventions; instead, the movements are designed to enhance and complement instruction. The manufacturers state that ideally, before implementing the program in the classroom, teachers become licensed Brain Gym® instructors or attend training sessions by a licensed instructor. After teachers master the movements, they can provide guided instruction to their students on how to correctly execute each movement. The website suggests that during the course of a typical school day, teachers can use the movements prior to instruction or utilize selected movements during instruction when students exhibit academic or behavioral difficulties. The movements can be performed as a whole-group activity, in small groups, as an individual intervention, or independently by students. The stated goal of the program is to assist students in self-monitoring their behavior and enable them to perform the requisite movement(s) to address their specific behavioral challenge.

The 26 Brain Gym® movements are organized into three categories: (a) Energy Exercises, (b) Lengthening Activities, and (c) Midline Movements (BGI, 2011). For each category, BGI provides broad descriptions with cursory discussion of their theoretical foundations. For instance, the Energy Exercises are described as follows:

> A series of Brain Gym activities designed to facilitate an awareness of the body as the central reference for all directional movement, thus providing a kinesthetic bridge for skills of organization and abstract thought; the ability to cross the top-bottom midline of the brain and postural system, thus integrating rational thinking with emotional responses. (BGI, 2011, p. 51)

The stated purpose of the Lengthening Activities is to "facilitate the ability to cross the back-front midline of the brain and postural system, thus integrating meaningful intention with habituated movement responses" (BGI, 2011, p. 52). Lastly, Midline Movements are defined as "activities designed to facilitate the ability to cross the midline of the body for improved reading, writing, listening, and coordination skills" (BGI, 2011, p. 52). Although BGI asserts that all 26 movements (or a combination of selected movements) improve academic and behavioral outcomes, for the purposes of this chapter we highlight a few of the movements from the Lengthening Activities and the Energy Exercises as these categories purportedly target attributes necessary to mitigate disruptive student behavior.

The Thinking Cap and Earth Buttons are movements intended to increase self-awareness and improve receptive and expressive communication skills (Dennison & Dennison, 2010). The Earth Button movement involves placing two fingers under the lower lip and placing the opposite hand on the stomach while breathing deeply and looking up and down several times. The Thinking Cap movement involves unrolling the ear cartilage from top to bottom several times; ostensibly, this action will improve a student's focus and concentration. Hook-ups and Calf Pumps are movements intended to increase students' self-esteem and their ability to be self-directed learners. To perform a Hook-up, students cross their arms and their wrists, interlace their fingers, and then fold their arms up towards their chins. Calf Pumps are a modified version of a runner's stretch; students are instructed to breathe deeply several times while stretching their calves. These examples demonstrate the unconventional use of movement to improve broad behavioral outcomes and are idiosyncratic of the Brain Gym® program. A complete listing of the 26 Brain Gym® is provided in Box 1.

Box 1. The 26 Brain Gym® Movements.

The Cross Crawl
Lazy 8s
The Double Doodle
Alphabet 8s
The Elephant
Neck Rolls
The Rocker
Belly Breathing
Cross Crawl Sit-ups
The Energizer
Think of an X
Hook-ups
The Positive Points
The Owl
Arm Activation
The Footflex
The Calf Pump
The Gravity Glider
The Grounder
Sipping Water
Brain Buttons
Earth Buttons
Balance Buttons
Space Buttons
The Energy Yawn
The Thinking Cap

In addition to Brain Gym® movements, the program also includes a learning readiness routine called PACE. This short physical movement routine addresses the four states deemed necessary for self-directed, whole-brain learning: (a) positive, (b) active, (c) clear, and (d) energetic (Dennison, 2006). Each state is activated by performing a specific Brain Gym® movement, and the combination of these movements enables individuals to find their unique rhythm and timing, or PACE. This movement routine allegedly helps students to achieve the mind/brain balance necessary for optimal learning (Dennison, 2006).

Theoretical Foundations and Critique

The Brain Gym® program is based upon an educational philosophy that promotes the interdependence of movement, cognition, and applied learning (BGI, 2015). The Dennisons postulate that individuals experience learning and behavioral challenges when both regions of the brain are not in sync or are not optimally coordinated with specific areas of the body (Dennison & Dennison, 1994). The purpose of the 26 physical movements is to address this mismatch and align an individual's brain and body to achieve academic and behavioral outcomes.

The theoretical foundation of Brain Gym® is based upon an imprecise and superficial understanding of the structure and function of the brain. As advances in neuroscience have revealed, the brain is composed of a minimum of 100 billion neurons, and each neuron is connected to approximately 10,000 other neurons. This results in an estimated 1,000 trillion neuronal connections in the brain (Purves et al., 2012). The Brain Gym® program's schema of brain structure and function does not accommodate the complexity of neurogenesis and synaptogenesis nor the phenomenally symbiotic interplay between various brain regions. Rather, Brain Gym® promotes a simplistic understanding of the brain, based upon three brain dimensions and functions: (a) laterality, (b) focusing, and (c) centering (BGI, 2011). Collectively, these are called the Three Dimensions of Whole-Brain Learning.

The Laterality Dimension refers to the communication pathways between the right and left hemispheres of the brain and the postural system. Effective communication within this dimension is considered necessary for speaking, listening, reading, writing, and the ability to think and move simultaneously. The Focusing Dimension refers to the ability to organize information between the front and back regions of the brain and is considered important for comprehension and executive function. The Centering Dimension refers to an individual's capacity to coordinate the top and bottom regions of the brain. This is considered necessary for regulating emotions and supporting abstract thought.

In addition to the Three Dimensions of Whole-Brain Learning, the foundation of the Brain Gym® program is based upon three theoretical assumptions: (a) perceptual motor training, (b) cerebral dominance, and (c) neurological repatterning. These three theories are evident throughout the Brain Gym® language, program, and rationale. Significantly, all three of these theoretical assumptions have been either invalidated or are not supported by empirical research.

Perceptual Motor Training
Much of Dennison's early research focused on the use of movement to enhance learning. His concept of *educational kinesiology* emerged from this research and is defined as follows:

> the study of movement and its relationship to whole-brain learning; a process for drawing out innate learning abilities through the understanding of movement and its relationship to whole-brain learning patterns; the application of kinesthetics (movement) to the study of whole-brain integration for purposes of alleviating stress and maximizing the full learning potential. (BGI, 2011, p. 50)

Dennison's belief that inefficient integration of visual, auditory, and motor skills can preclude academic and behavioral success is closely aligned with the theory of perceptual motor training. Essentially, perceptual motor training – and the many commercial perceptual motor programs – claim to ameliorate academic and behavioral challenges through physical activities and exercises that target fine and gross motor skills (Stephenson, Carter, & Wheldall, 2007). Some of the most popular strategies used in perceptual motor programs involve walking on a balance beam, throwing beanbags, crawling, and bouncing balls (Hyatt, 2007). Ostensibly, these activities improve students' visual-motor coordination, resulting in improved reading ability and overall behavior.

Perceptual motor training has a rich research history within the field of special education. Research articles on perceptual motor training date back more than fifty years (Frostig & Maslow, 1973; Getman, 1965; Kephart, 1960). Although perceptual motor programs were initially very popular for use with students with disabilities, research studies quickly challenged the efficacy of this practice (Arter & Jenkins, 1979; Balow, 1971; Bochner, 1978; Kavale & Forness, 1987; Kavale & Mattson, 1983; Sullivan, 1972).

In a meta-analysis of 180 studies on perceptual motor programs, Kavale and Mattson (1983) found their effect to be near zero ($d = .08$). Catalyzed by the flurry of research publications denouncing this intervention, the Council for Learning Disabilities issued a position paper opposing the use of perceptual motor programs as interventions for students with disabilities (Board of Trustees of the Council for Learning Disabilities, 1986). Despite the rather large amount of empirical studies invalidating the effectiveness of perceptual motor training, BGI continues to utilize it as a theoretical support for its trademarked 26 movements.

Cerebral Dominance
In pop vernacular, cerebral dominance is commonly referred to as the left brain versus right-brain phenomenon in which left-brain individuals are logical and systematic, and right-brain individuals tend to be more artistic and creative. This generally accepted construct is, in fact, a gross oversimplification of brain lateralization. The brain, indeed, is divided into two discrete hemispheres that are connected by the corpus callosum. However, the notion that we use the right side of our brain for specific activities, and the left side of our brain for others is simply not true. The importance of inter-hemispheric interaction for cognition and attention is well documented (Banich,1998; Christman, Propper, & Dion, 2004). Specific brain regions do have functional correlates. For instance, the prefrontal cortex is associated with executive processes and the occipital cortex is the primary visual area of the brain. However, the theory that students may excel in some areas or be deficient in others due to hemispheric dominance has not been proven.

Within educational research, the provenance of cerebral dominance can be traced to the work of neuropsychiatrist and pathologist Orton (1937). Orton's research was initially based upon his observations that left-handed students encountered reading difficulties not apparent in right-handed students. Accordingly, he postulated that reading interventions should incorporate kinesthetic and tactile elements in order to integrate and balance left- and right-brain functions. Orton's theories of cerebral dominance are evident in the rationale of the Brain Gym® program and its 26 movements despite the empirical evidence invalidating the significance of cerebral dominance related to learning difficulties (Goswami, 2006; Kavale & Forness, 1995; Kavale & Mostert, 2004; Stichter, Conroy, & Kauffman, 2008).

A growing body of research challenges this conceptualization of the brain and behavior. In general, researchers are demonstrating that effective interventions and remediation are founded upon neural plasticity – the reorganization of neural pathways in the brain – along with an increase in the number of synapses between neurons (Garvert, Moutoussis, Kurth-Nelson, Behrens, & Dolan, 2015; Kilgard, 2012; Ylinen & Kujala, 2015). These processes are responsible for learning and retaining new behaviors, not the "integration" of the left- and right-brain hemispheres (Nielsen, Zielinski, Ferguson, Lainhart, & Anderson, 2013). Unfortunately, the Brain Gym® program is founded upon the assumption that cerebral dominance contributes to academic and behavioral challenges. The Brain Gym® movements strive to coordinate the right and left hemispheres of the brain (along with the front, back, top, and bottom regions). These theorized distinct regional partitions do not accurately reflect the physiology of the human brain. As Hyatt (2007) suggested, "the Brain Gym literature has made it sound as if the brain could be easily partitioned into different sections, and that simple movement activities would result in improved neurological development and learning for people of all ages" (p. 118).

Neurological Repatterning
Neurological repatterning is another specious theoretical assumption of the Brain Gym® program (Dennison & Dennison, 1994). Based primarily upon the Doman-Delacato theory of development, neurological repatterning suggests children must acquire specific motor skills at certain developmental stages, from the simple to the complex. If this fails to happen, children will experience learning and psychological challenges that will impede academic and behavioral success (Doman, 1968; Doman, Spitz, Zucman, Delacato, & Doman, 1960). For example, if a child begins talking before mastering walking, that child is considered to have missed a critical developmental stage in motor development that will have adverse effects on more complex neurological processes. Allegedly, this phenomenon will affect the overall psychological and cognitive well-being of the child. According to the Doman-Delacato theory of development, children who skip developmental stages in motor development need to be provided with opportunities to master the undeveloped skills to ensure all stages are mastered. Purportedly, this intervention retroactively repatterns neural pathways in the brain, addressing the neurological pathology responsible for behavioral or learning challenges.

The practice of neurological repatterning was invalidated *prior* to the development of the Brain Gym® program (Robbins, 1966; Stone & Pielstick, 1969). Due to the widespread popularity of neurological repatterning, several professional organizations – including the American Academy for Cerebral Palsy, the American Academy of Physical Medicine and Rehabilitation, the American Association on Mental Deficiency, the Canadian Association for Retarded Children, the Canadian Rehabilitation Council for the Disabled, and the National Association for Retarded Children – issued a joint statement cautioning against the practice (American Academy for Cerebral Palsy et al., 1968). More recently, the American Academy of Pediatrics (1999) published a similar cautionary statement. Nonetheless, the Brain Gym® program continues to endorse neurological repatterning.

Review of Research

Considering the popularity of the Brain Gym® program, the lack of empirical research supporting this intervention should alarm education professionals. In our review of research of the Brain Gym® program, we found two published reviews (Hyatt, 2007; Spaulding, Mostert, & Beam, 2010) and did not uncover any studies that were not included in these reviews. Hyatt (2007) identified only five peer-reviewed journal studies examining the effectiveness of Brain Gym®. One of the studies was eliminated from the review because the author of the study was also a participant in the study (Wolfsont, 2002). None of the studies reviewed could be considered true experiments and all of the studies "contained serious methodological flaws" (Hyatt, 2007, p. 120). Hyatt therefore concluded that the research reviewed did not demonstrate that the Brain Gym® program was "superior to no treatment at all" (p. 121).

The de los Santos, Hume, and Cortes study (2002) included the most participants ($N = 986$). The sample was comprised of students in pre-K to Grade 5. The experimental group participated in Brain Gym® activities and also listened to Mozart throughout the school day. Measures consisted of teacher ratings and scores on academic achievement tests. The author concluded the intervention was effective, although there was no analysis of statistically significant differences between the control and experimental groups. Based on the research findings, the author suggested that Brain Gym® is an effective strategy for improving test scores of Latino university students. However, the research study was conducted with elementary students, not university students. Additionally, the authors did not discuss the reliability of their research instrument, treatment fidelity, or threats to validity.

The remaining three studies in Hyatt's (2007) review of research also contained serious methodological flaws. Sifft and Khalsa (1991) conducted a study to examine whether Brain Gym® was an effective intervention for improving response time of college students to visual stimuli. Khalsa, Morris, and Sifft (1988) conducted a study to determine if Brain Gym® activities improved the static balance of elementary school students. The data from both of these studies are difficult to interpret due to the quality of the research designs, including threats to reliability and validity, along with questionable statistical procedures to determine significance. The fourth and final study in Hyatt's review (Cammisa, 1994) examined the correlation between the use of the Brain Gym® program for one year and perceptual motor and academic skills. The study indicated a positive effect for perceptual motor activities but not academic skills. The study did not detail the specific Brain Gym® movements used in the intervention, did not account for maturation effects or extraneous variables, and used assessments that did not include children with disabilities in the standardization sample.

Spaulding et al. (2010) conducted a subsequent review of research for Brain Gym®. These authors did not uncover any peer-reviewed research studies not already included in Hyatt's review. This is not surprising, given the historical paucity of empirically based research on the Brain Gym® intervention. In their review, Spaulding et al. first discussed and outlined the established quality indicators for evaluating experimental and quasi-experimental research (Gersten et al., 2005). The authors then applied the standards to the same four Brain Gym® studies reviewed by Hyatt. According to Spaulding et al., none of the studies can be considered *high quality* or *acceptable* research based upon the quality indicators for experimental and quasi-experimental research.

BGI provides an internal research summary guide on their website; all of the studies included are weak in demonstrating validity or reliability. The summary guide also contains anecdotal accounts submitted by teachers or other Brain Gym® advocates that do not apply rigorous or experimental design. Nothing included in the research summary guide provides meaningful support for the effectiveness of this program to target disruptive student behavior.

Discussion

Brain Gym® is founded upon invalidated theoretical assumptions and has not been demonstrated to be an effective intervention by any methodologically sound empirical studies. We do not encourage professionals to use the program in their classroom, or for administrators to spend money purchasing Brain Gym® teacher handbooks or trainings. Education professionals should strive to implement evidence-based strategies in the classroom to assist students in making significant gains throughout each school year. There is minimal evidence supporting the effectiveness of Brain Gym® and teachers should not waste valuable instructional time or resources exposing their students to this program.

Given the dearth of research on the effectiveness of Brain Gym® coupled with the growing amount of publications invalidating the theoretical foundation of the program, one must wonder why Brain Gym® has enjoyed such sustained popularity amongst educators. Weisberg, Keil, Goodstein, Rawson, and Gray (2008) explored what they term the seductive allure of neuroscience. According to the authors, people are much more likely to embrace psychological explanations as significant and meaningful if they are accompanied with neuroscientific information. In fact, Weisberg et al. reported that study participants found behavioral explanations that included illogical or irrelevant neuroscientific information more satisfying than explanations without the additional, specious information. This phenomenon complicates teachers' selection of classroom interventions because, in general, individuals tend to find programs more valuable when coupled with alleged "hard" biological evidence. Teacher preparation programs should provide their candidates with the necessary training to become critical consumers of educational research *and* popular science. This will help in-service teachers recognize pseudoscience and avoid empirically unsubstantiated programs packaged as "brained-based" interventions.

Although research does not suggest that the specific movements associated with the Brain Gym® program improve student behavior, empirical evidence indicates the positive effect more intensive physical activity can have on student behavior. The following section provides the background, theory, and research behind the use of antecedent bouts of exercise as a discrete intervention to address disruptive student behavior.

ANTECEDENT BOUTS OF EXERCISE

Considerable and longstanding anecdotal support suggests that exercise is associated with positive outcomes in non-physical domains, as reflected in the Latin phrase *mens sana in corpore sano* (a sound mind in a sound body). A body of evidence is emerging that empirically supports exercise as an effective educational intervention. In this section, we review the effects of bouts of antecedent exercise on behavior-related outcomes (e.g., on-task behavior, disruptive behavior) for children and youth with learning and behavioral disabilities.

Best (2010) noted that research has examined the effects of two types of exercise interventions: (a) habitual (i.e., chronic) exercise programs (e.g., a 10-week program of exercising five days a week) and (b) acute (e.g., individual) bouts of moderate or vigorous exercise (e.g., a single 20-minute jog). Although research suggests that both acute exercise and habitual exercise programs have positive effects, the evidence appears to more strongly support the effectiveness of acute, vigorous exercise bouts (Tomporowski, 2003). It is also important to clarify that the studies and reviews described in this chapter use exercise as an antecedent to bring about positive changes in participants' behavior. That is, exercise is not being used to punish or reward behaviors after they occur. Rather, exercise is implemented prior to instruction to "set the stage" for appropriate behavior. Although research also supports a positive association between antecedent exercise and outcomes in other domains (e.g., academic performance, executive function, cognition; Chang, Labban, Gapin, & Etnier, 2012; Tomporowski, Davis, Miller, & Naglieri, 2008; Verburgh, Königs, Scherder, & Oosterlaan, 2014), in this chapter we focus on using exercise to improve outcomes related to classroom behavior.

Though evidence suggests that exercise is effective for improving behavioral outcomes for students with learning and behavioral disabilities, the causal mechanism for these improvements is not clear. Indeed, scholars have posed a number of possible explanations (Allison, Faith, & Franklin, 1995; Ogg-Groenendaal, Hermans, & Claessens, 2014). For example, fatigue might explain decreases in disruptive behaviors subsequent to exercise. However, Lang et al. (2010) noted this would not explain increases in behaviors such as attention and academic performance also associated with antecedent exercise. A sense of mastery or achievement from completing exercise might also improve self-esteem and self-concept, which could in turn reduce the occurrence of challenging behaviors (Allison et al., 1995; Ogg-Groenendaal et al., 2014). Perhaps most significantly, exercise influences the central serotonergic, noradrenergic, and dopaminergic systems, and triggers the release of neurotransmitters associated with improved affective, cognitive, and meta-cognitive functioning. In this manner, exercise can potentially target some of the physiological causes of disruptive behaviors (Barclay et al., 2014; Ratey, 2008).

Regardless of the specific causal mechanism, exercise may be an attractive option for educators seeking to improve the behavior of students with disabilities for a number of reasons (Allison et al., 1995). For one, there is at least anecdotal support for treatment acceptability. Most students enjoy some form of exercise, many forms of exercise require little to no expense or equipment (e.g., running), and exercise doesn't require rigid adherence to a particular protocol and can be easily adapted and individualized. Moreover, unlike interventions such as psychopharmacological treatments (medication), exercise is associated with positive (e.g., improved health) rather than negative side effects. Additionally, exercise can be readily combined and should not interfere with other interventions (e.g., medication, reinforcement, self-monitoring).

Reviews of Research

Reviews across Disabilities

Allison et al. (1995) reviewed 16 group studies and 26 single-case design studies investigating the impact of antecedent exercise on disruptive behavior. Although the review included participants who were children and adults as well as those with and without disabilities, many studies included youth with disabilities. The effect size for the group studies was relatively small ($d = 0.33$). However, most of the group studies examined the cumulative effects of chronic exercise programs rather than bouts of exercise. The effect size of the single-case design studies, which primarily investigated the effects of acute exercise bouts, was much larger ($d = 1.99$). Participants in studies included students with learning disabilities, intellectual disabilities, emotional and behavioral disorders (EBD), and autism spectrum disorder (ASD) (as well as adults and youth without disabilities in some studies). The most common exercise activity in the single-case studies was jogging; interventions also involved weight lifting, outdoor activities, games, swimming, walking, and an obstacle course; and lasted between 3 and 60 minutes. Correlational analyses indicated disability status was not related to the effect of antecedent exercise across the single-case studies, suggesting that bouts of exercise were similarly effective for participants with and without disabilities.

Tomporowski (2003) conducted a review of research examining the effects of acute exercise on cognitive and behavioral outcomes in youth. Specific to youth with disabilities and behavioral outcomes, the author identified seven studies related to autism, four on students with EBD, and two for youth with intellectual disabilities. The studies all found positive effects of exercise bouts (e.g., jogging, ball play, roller skating), which ranged from 6 to 45 minutes, on outcomes such as self-stimulation, stereotypic behavior, attention, on-task behavior, disruptive behavior, and aggression. The author concluded that "the research on the effects of acute bouts of exercise on children who have clinical disorders that are characterized by poor impulse control and attention indicates that exercise interventions are associated with reductions in disruptive behaviors and improvements in desirable behaviors" (p. 354). Interestingly, one study showed that exercise resulted in a higher level of disruptive behaviors for a three-year with ADHD than did a medication treatment (Silverstein & Allison, 1994). However, the participant found the vigorous exercise intervention aversive and attempted to escape the intervention, indicating the importance of matching the intervention approach to individual preferences.

Autism Spectrum Disorders
Lang et al. (2010) reviewed 18 studies, the majority of which were single-case designs, investigating the effects of antecedent exercise on 64 individuals with ASD. Although some studies included adult participants, most participants were school age youth (participants' mean age = 12.5). The most common settings for exercise were "a school track, in the school gym, or on a school sports field" (p. 568). The majority of studies used jogging/ running as the intervention, whereas other studies used activities such as water-based exercises, stationary bike riding, lifting weights, treadmill walking, roller skating, muscle toning with stretching, and snow shoeing. The authors reported that all studies reviewed reported improved outcomes associated with antecedent exercise, including behavioral outcomes such as reduced stereotypy, aggression, and self-injury, as well as increased time-on-task. The authors noted that four reviewed studies compared more and less strenuous exercises. In each case, the more vigorous exercises had larger effects on participant outcomes. Furthermore, the positive effects of exercise bouts were found to be temporary. Three studies investigated the length of benefits and showed the behavior returned to baseline rates in 40−90 minutes after cessation of exercise.

The National Professional Development Center on Autism Spectrum Disorders has classified exercise as one of 27 evidence-based practices for individuals with ASD (Wong et al., 2014). By virtue of positive effects demonstrated by three group experimental and three single-case studies that met rigorous standards for methodological quality, exercise was identified as an evidence-based practice to improve behavior (as well as school-readiness, academic, and motor skills) for individuals with ASD from pre-school to middle school. In contrast, the National Autism Center (2015) classified exercise as an emerging (or promising) practice (rather than an established practice) for individuals with ASD under the age of 22 based on the amount, type, and quality of research support.

Intellectual Disabilities
Ogg-Groenendaal et al. (2014) identified 20 studies examining the effects of exercise on challenging behaviors exhibited by individuals with intellectual disabilities. Although the 91 participants across studies included some adults, participants in the majority of studies were children and youth. For studies involving children and youth, exercise interventions included jogging, running, walking, basketball, soccer, trampoline, calisthenics, and roller skating, with the duration of exercise lasting from 1 to 90 minutes. Outcomes included stereotypical behavior, total challenging behavior, self-injurious behavior, and aggressive behavior. Across all studies, Ogg-Groenendaal et al. reported that exercise was associated with a 30.9% reduction in challenging behaviors, which was statistically significant. The authors reported that the effects of low- and high-intensity exercise did not differ significantly, though high-intensity exercises were, on average, associated with a greater reduction in challenging behaviors (32.2%) than low-intensity exercises (22.9%). Consistent with Lang et al.'s (2010) findings, the effects of exercise were found to dissipate over time. Ogg-Groenendaal et al. reported that measures taken within two hours of exercising resulted in a 43.4% reduction in challenging behavior, whereas measure taken more than two hour but within 24 hours of exercising were associated with only a 20.8% reduction. Interestingly, measures taken more than one day after exercising indicated a 49.2% reduction in challenging behaviors.

Attention-Deficit/Hyperactivity Disorder and Emotional and Behavioral Disorders
Halperin, Berwid, and O'Neill (2014) reviewed the research investigating the effects of exercise on children with ADHD. The authors concluded that although the literature is limited, study findings indicated that acute bouts of exercise positively impacted the outcomes of children with ADHD. However, most of the studies investigated neurobiological, cognitive, meta-cognitive, and academic outcomes. For instance, Medina et al. (2010) reported significant improvements in vigilance and impulsivity (among other outcomes) among 25 boys with ADHD following a 30-minute bout of exercise on a treadmill. However, these outcomes were measured by

performance on a computer-based performance test rather than by class-room observations.

We could not locate a systematic review of studies examining the effects of acute, antecedent exercise on children and youth with EBD. However, a number of studies in the reviews summarized in the previous paragraphs included studies demonstrating positive effects of bouts of exercise on the behaviors of students with EBD. For example, Cannella-Malone, Tullis, and Kazee (2011) examined the effects of multiple bouts of antecedent exercise throughout the school day (i.e., 20 minutes of exercise when arriving at school and after lunch, 1- to 5-minute exercise breaks every hour) involving a variety of aerobic exercises on three boys with EBD and comorbid conditions (e.g., intellectual disability, autism) using a multiple baseline across participants design. Findings indicated the frequent bouts of exercise reduced challenging behaviors (i.e., aggression, property destruction) to zero or near-zero levels for all participants.

Limitations

Although we consider antecedent bouts of exercise to be an empirically validated approach for improving challenging behaviors of students with learning and behavioral disabilities, it is important to contextualize this recommendation with some important limitations. Our review of research on antecedent bouts of exercise in this chapter is neither comprehensive nor systematic. We primarily summarized research reviews that were conducted systematically, but we did not attempt to identify and review all relevant studies. Furthermore, though antecedent bouts of exercise generally improved behavioral outcomes for children and youth across the studies reviewed, there is insufficient research to draw firm conclusions about what types of exercise are most effective, how lengthy and vigorous exercise should be, and the degree to which the effects of exercise interact with learner characteristics (e.g., age, gender, disability) and behaviors (e.g., are some types of exercise more effective for certain behaviors than others?) (Tomporowski, 2003). Research addressing these issues is beginning to be conducted. For example, Folino, Ducharme, and Greenwald (2014) examined the effects of 30 minutes of jogging on disruptive behaviors, prosocial behaviors, and compliance for four boys with LD and EBD. The researchers measured outcomes within 30 minutes of exercise completion, and again at 30−60 minutes, 60−90 minutes, and 90−120 minutes. Findings indicated that exercise positively impacted all outcomes, but that improvement dissipated over time, returning to baseline levels after 90 minutes. More research of this type will help flesh out specific guidelines regarding the duration, intensity, frequency, and type of exercises needed to improve specific behaviors. Additionally, though many of the studies reviewed used experimental designs and were considered to be internally valid and of high methodologically quality (Wong et al., 2014), many reviewers noted that a number of studies in the research base used research designs that did not establish causality and had important methodological limitations (Halperin et al., 2014; Ogg-Groenendaal et al., 2014). Therefore, additional, high-quality research is needed to (a) replicate findings that antecedent bouts of exercise are an effective intervention and (b) provide evidence-based guidelines related to type, frequency, duration, and intensity of exercise needed to bring about improved behavior.

Recommendations for Implementation

Research suggests that many different types of exercise of different lengths and levels of intensity have been effective in improving the behaviors of students with learning and behavioral disabilities. Thus, there is not one "right way" to implement antecedent bouts of exercise. Nonetheless, scholars have suggested guidelines that appear important for successfully implementing antecedent bouts of exercise. The following recommendations are based largely on two sets of implementation guidelines (Austin, 2014; Srinivasan, Pescatello, & Bhat, 2014), both of which target learners with ASD but seem to apply to other groups of students with disabilities as well.

First, before implementing antecedent bouts of exercise, determine student behaviors to target, operationally define the target behaviors, and collect baseline data. Baseline data will provide a comparison to reliably determine whether the intervention is working. Consider involving the student and/or the student's family in selecting a socially important target behavior. Teachers may target different behaviors for different students in a class, or select a common behavior for the whole class. To operationally define the target behaviors, clearly, objectively, and completely describe what the behavior looks like. Finally, measure the occurrence of the behavior (depending on the behavior, you may want to measure frequency, duration, or latency of the behavior) across multiple days in the absence of the intervention (i.e., baseline data).

In terms of the intervention, teachers need to decide what type of exercise students will engage in, the duration of exercise bouts, the frequency of exercise bouts, the intensity of exercise, and the location of exercise. A number of different exercises have been shown in the research to improve student behavior. For example, see Cannella-Malone et al. (2011) for descriptions of a number of exercise activities used in their study. We encourage teachers to provide choices for students as to what type of exercise they would like to engage in. Choices should be limited to exercises that the student can reasonably perform and that the teacher/school has the resources/equipment for. In terms of duration and intensity, research indicates that vigorous exercise that raises students' heart rates is more effective than moderate or light activities (Lang et al., 2010). Duration of exercise bouts varies considerably in the literature. Thus, we recommend that teachers select a vigorous exercise activity and allot sufficient time for students to warm up, raise their heart rate/breath hard, and cool down. Research also suggests that the effects of exercise dissipate over time (Ogg-Groenendaal et al., 2014). Thus, if possible, we recommend that teachers plan for multiple bouts of exercise throughout the day. Any location is fine so long as it is accessible and permits students to engage in the exercise safely. Especially for students with ASD, predictability is important, so exercise bouts should follow a consistent schedule and routine, and take place in a familiar and consistent environment.

Lang et al. (2010) noted that teachers will need to teach the exercise activities to many students. Both Austin (2014) and Srinivasan et al. (2014) recommended using visual prompts to guide exercise activities (e.g., pictures of the different steps of exercise activity) rather than engage in lengthy verbal directions. Consider task analyzing the exercise activity to identify critical components of the activity for which to provide visual cues. Furthermore, many students will need supports to successfully complete exercise activities. To maintain motivation, teachers should consider using empirically validated behavioral approaches such as behavior-specific praise, token economies, and self-monitoring (Alberto & Troutman, 2013). For students with physical limitations, consider working with an expert in adaptive physical education on how to adapt and support student participation.

During the exercise activity, teachers should actively monitor, reinforce, and prompt (as needed) student participation. Teachers may wish to use a heart rate monitor and target a particular heart rate. The target heart rate for vigorous exercise is typically considered to be 70–85% of one's maximum heart rate (220 − age). Thus, a target heart rate for a 10-year old might be 147 beats per minute ([220 − 10] x .70). Generally, we recommend monitoring other, more readily observable indicators of physical exertion, such as sweating and increased breathing rate. During the exercise activity, teachers should provide warm-up and cool-down activities, and make sure students are hydrated and not over-heated. Teachers should also monitor students for escape-related behaviors and other indications that students find the selected exercise activity punishing. If this occurs, an alternative exercise activity should be selected.

After completing the exercise activity, take data on the target behavior at different time intervals. These data will provide guidance as to when students should engage in another bout of exercise (i.e., when data show behavior returning to unacceptable or baseline levels). More generally, these data will indicate the effectiveness of the exercise bouts. If the exercise bouts are not improving behavior meaningfully, consider adapting the intervention (Torres, Farley, & Cook, 2012). For example, the teacher might change the exercise activity, make an exercise activity more intense or of longer duration, or provide more supports for students to be successful in the activity. Whatever changes are made, it is important to continue taking data to determine the effects of the changes and decide whether further adaptations are needed.

CONCLUSION

A research review of Brain Gym® reveals there is scarce empirical evidence demonstrating the effectiveness of this program. Moreover, the program is founded upon invalidated and unsubstantiated theoretical assumptions. We do not recommend that educators use Brain Gym® as an intervention to target disruptive behavior or that administrators allocate resources for training or materials. Alternatively, there is a growing body of research supporting the effectiveness of antecedent bouts of exercise as an intervention for ameliorating disruptive behaviors for students with a variety of learning and behavioral disabilities. Although further research should be done to develop discrete program protocols, there is ample evidence to support the implementation of this research-based, free, and socially acceptable intervention in classrooms and schools.

REFERENCES

Alberto, P. A., & Troutman, A. C. (2013). *Applied behavioral analysis for teachers* (9th ed.). Boston, MA: Pearson.

Allison, D. B., Faith, M. S., & Franklin, R. D. (1995). Antecedent exercise in the treatment of disruptive behavior: A meta-analytic review. *Clinical Psychology: Science and Practice, 2*, 279–303.

American Academy for Cerebral Palsy and others. (1968). *Neurology, 18*, 1214–1215. doi:10.1212/WNL.18.12.1214

American Academy of Pediatrics. (1999). The treatment of neurologically impaired children using patterning. *Pediatrics, 104*, 1149–1151.

Arter, J. A., & Jenkins, J. R. (1979). Differential diagnosis—Prescriptive teaching: A critical appraisal. *Review of Educational Research, 49*, 517–555.

Austin, K. (2014). Exercise for students with autism spectrum disorder: More than just a passing fad. Innovations & Perspectives, November 5. Virginia Department of Education's Training & Technical Assistance Center. Retrieved from http://www.ttacnews.vcu.edu/2014/11/exercise-for-students-with-autism-spectrum-disorder-more-than-just-a-passing-fad/

Balow, B. (1971). Perceptual-motor activities in the treatment of severe reading disability. *The Reading Teacher, 24*, 513–542.

Banich, M. T. (1998). The missing link: The role of interhemispheric interaction in attentional processing. *Brain and Cognition, 36*(2), 128–157.

Barclay, T. H., Richards, S., Schoffstall, J., Magnuson, C., McPhee, C., Price, J., … Price, J. (2014). A pilot study on the effects of exercise on depression symptoms using levels of neurotransmitters and EEG as markers. *European Journal of Psychology and Educational Studies, 1*(1), 30–35.

Best, J. R. (2010). Effects of physical activity on children's executive function: Contributions of experimental research on aerobic exercise. *Developmental Review, 30*, 331–351.

Board of Trustees of the Council for Learning Disabilities. (1986). Measurement and training of perceptual and perceptual-motor functions: A position statement by the Board of Trustees of the Council for Learning Disabilities. *Learning Disability Quarterly, 9*, 247.

Bochner, S. (1978). Ayres, sensory integration and learning disorders: A question of theory and practice. *Australian Journal of Mental Retardation, 5*, 41–45.

Bradley, R., Doolittle, J., & Bartolotta, R. (2008). Building on the data and adding to the discussion: The experiences and outcomes of students with emotional disturbance. *Journal of Behavioral Education, 17*(1), 4–23. doi:10.1007/s10864-007-9058-6

Brain Gym International. (2015). Brain Gym about. Retrieved from http://www.braingym.org/about

Brain Gym International. (2011). *Edu-K style guide: The style and standards of educational kinesiology*. Ventura, CA: The Educational Foundation. Retrieved from http://www.braingym.org/brochures/Edu-K%20Style%20Guide%202011.pdf

Bru, D. (2009). Academic outcomes in school classes with markedly disruptive pupils. *Social Psychology of Education, 12*, 461–479.

Cammisa, K. M. (1994). Educational kinesiology with learning disabled children: An efficacy study. *Perceptual and Motor Skills, 78*(1), 105–106.

Cannella-Malone, H. I., Tullis, C. A., & Kazee, A. R. (2011). Using antecedent exercise to decrease challenging behavior in boys with developmental disabilities and an emotional disorder. *Journal of Positive Behavior Interventions, 13*, 230–239.

Chang, Y. K., Labban, J. D., Gapin, J. I., & Etnier, J. L. (2012). The effects of acute exercise on cognitive performance: A meta-analysis. *Brain Research*, *1453*, 87−101.

Christman, S. D., Propper, R. E., & Dion, A. (2004). Increased interhemispheric interaction is associated with decreased false memories in a verbal converging semantic associates paradigm. *Brain and Cognition*, *56*(3), 313−319.

De Los Santos, G., Hume, E. C., & Cortes, A. (2002). Improving the faculty's effectiveness in increasing the success of Hispanic students in higher education—Pronto! *Journal of Hispanic Higher Education*, *1*(3), 225−237.

Dennison, P. E. (2006). *Brain Gym® and me: Reclaiming the pleasure of learning*. Ventura, CA: Edu-Kinesthetics.

Dennison, P. E., & Dennison, G. E. (1994). *Brain Gym® teachers'* (Rev. ed.). Ventura, CA: Edu-Kinesthetics.

Dennison, P. E., & Dennison, G. E. (2010). *Brain Gym® teachers'* (Rev. ed.). Ventura, CA: Edu-Kinesthetics.

Doman, C. H. (1968). *The diagnosis and treatment of speech and reading problems*. Springfield, IL: Thomas.

Doman, R. J., Spitz, E. B., Zucman, E., Delacato, C. H., & Doman, G. (1960). Children with severe brain injuries: Neurological organization in terms of mobility. *Journal of the American Medical Association*, *174*(3), 257−262.

Emmer, E. T., & Stough, L. M. (2001). Classroom management: A critical part of educational psychology, with implications for teacher education. *Educational Psychologist*, *36*(2), 103−112.

Folino, A., Ducharme, J. M., & Greenwald, N. (2014). Temporal effects of antecedent exercise on students' disruptive behaviors: An exploratory study. *Journal of School Psychology*, *52*, 447−462.

Frostig, M., & Maslow, P. (1973). *Learning problems in the classroom*. New York, NY: Grune & Stratton.

Garvert, M. M., Moutoussis, M., Kurth-Nelson, Z., Behrens, T. E., & Dolan, R. J. (2015). Learning-induced plasticity in medial prefrontal cortex predicts preference malleability. *Neuron*, *85*, 418−428.

Gersten, R., Fuchs, L. S., Compton, D., Coyne, M., Greenwood, C., & Innocenti, M. S. (2005). Quality indicators for group experimental and quasi-experimental research in special education. *Exceptional Children*, *71*, 149−164.

Getman, G. N. (1965). The visuomotor complex in the acquisition of learning skills. In J. Hellmuth (Ed.), *Learning disorders* (Vol. 1, pp. 49−76). Seattle, WA: Special Child Publications.

Goswami, U. (2006). Neuroscience and education: From research to practice? *Nature Reviews Neuroscience*, *7*(5), 406−413.

Halperin, J. M., Berwid, O. G., & O'Neill, S. (2014). Healthy body, healthy mind? The effectiveness of physical activity to treat ADHD in children. *Child and Adolescent Psychiatric Clinics of North America*, *23*, 899−936.

Henricsson, L., & Rydell, A. M. (2004). Elementary school children with behavior problems: Teacher-child relations and self-perception. A prospective study. *Merrill-Palmer Quarterly*, *50*(2), 111−138.

Hyatt, K. J. (2007). Brain Gym® building stronger brains or wishful thinking? *Remedial and Special Education*, *28*(2), 117−124.

Kavale, K., & Mattson, P. D. (1983). "One jumped off the balance beam": Meta-analysis of perceptual-motor training. *Journal of Learning Disabilities*, *16*, 165−173.

Kavale, K. A., & Forness, S. R. (1987). Substance over style: Assessing the efficacy of modality testing and teaching. *Exceptional Children, 54*, 228−239.

Kavale, K. A., & Forness, S. R. (1995). *The nature of learning disabilities: Critical elements of diagnosis and classification.* Abingdon: Routledge.

Kavale, K. A., & Mostert, M. P. (2004). *The positive side of special education: Minimizing its fads, fancies, and follies.* Lanham, MD: R&L Education.

Kephart, N. C. (1960). *The slow learner in the classroom.* Columbus, OH: Merrill.

Khalsa, G. K., Morris, G. D., & Sifft, J. M. (1988). Effect of educational kinesiology on static balance of learning disabled students. *Perceptual and Motor Skills, 67*(1), 51−54.

Kilgard, M. P. (2012). Harnessing plasticity to understand learning and treat disease. *Trends in Neurosciences, 35*(12), 715−722.

Lang, R., Koegel, L. K., Ashbaugh, K., Regester, A., Ence, W., & Smith, W. (2010). Physical exercise and individuals with autism spectrum disorders: A systematic review. *Research in Autism Spectrum Disorders, 4*, 565−576.

McCarthy, C. J., Lambert, R. G., O'Donnell, M., & Melendres, L. T. (2009). The relation of elementary teachers' experience, stress, and coping resources to burnout symptoms. *The Elementary School Journal, 109*(3), 282−300.

Medina, J. A., Netto, T. L., Muszkat, M., Medina, A. C., Botter, D., Orbetelli, R., & Miranda, M. C. (2010). Exercise impact on sustained attention of ADHD children, methylphenidate effects. *Attention Deficit and Hyperactivity Disorders, 2*(1), 49−58.

National Autism Center. (2015). *Findings and conclusions: National standards project, phase 2.* Randolph, MA: Author. Retrieved from http://www.nationalautismcenter.org/resources/

Nielsen, J. A., Zielinski, B. A., Ferguson, M. A., Lainhart, J. E., & Anderson, J. S. (2013). An evaluation of the left-brain vs. right-brain hypothesis with resting state functional connectivity magnetic resonance imaging. *PloS One, 8*(8), e71275.

Ogg-Groenendaal, M., Hermans, H., & Claessens, B. (2014). A systematic review on the effect of exercise interventions on challenging behavior for people with intellectual disabilities. *Research in Developmental Disabilities, 35*, 1507−1517.

Orton, S. T. (1937). *Reading, writing and speech problems in children.* New York, NY: W.W. Norton & Company.

Purves, D., Augustine, G. J., Fitzpatrick, D., Hall, W. C., LaMantia, A. S., & White, L. E. (2012). *Neuroscience* (5th ed.). Sunderland, MA: Sinauer.

Ratey, J. J. (2008). *Spark: The revolutionary new science of exercise and the brain.* New York, NY: Little, Brown.

Robbins, M. P. (1966). The Delacato interpretation of neurological organization. *Reading Research Quarterly, 1*(3), 57−78.

Sifft, J. M., & Khalsa, G. C. K. (1991). Effect of educational kinesiology upon simple response times and choice response times. *Perceptual and Motor Skills, 73*(3), 1011−1015.

Silverstein, J. M., & Allison, D. B. (1994). The comparative efficacy of antecedent exercise and methylphenidate: A single-case randomized trial. *Child: Care, Health and Development, 20*(1), 47−60.

Spaulding, L. S., Mostert, M. P., & Beam, A. P. (2010). Is Brain Gym® an effective educational intervention? *Exceptionality, 18*(1), 18−30.

Srinivasan, S. M., Pescatello, L. S., & Bhat, A. N. (2014). Current perspectives on physical activity and exercise recommendations for children and adolescents with autism spectrum disorders. *Physical Therapy, 94*, 875−889.

Stephenson, J., Carter, M., & Wheldall, K. (2007). Still jumping on the balance beam: Continued use of perceptual motor programs in Australian schools. Australian *Journal of Education, 51*(1), 6−18.

Stichter, J. P., Conroy, M. A., & Kauffman, J. M. (2008). An introduction to students *with high-incidence disabilities*. Upper Saddle River, NJ: Prentice Hall.

Stone, M., & Pielstick, N. L. (1969). Effectiveness of Delacato treatment with kindergarten children. *Psychology in the Schools, 6*(1), 63−68.

Sullivan, J. (1972). The effects of Kephart's perceptual motor-training on a reading clinic sample. *Journal of Learning Disabilities, 5*(9), 545−551.

Sutherland, K. S., & Oswald, D. P. (2005). The relationship between teacher and student behavior in classrooms for students with emotional and behavioral disorders: Transactional processes. *Journal of Child and Family Studies, 14*(1), 1−14.

Tomporowski, P. D. (2003). Cognitive and behavioral responses to acute exercise in youths: A review. *Pediatric Exercise Science, 15*, 348−359.

Tomporowski, P. D., Davis, C. L., Miller, P. H., & Naglieri, J. A. (2008). Exercise and children's intelligence, cognition, and academic achievement. *Educational Psychology Review, 20*, 111−131.

Torres, C., Farley, C. A., & Cook, B. G. (2012). A special educator's guide to successfully implementing evidence-based practices. *Teaching Exceptional Children, 45*(1), 64−73.

Verburgh, L., Königs, M., Scherder, E. J. A., & Oosterlaan, J. (2014). Physical exercise and executive functions in preadolescent children, adolescents and young adults: A meta-analysis. *British Journal of Sports Medicine, 48*, 973−979.

Wagner, M., & Davis, M. (2006). How are we preparing students with emotional disturbances for the transition to young adulthood? Findings from the national longitudinal transition study 2. *Journal of Emotional and Behavioral Disorders, 14*(2), 86−98.

Weisberg, D. S., Keil, F. C., Goodstein, J., Rawson, E., & Gray, J. R. (2008). The seductive allure of neuroscience explanations. *Journal of Cognitive Neuroscience, 20*, 470−477.

Wolfsont, C. (2002). Increasing behavioral skills and level of understanding in adults: A brief method integrating Dennison's Brain Gym balance with Piaget's reflective processes. *Journal of Adult Development, 9*, 187−203.

Wong, C., Odom, S. L., Hume, K., Cox, A. W., Fettig, A., Kucharczyk, S., … Schultz, T. R. (2014). *Evidence-based practices for children, youth, and young adults with autism spectrum disorder*. Chapel Hill, NC: The University of North Carolina, Frank Porter Graham Child Development Institute, Autism Evidence-Based Practice Review Group. Retrieved from http://autismpdc.fpg.unc.edu/sites/autismpdc.fpg.unc.edu/files/imce/documents/2014-EBP-Report.pdf

Ylinen, S., & Kujala, T. (2015). Neuroscience illuminating the influence of auditory or phonological intervention on language-related deficits. *Frontiers in Psychology, 6*, 1−8. doi:10.3389/fpsyg.2015.00137

CHAPTER 7

LEARNING STYLES, LEARNING PREFERENCES, AND STUDENT CHOICE: IMPLICATIONS FOR TEACHING

Timothy J. Landrum and Kimberly M. Landrum

ABSTRACT

We consider the theory and evidence supporting learning styles, and contrast these with the related concepts of learning preferences and student choice. Although the theory of learning styles remains popular in the field of education as one guidepost teachers might use to maximize the effectiveness of instruction for individual students, including students with learning and behavioral disabilities, a review of the evidence supporting a learning styles approach suggests that it offers little benefit to students with disabilities. In contrasting learning styles with the related concept of learning preferences, we posit that interventions based on student choice may offer a more parsimonious and evidence-driven approach to enhancing instruction and improving outcomes for students with learning and behavioral disabilities.

Keywords: Learning styles; differentiated instruction; student choice; choice and preferred activities

Instructional Practices with and without Empirical Validity
Advances in Learning and Behavioral Disabilities, Volume 29, 135–152
Copyright © 2016 by Emerald Group Publishing Limited
All rights of reproduction in any form reserved
ISSN: 0735-004X/doi:10.1108/S0735-004X20160000029006

Among the fundamental questions teachers face as they prepare to teach, few would seem as critical as this: on what should instruction be based? Put simply, planning instruction involves at least two basic tasks: deciding what to teach then deciding how to teach it. The move toward standards-based reforms and accountability (e.g., *A Nation at Risk*, U.S. Department of Education, 1983) might suggest that state standards, or more recently the Common Core (National Governors Association Center for Best Practices, 2010), should dictate curricular content. But much less clear is how to select from the array of approaches teachers might use in the delivery of instruction. While standards-based reforms increasingly drive curricular content in the United States, and emphasis increases for students with disabilities to gain meaningful access to the general curriculum, we note that a hallmark of special education for students with learning and behavioral disabilities since it earliest days has been individualization (Hallahan, Kauffman, & Pullen, 2015). Importantly, this individualization presumably involves both what is to be taught and how it is to be taught. Special education teachers have been encouraged to figure out through systematic observation and data collection where students' strengths and needs lie, and to target instruction toward the next skill or curricular component a student must master in order to progress along on their individual learning trajectory. Whether discussing academic instruction or social/behavioral interventions, concepts like targeting just manageable difficulties (Hobbs, 1974) seem quite relevant in planning instruction for students with learning or behavioral disabilities. Additionally, students with disabilities, by definition (Hallahan et al., 2015), require specially designed instruction. In other words, students with identified disabilities may be taught different or modified curriculum, but will almost always require different instructional approaches.

For the purposes of this chapter, we set aside discussions of what to teach (which should not imply that such decisions are any less critical for students with disabilities), and focus instead on how teachers might best plan and deliver instruction. Approaches to instruction are often discussed in their extremes: teacher-led versus student-centered instruction, for example, or constructivist versus direct-instruction orientations. Debates about these competing instructional paradigms have persisted for decades, and indeed may be even more pointed as the lines between general education and special education have blurred, and models such as co-teaching (Friend & Cook, 2003) become increasingly common as service delivery options for special education services. Within an inclusive or co-teaching framework, distinctions among instructional theories and models create critical decision points for educators who may have different perspectives and training regarding how best to teach but who must nonetheless work collaboratively to provide instruction for students with disabilities. The weight of these decisions, and the impact of educators' choices regarding them, is enormous. Consider the potential influence of constructivism (Vygotsky, 1978, 1986) or whole language theories (Goodman & Goodman, 2009), or models like direct instruction (Carnine, Silbert, Kame'enui, Slocum, & Travers, 2017) on the nature of instruction in an inclusive classroom.

We focus in this chapter on one element of the how-to-teach question, considering specifically what guidance teachers might derive from students' perspectives on the content and delivery of instruction they will be exposed to. Given the general focus of this volume on discrepancies between practices supported by more versus less evidence, we consider what might be described as a continuum teachers may think of when deciding how best to design and deliver instruction to a particular student or group. We consider in turn (a) learning styles, (b) learning preferences, and (c) student choice. As we discuss in the next section, references to teaching to students' learning styles have appeared consistently in the professional and trade literature in education since at least the 1970s (Canfield & Lafferty, 1970; Dunn, 1983; Dunn & Dunn, 1993; Lovelace, 2005), despite little to no empirical support for basing instruction on purported learning styles (Willingham, Hughes, & Dobolyi, 2015). The concept of learning *preferences* has received significant visibility in the context of differentiated instruction (Tomlinson, 1999, 2009). Many descriptions of differentiation include calls to assess and use students' learning preferences when planning differentiated instruction, and in some cases learning styles seem to have been used interchangeably with, or explicitly subsumed within, students' learning preferences (Tomlinson et al., 2003). As we outline in this chapter, while the evidence supporting learning styles is quite limited, the notion of identifying students' learning preferences — often as simple as asking students what they prefer in a given instructional context — has both logical and empirical support. We conclude however, that there is a fundamental and essential distinction between a learning style and a learning preference, and we argue that it is really student choice that may drive any effects of interventions based on a purported learning style or preference. Critically, we note that arguments that students learn better, or learn more, when taught toward a learning style are not supported by empirical evidence, whereas the use of student choice has been associated with improved student compliance and engagement, both of which are known correlates of achievement.

LEARNING STYLES

We noted that the term "learning styles" has appeared in the education literature since at least the 1970s (Dunn & Dunn, 1979), but it is important to acknowledge that the very concept of a learning style has been controversial for nearly as long, and especially so related to students who may have learning or behavioral disabilities (Dunn, 1983, 1990; Kavale & Forness, 1987; Kavale, Hirshoren, & Forness, 1998; Kavale & LeFever, 2007; Lovelace, 2005; Stahl, 1999). In this section we provide (a) an overview of the definition of learning styles; (b) a brief discussion of the ways that learning styles have been assessed, and how a learning style is established for an individual student; and (c) a summary of literature on whether evidence supports matching instruction to a purported learning style.

A Definition and Description of Learning Styles

Any general definition of learning styles would undoubtedly include the simple notion that individuals differ in how they learn, but even this brief phrase raises a number of questions. For example, is the difference between individuals merely a self-reported preference regarding learning, such as would be obtained by simply asking a learner what type of instructional environment they would prefer? Or, conversely, does "learning differently" imply that more or better learning takes place when a preference is addressed? In fact, although the idea that learning styles exist (i.e., that we all learn differently) appears to have broad appeal and popularity (Willingham, 2005), there is no standard definition of learning styles. Instead, definitions are often unique to a given model or method for assessing learning style. As Coffield, Moseley, Hall, and Ecclestone (2004) noted, "the learning styles field is not unified, but instead is divided into three linked areas of activity: theoretical, pedagogical and commercial" (p. 1). To highlight the complexity of this point, consider that Coffield et al. identified 71 separate learning styles models, though in their comprehensive review of learning styles models and inventories they identified 13 "major" models, with the remaining 58 consisting of models that differed only slightly from, or were deemed to be derivative of, one of the 13 major models.

Many models of learning styles focus on adults, and much of the literature and corpus of assessment tools available were designed for use with students in college or other adult learning environments (e.g., management training, nursing; Hauer, Straub, & Wolf, 2005; Kolb & Kolb, 2005). In terms of students with learning and behavioral disabilities, far and away the most prominent model is that proposed by Dunn and colleagues (Dunn, 1983; Dunn & Dunn, 1979). This model gained particular prominence in special education with Dunn's (1983) publication, "Learning style and its relation to exceptionality at both ends of the spectrum," published in *Exceptional Children*, arguably the most prominent journal in special education at the time, and the research journal of the Council for Exceptional Children, the United States's largest professional organization representing professionals who work with or on behalf of students with disabilities. The prominence of this paper no doubt established considerable credibility for the concept and its applicability to instruction in special education.

In Dunn's (1983) model, learning styles capture the ways individuals differ in how they concentrate on, absorb, and retain new information. Dunn proposed that a learning style "comprises a combination of environmental, emotional, sociological, physical, and psychological elements that permit individuals to receive, store, and use knowledge" (p. 496). Critical to our analysis in this chapter is the idea conveyed here that students learn better when instruction is matched to their learning style. Dunn and Dunn (1979) offered descriptions of 18 separate elements across five domains that should be examined in assessing and identifying an individual's learning style (Table 1); they further claimed that for most individuals, learning style is strongly influenced by between 6 and 14 of these elements (Dunn, 1983). With regard to physical elements, Dunn and Dunn (1979) and Dunn (1983) argued, for example, that the temperature and lighting of a room, or the formality of the learning environment might differentially impact students based on distinct learning styles. Similar arguments were offered regarding emotional elements; Dunn (1983) argued that motivation, persistence, responsibility, and structure differentially affect the way students respond

Table 1. Domains and Elements of the Dunn Model of Learning Styles.

Domain	Elements
Environmental	Sound, light, temperature
Emotional	Motivation, task persistence, structure
Sociological	Alone, pairs, peers, team, with an adult
Physical/Physiological	Auditory, visual, tactual, kinesthetic, time of day, mobility
Psychological	Analytic/global, impulsive/reflective

Source: Dunn and Dunn (1979), see also www.learningstyles.net

to instruction. Dunn (1983) noted, for example, "impersistent students often need 'breaks' while they are learning" (p. 498). Elements of the sociological domain included the notion that some students might work better alone, while others may work better with a peer or adult, or in a small group. In the perceptual domain, Dunn and Dunn (1979) argued that 20% to 30% of students appear to prefer and respond better to instruction that emphasizes an auditory channel, 40% prefer visual, and 30–40% have learning styles that are grounded in either tactual/kinesthetic, visual tactual, or some combination of these four sensory pathways. Dunn and Dunn (1979) noted that when teachers teach only one way, or instruction is delivered primarily through a single mode (e.g., lecture) educators should not be surprised that "so few students achieve as well as we believe they should" (p. 240). Therefore, Dunn (1983) stressed the importance of matching instruction to students' perceptual strengths.

Finally, the psychological elements of learning style include global versus analytic learners, left- versus right-brain learners, and impulsive versus reflective learners. Accordingly, the structure of lessons should presumably differ based on learner's preferred styles (e.g., a sequential lesson might suit an analytic learner, while a global learner might prefer and benefit more from a lesson focusing on big picture concepts). Further, teachers must differ in how responses and feedback from students are sought; impulsive students, prone to calling out answers, and reflective students, who might seldom offer responses, would in theory require significantly different instructional approaches according to Dunn (1983).

A critical point we draw from these early descriptions of learning styles is that they were offered with very explicit claims that students learn better when teachers identify learning styles and tailor instruction toward them. That is, early proponents argued more than a simple relationship between students' preferences and willingness to engage in an activity – a concept we elaborate on in a subsequent section.

Assessing Learning Styles

The assessment of learning styles is possible through dozens of commercially available checklists and inventories. The *Kolb Learning Style Inventory* (Version 4) (Kolb, n.d.) is regarded as among the most popular learning style models (Coffield et al., 2004), but as we noted earlier this assessment tool is designed primarily for use in higher education and for training for adults, managers, or other executives. The Dunn and Dunn model is undoubtedly among the most popular learning style assessments geared toward struggling learners. This model includes several separate online assessment tools geared toward different age levels. The *Elementary Learning Style Assessment* (ELSA, Dunn & Burke, 2007; available at www.learningstyles.net), for example, is for use with students age 7–9 (grades 3–5 in the United States). Additional versions are also available (for ages 10–13, or grades 6–8; ages 14–18, or grades 9–12; and ages 17 and up). These learning style inventories include items that ask students about their learning preferences. For example, a sample item on the ELSA, for students aged 7–9, asks students to choose from (a) "I like the light to be low when I am learning new things," (b) "I like bright light when I am learning new things," or (c) "it doesn't matter to me" (Dunn & Burke, 2007).

Scholars who have examined learning style assessment tools generally agree that there are concerns with the basic psychometric properties (i.e., reliability and validity) of most learning style inventories. Reliability is of course a particularly fundamental problem; if a learning style cannot be reliably established, teaching toward any purported learning style in instructional contexts is unlikely to result in any benefit. Logically, the idea that a learning style might be static is particularly problematic, and on balance this has been borne out by research. In a seminal meta-analysis of modality-based instruction (importantly, *not* a critique of any particular learning style model or assessment tool), Kavale and Forness (1987) found that a clear modality preference was established only about 70% of the time for individual students across the 39 studies they reviewed. Willingham et al. (2015) suggested that the general lack of reliability among learning styles assessment tools is both well-established (Coffield et al., 2004), and further is well-known even among researchers in the field of learning styles (Peterson, Rayner, & Armstrong, 2009). In an exhaustive review of learning styles models and instruments, Coffield et al. (2004) noted problems with internal consistency, and particular problems with test-retest reliability, in Dunn's *Learning Styles Inventory* (Price & Dunn, 1997). Addressing the application of a learning styles approach to the teaching of reading specifically, Stahl (1999) concluded from an overview of research reviews that "one cannot reliably measure children's reading styles and even if one could, matching children to reading programs by learning styles does not improve their learning" (p. 2).

The association between reliability and validity – that reliability is a necessary but not sufficient criterion for any claim of validity – consequently raises questions about the utility of the entire learning styles enterprise, at least in terms of school-aged children, and especially among those with or suspected of having learning or behavioral disabilities. Coffield et al. (2004) were direct and blunt with their assessment, noting "with regard to Dunn and Dunn ..., our examination of the reliability and validity of their learning style instruments strongly suggests that they should not be used in education" (p. 119).

Matching Instruction to a Learning Style

The concepts of modality preferences and modality-based instruction were popular in the literature of the 1970s in special education, but early reviews found little support for matching instruction to any such preference in students (Arter & Jenkins, 1977, 1979; Kampwirth & Bates, 1980). An important contribution to this debate was the meta-analysis of 39 studies of modality-based instruction in special education by Kavale and Forness (1987). Among the results of the Kavale and Forness meta-analysis were that (a) a clear modality preference was established for only about 70% of participants and (b) the average effect size resulting from teaching to a preferred modality was .144, or a change in approximately 6 percentile ranks. Kavale and Forness concluded "no appreciable gain was found by differentiating instruction according to modality preference" (p. 238).

We emphasize that Kavale and Forness (1987) did not set out to evaluate the Dunn and Dunn model of learning styles, but the exchange that followed between Dunn et al. and Kavale and Forness et al. regarding the utility of a learning styles approach would come to be called "blistering" (O'Neil, 1990, p. 7). Landrum and McDuffie (2010) summarized this debate, which included a response to Kavale and Forness by Dunn (1990), a rejoinder to Dunn by Kavale and Forness (1990); and subsequent papers that included a meta-analysis by Dunn, Griggs, Olson, Beasley, and Gorman (1995), a critique of this meta-analysis by Kavale et al. (1998), a meta-analysis by Lovelace (2005), and a critique of Lovelace by Kavale and LeFever (2007). Though Dunn et al. consistently defended their claims regarding the usefulness of a learning styles approach, and the use of their model specifically, perhaps the major criticism offered of their reviews and meta-analyses was a reliance on a preponderance of unpublished literature, including dissertations from a single university. In critiquing the Dunn et al. (1995) meta-analysis, Landrum and McDuffie pointed out "the literature ultimately retained for review included 35 dissertations and 1 published study" (p. 12), and further that 20 of the dissertations reviewed were from a single university. Landrum and McDuffie also noted that the one published study included in this meta-analysis was published in *Human Resource Quarterly* and focused on employee training.

Finally, Pashler, McDaniel, Rohrer, and Bjork (2009) provided a review of studies of the effectiveness of a learning styles-based approach to instruction, but found only four studies that met their criteria for inclusion. In three of the four studies, no positive effects were noted for matching instruction to a learning style; in the fourth study (Sternberg, Grigorenko, Ferrari, & Clinkenbeard, 1999), gifted high school students performed better, according to ratings of their performance in courses, when summer psychology classes were matched to their analytical, creative, or practical aptitudes.

In summary, the available literature lacks support for the general matching of instruction to a preferred learning style. Landrum and Landrum (2014) noted specifically

> there is simply a dearth of published research that applies rigorous methodology to the evaluation of (a) whether a learning style can be reliably established for an individual student, and if so (b) whether matching instruction to learning styles result in improved learning outcomes. (p. 3)

They further noted that this is especially the case for students who may have learning disabilities, but importantly suggested that a fruitful line of research may lie be in examining the importance of examining learning preferences, rather than learning styles specifically.

LEARNING PREFERENCES

The notion of a learning preference may have achieved prominence in the educational literature primarily through conceptualizations of differentiated instruction, and specifically through the models of differentiation described by Tomlinson (1999). In her models, instruction to meet the needs of diverse learners must be differentiated based on students' readiness, interests, and learning profiles. The latter element, learning profile, has been further described as including students' intelligence preferences, gender, culture, and learning style (Tomlinson, 1999). We have described elsewhere (Landrum & McDuffie, 2010) some significant and positive consistencies between differentiated instruction broadly defined and the conceptual foundations of special education. Our point here is to draw the distinction between what we view as appropriate guideposts for planning instruction, and the unnecessary consideration of learning style. Even in Tomlinson and colleagues' work summarizing theoretical and empirical support for differentiated instruction generally (Tomlinson et al., 2003), there is little support for the specific inclusion of learning styles in the planning and delivery of differentiated instruction. For example, in their 2003 literature review on differentiated instruction, Tomlinson et al. cited only a single unpublished doctoral dissertation to support the idea of learning styles. This dissertation (Sullivan, 1993) reported a meta-analysis of studies that examined the effects of applying the Dunn model on student achievement and performance, and was conducted at the same university where a majority of the unpublished studies included in the review were conducted (Landrum & McDuffie, 2010).

Despite concerns with learning styles, many of the elements or domains on which Tomlinson (1999) has encouraged teachers to base differentiated instruction are in fact highly consistent with core tenets of special education for students with disabilities. Readiness, for example, is critical in that instruction must take into account students' current skill and developmental levels, and requires some level of observation and data collection on the part of teachers so they know where to begin instruction. Similarly, addressing students' interests in instruction has been a focus of special education teacher preparation for decades; this is especially true in the context of literacy instruction, for example, where the concept of "high interest, low vocabulary" texts has been prominent for decades (Chall, 1953). A significant part of this theory is the simple connection between motivation to engage in a given task and the ability to choose a preferred task. When asked to engage in independent silent reading, for example, a student with a keen interest in dinosaurs but no interest in the American Revolutionary War would seem more likely to engage in reading, and perhaps to sustain reading, when allowed to choose a book on dinosaurs instead of being told to read about the Revolutionary War.

We argue that the connection described above has little to do with a learning preference, but in fact is as simple as allowing students choice. Moreover, the idea extends well beyond choosing a book or assignment on a topic of interest. As we describe in the subsequent section, student choice can take into account when to do assignments, where to work, and with what material to complete an assignment. Importantly, and quite distinct from learning styles, there is evidence that students can readily identify a preference (Willingham, 2005), and such preferences are not characteristic of any given individual trait or style of learning. Nor are preferences static; they simply involve presenting students with a choice, which is generally as easy as posing a question (e.g., "would you like to do your math homework or your vocabulary review first?").

STUDENT CHOICE

In the previous sections we offered an analysis of learning styles, which we characterized as a broad, tenuous concept (Willingham et al., 2015) that has been defined in multiple ways, and toward which dozens of measures have been promulgated (Coffield et al., 2004). We then described the more specific concept of learning preference, which we argue (a) represents a more distinct concept that can be measured in a relatively straightforward manner but (b) has been defined in popular literature, especially in the context of models of differentiated instruction, as including learning style (Tomlinson, 2003, 2009). We transition now to what we view as the more concrete, measureable, and instructionally relevant end of this continuum, where we focus on the growing body of literature that supports student choice as a potentially powerful intervention for students with learning and behavioral disabilities. We noted previously that learning preference and student choice might be viewed as highly overlapping constructs if the terms are merely examined semantically, but in this chapter we use the term student choice to refer to a very specific intervention that has been tested in dozens of studies.

Student choice (sometimes referred to in the intervention literature as choice and preferred activities; Kern & State, 2009) takes advantage of the idea that motivation and persistence are increased when individuals are allowed to make choices about what to do, or when and how to do it. Skinner (1971) referred to this concept in a behavioral context, suggesting that an individual makes a choice whenever he or she engages in a given behavior in order to obtain a particular reinforcer. The application of choice as an explicit intervention evolved significantly in the 1980s, primarily with regard to individuals with severe disabilities or developmental delay. Choice-making interventions were shown to be effective both in increasing engagement and reducing problem behavior. Dattilo and Rusch (1985) for example, showed that student choice resulted in greater participation in leisure activities among children aged 8–12 with severe intellectual disabilities, compared to participation in a leisure activity under a no-choice condition. Dyer, Dunlap, and Winterling (1990) demonstrated positive effects of choice on problem behavior. In this study, participants were three children aged 5–11 identified with developmental delay or severe intellectual disabilities who engaged in high rates of serious disruptive behavior, including aggression, self-injury, and tantrums. When students were provided a choice of both task (from among three to four options) and reinforcers (from among four to five options), rates of problem behavior decreased dramatically for all participants, and reversal phases indicated a clear functional relationship between the intervention (choice condition versus no-choice condition) and rates of problem behavior.

Whereas much of the earlier literature on choice focused on learners with more severe disabilities, and often addressed how to assess choice, whether choice could be assessed reliably, and how to infuse choice into daily routines (Lancioni, O'Reilly, & Emerson, 1996), more recent studies have assessed the impacts of choice on student behavior and compliance, and have included students with learning and behavioral (i.e., high incidence) disabilities as well. In traditional classrooms, virtually all aspects of students' experiences are dictated by teachers: where to sit, what to do first, what to do next, the order in which tasks are to be undertaken, and the consequences associated with student behavior. But according to a growing body of research, students are more motivated when they are allowed some level of choice about any of these variables, including which task to work on (Dunlap et al., 1994), the sequence of completing tasks or items on a task (Kern, Mantegna, Vorndran, Bailin, & Hilt, 2001; Ramsey, Jolivette, Patterson, & Kennedy, 2010), where to complete the task, and what materials are used (Harding, Wacker, Cooper, Millard, & Jensen-Kovalan, 1994; Rispoli et al., 2013; Ulke-Kurkcuoglu & Kircaali-Iftar, 2010). This can mean something as simple as allowing a student to choose whether to do a math problem set or a vocabulary exercise first, or to complete their writing assignment at their desk with pen and paper, or on a computer. Simple logic suggests that choice making can have a positive impact on compliance. For example, a student would seem far more likely to begin working on an assignment if he's asked whether he wants to do math or spelling first, and then is allowed to choose which to work on, rather than simply being told "time for spelling." But among the most validated outcomes of choice-making interventions is a reduction in problem behavior (Shogren, Faggella-Luby, Bae, & Wehmeyer, 2004), especially behavior maintained by escape from tasks (Romaniuk et al., 2002). The main targets for intervention we have described are no doubt highly interrelated: complying with teacher requests and engaging in appropriate tasks by definition will result in a reduction in off-task and problem behavior.

A number of authors have described the implementation of choice (Kern & State, 2009; Landrum & Sweigart, 2014) or summarized the effectiveness of choice interventions for students with learning and behavioral disabilities (Kern & Parks, 2012). We provide a brief listing of the types of choices that can be provided in Table 2. As can be seen, choice can cut across tasks themselves, or task preferences, such as allowing students to choose which task to complete first (e.g., working on a math assignment or a spelling

Table 2. Variables to Consider in Implementing Choice Interventions.

Context	Potential Choices
Tasks	Order of tasks
	Time of day
Nature/form of tasks	Tasks in different forms (flash cards vs. worksheets)
	Tasks with different materials (pen, pencil, electronic)
	Where in classroom to work on task
	With whom to work on a given task
Consequence	Activity reinforcer from among two or more options

assignment first), or which form of a task to choose (e.g., reviewing science vocabulary words by using flash cards with a peer, or by completing a science vocabulary worksheet independently). Simple topographical elements of tasks can provide choices: whether to use pen or pencil, or a choice among different colored pencils. Where in the classroom to work, within well-defined and predetermined options acceptable to the teacher, provides appealing choices for many students. Separate from choices regarding the tasks themselves, or features of the tasks and response options, are choices teachers may provide regarding consequences. Even within the context of existing classroom management structures, a simple choice of reinforcer (e.g., "when you're finished with your math assignment you may choose from 10 minutes in the gym to play basketball or 10 minutes in the computer lab to play a game of your choice") can result in enhanced compliance (Schmidt, Hanley, & Layer, 2009).

As Landrum and Sweigart (2014) and others have argued, choice provides a low-intensity antecedent strategy that has potentially powerful effects on compliance, engagement, and, consequently, achievement (Kern & State, 2009). While implementing choice requires forethought and planning, and evaluating its effects demands basic data collection on students' rates of compliance, engagement, or assignment completion (as would be true with any intervention), choice is low intensity in that virtually no additional materials, resources, or advanced training are needed. By and large, teachers can easily implement choice interventions in the context of existing curricula and management systems with minimal effort.

CONCLUSION

We have tried to provide some dissection of the student-centric concepts to which teachers might most profitably attend in planning and delivering instruction. We argued that learning styles may represent a misguided conceptual orientation, especially as applied to students with learning and behavioral disabilities. The reasons for this include that learning styles are difficult to assess reliably, but even more importantly that there appears to be virtually no published, peer-reviewed research supporting the effectiveness of learning styles-based instruction on outcomes for students with learning and behavioral disabilities. We further discussed the idea of learning preferences, specifically in the context of models of differentiated instruction that stress learning preferences as one driver of how specifically to differentiate instruction. We also noted that students' learning style is included within the definition of learning preferences in perhaps the most prominent models of differentiated instruction (Tomlinson, 2003, 2009). Finally, we argued that the more parsimonious, data-supported way to use these concepts to improve student outcomes might lie in student choice. In contrast to learning styles and learning preferences, choice has been studied and validated in literally dozens of empirical investigations appearing in peer-reviewed journals.

Choice addresses at least two critical elements of students' perspective on the nature of learning experiences they encounter. First and most simply, choice appears to provide significant motivation for students to engage and persist in a given task or activity. Second, and especially important for students with learning and behavioral disabilities, choice addresses a fundamental concern with autonomy. Effective special education instruction for students with disabilities carries explicit structure, and includes elements that are clearly teacher-directed. Effective instructional approaches such as opportunities to respond (OTRs; Sutherland & Wehby, 2001), prompting (Simonsen, Myers, & DeLuca, 2010), behavior specific praise (Sutherland, Wehby, & Copeland, 2000), and corrective feedback (Chard, Vaughn, & Tyler, 2002), to name only a few, are teacher-driven. But in the context of effective, explicit instruction, there are many opportunities for teachers to provide students with choices. As we have described, offering students choice regarding such simple things as the order of assignments, the methods or materials they will use to complete a task, where to complete a task, or a reinforcer they will receive can have a significant positive impact on their engagement and learning.

We recognize that our arguments in this chapter may be interpreted as little more than a semantic analysis of three highly similar concepts that rely on definitions and terminology that are muddied by both vague terminology and overlapping elements. Nonetheless, we find that learning styles remain hugely popular in the professional literature, the popular press, and the lore of teaching and teacher education. The same can be said of differentiated instruction, and the concern, as we have noted elsewhere (Landrum & McDuffie, 2010), is that confusing terminology and overlapping constructs may lead teachers to include learning styles in their planning and delivery of instruction. Returning to the guiding framework of this volume, that some practices are more effective than others, it appears that the utility of basing instruction for students with disabilities on a purported learning style is not supported by empirical evidence. In contrast, a significant body of empirical evidence supports the use of student choice for enhancing both engagement and outcomes for students with learning and behavioral disabilities.

REFERENCES

Arter, J., & Jenkins, J. R. (1979). Differential diagnosis: Prescriptive teaching – A critical appraisal. *Review of Educational Research*, *49*, 517–555. doi:10.3102/00346543049004517

Arter, J. A., & Jenkins, J. R. (1977). Examining the benefits and prevalence of modality considerations in special education. *Journal of Special Education*, *11*, 281–298. doi:10.1177/002246697701100304

Canfield, A. A., & Lafferty, J. C. (1970). *Learning styles inventory*. Detroit, MI: HumanicsMedia.

Carnine, D. W., Silbert, J., Kame'enui, E. J., Slocum, T. A., & Travers, P. A. (2017). *Direct instruction reading* (6th ed.). Upper Saddle River, NJ: Pearson.

Chall, J. (1953). Ask him to try on the book for fit. *The Reading Teacher*, *7*(2), 83–88. Retrieved from http://www.jstor.org/stable/20140178

Chard, D. J., Vaughn, S., & Tyler, B. J. (2002). A synthesis of research on effective interventions for building reading fluency with elementary students with learning disabilities. *Journal of Learning Disabilities*, *35*, 386–406. doi:10.1177/00222194020350050101

Coffield, F., Moseley, D., Hall, E., & Ecclestone, K. (2004). *Learning styles and pedagogy in post-16 learning: A systematic and critical review*. Learning and Skills Research Centre & Dept. for Education and Skills, London.

Dattilo, J., & Rusch, F. R. (1985). Effects of choice on leisure participation for persons with severe handicaps. *Journal of the Association for Persons with Severe Handicaps*, *10*, 194–199. doi:10.1177/154079698501000402

Dunlap, G., dePerczel, M., Clarke, S., Wilson, D., Wright, S., White, R., & Gomez, A. (1994). Choice making to promote adaptive behaviors for students with emotional and behavioral challenges. *Journal of Applied Behavior Analysis*, *27*, 505–518. doi:10.1901/jaba.1994.27-505

Dunn, R. (1983). Learning style and its relation to exceptionality at both ends of the spectrum. *Exceptional Children*, *49*, 496–506. doi:10.1177/001440298304900602

Dunn, R. (1990). Bias over substance: A critical analysis of Kavale and Forness' report on modality-based instruction. *Exceptional Children*, *56*, 352–356.

Dunn, R., & Burke (2007). *Learning style: Elementary learning style assessment (ELSA)*. Retrieved from http://www.learningstyles.net/images/stories/documents/samples/ELSA %20Survey%20Screen%20Caps.pdf

Dunn, R., Griggs, S. A., Olson, J., Beasley, M., & Gorman, B. S. (1995). A meta-analytic validation of the Dunn and Dunn model of learning-style preferences. *The Journal of Educational Research, 88*, 353–362. doi:10.1080/00220671.1995.9941181

Dunn, R. S., & Dunn, K. J. (1979). Learning styles/teaching styles: Should they ... can they ... be matched? *Educational Leadership, 36*, 238–244.

Dunn, R. S., & Dunn, K. J. (1993). *Teaching secondary students through their individual learning styles: Practical approaches for grades 7–12*. Boston, MA: Allyn & Bacon.

Dyer, K., Dunlap, G., & Winterling, V. (1990). Effects of choice making on the serious problem behaviors of students with severe handicaps. *Journal of Applied Behavior Analysis, 23*, 515–524. doi:10.1901/jaba.1990.23-515

Friend, M., & Cook, L. (2003). *Interactions: Collaboration skills for school professionals* (4th ed.). New York, NY: Longman.

Goodman, K. S., & Goodman, Y. M. (2009). Helping readers make sense of print: Research that supports a whole language pedagogy. In S. E. Israel & G. G. Duffy (Eds.), *Handbook of research on reading comprehension* (pp. 91–114). New York, NY: Routledge.

Hallahan, D. P., Kauffman, J. M., & Pullen, P. C. (2015). *Exceptional learners: An introduction to special education* (13th ed.). Upper Saddle River, NJ: Pearson.

Harding, J., Wacker, D. W., Cooper, L. J., Millard, T., & Jensen-Kovalan, P. (1994). Brief hierarchical assessment of potential treatment components with children in an outpatient clinic. *Journal of Applied Behavior Analysis, 27*, 291–300. doi:10.1901/jaba.1994.27-291

Hauer, P., Straub, C., & Wolf, S. (2005). Learning styles of allied health students using Kolb's LSI-IIa. *Journal of Allied Health, 34*, 177–182.

Hobbs, N. (1974). A natural history of an idea. In J. M. Kauffman & C. D. Lewis (Eds.), *Teaching children with behavior disorders: Personal perspectives* (pp. 145–167). Columbus, OH: Charles E. Merrill.

Kampwirth, T. J., & Bates, M. (1980). Modality preference and teaching method: A review of the research. *Academic Therapy, 15*, 597–605.

Kavale, K. A., & Forness, S. R. (1987). Substance over style: Assessing the efficacy of modality testing and teaching. *Exceptional Children, 54*, 228–239. doi:10.1177/001440298705400305

Kavale, K. A., & Forness, S. R. (1990). Substance over style: A rejoinder to Dunn's animadversions. *Exceptional Children, 56*, 357–361.

Kavale, K. A., Hirshoren, A., & Forness, S. R. (1998). Meta-analytic validation of the Dunn and Dunn model of learning-style preferences: A critique of what was Dunn. *Learning Disabilities Research and Practice, 13*, 75–80.

Kavale, K. A., & LeFever, G. B. (2007). Dunn and Dunn model of learning-style preferences: Critique of Lovelace meta-analysis. *The Journal of Educational Research, 101*, 94–97. doi:10.3200/JOER.101.2.94-98

Kern, L., Mantegna, M. E., Vorndran, C. M., Bailin, D., & Hilt, A. (2001). Choice of task sequence to reduce problem behaviors. *Journal of Positive Behavioral Interventions, 3*, 3–10. doi:10.1177/109830070100300102

Kern, L., & Parks, J. K. (2012). *Choice making opportunities for students*. Module 4. Virginia Department of Education. Retrieved from http://ttac-esd.gmu.edu/my_files/Choice_Making_Opportunities_Sup_Doc.pdf

Kern, L., & State, T. (2009). Incorporating choice and preferred activities into classwide instruction. *Beyond Behavior, 18*(2), 3–11.

Kolb, A. Y., & Kolb, D. A. (2005). Learning styles and learning spaces: Enhancing experiential learning in higher education. *Academy of Management Learning & Education, 4*, 193–212. doi:10.5465/AMLE.2005.17268566

Kolb, D. A. (n.d.). The Kolb learning style inventory. (Version 4). Hay Group, Boston, MA.

Lancioni, G. E., O'Reilly, M. F., & Emerson, E. (1996). A review of choice research with people with severe and profound developmental disabilities. *Research in Developmental Disabilities, 17*, 391–411. doi:10.1016/0891-4222(96)00025-X

Landrum, T. J., & Landrum, K. M. (2014). *Current practice alert: Learning styles.* Division for Learning Disabilities (DLD) and Division for Research (DR), Council for Exceptional Children. Retrieved from http://teachingld.org/alerts#learning-styles

Landrum, T. J., & McDuffie, K. A. (2010). Learning styles in the age of differentiated instruction. *Exceptionality, 18*, 6–17. doi:10.1080/09362830903462441

Landrum, T. L., & Sweigart, C. A. (2014). Simple, evidence-based interventions for classic problems of emotional and behavioral disorders. *Beyond Behavior, 23*(3), 3–9.

Lovelace, M. K. (2005). Meta-analysis of experimental research based on the Dunn and Dunn model. *The Journal of Educational Research, 98*, 176–183. doi:10.3200/JOER.98.3.176-183

National Governors Association Center for Best Practices. (2010). *Common core state standards.* Washington, DC: Author. Retrieved from http://www.corestandards.org/

O'Neil, J. (1990). Making sense of style. *Educational Leadership, 48*(2), 4–9.

Pashler, H., McDaniel, M., Rohrer, D., & Bjork, R. (2009). Learning styles: Concepts and evidence. *Psychological Science in the Public Interest, 9*, 105–119. doi:10.1111/j.1539-6053.2009.01038.x

Peterson, E. R., Rayner, S. G., & Armstrong, S. J. (2009). Researching the psychology of cognitive style and learning style: Is there really a future? *Learning and Individual Differences, 19*, 518–523. doi:10.1016/j.lindif.2009.06.003

Price, G. E., & Dunn, R. (1997). *The learning style inventory: LSI manual.* Lawrence, KS: Price Systems, Inc.

Ramsey, M. L., Jolivette, K., Patterson, D., & Kennedy, C. (2010). Using choice to increase time on task, task completion, and accuracy for students with emotional/behavior disorders in a residential facility. *Education and Treatment of Children, 33*, 1–21.

Rispoli, M., Lang, R., Neely, L., Camargo, S., Hutchins, N., Davenport, K., & Goodwyn, F. (2013). A comparison of within-and across-activity choices for reducing challenging behavior in children with autism spectrum disorders. *Journal of Behavioral Education, 22*, 66–83. doi:10.1007/s10864-012-9164-y

Romaniuk, C., Miltenberger, R., Conyers, C., Jenner, N., Jurgens, M., & Ringenberg, C. (2002). The influence of activity choice on problem behaviors maintained by escape versus attention. *Journal of Applied Behavioral Analysis, 35*, 349–362. doi:10.1901/jaba.2002.35-349

Schmidt, A. C., Hanley, G. P., & Layer, S. A. (2009). A further analysis of the value of choice: Controlling for illusory discriminative stimuli and evaluating the effects of less preferred items. *Journal of Applied Behavior Analysis, 42*, 711–716. doi:10.1901/jaba.2009.42-711

Shogren, K. A., Faggella-Luby, M. N., Bae, S., & Wehmeyer, M. L. (2004). The effect if choice making as an intervention for problem behavior: A meta-analysis. *Journal of Positive Behavior Interventions, 6*, 228–237. doi:10.1177/10983007040060040401

Simonsen, B., Myers, D., & DeLuca, C. (2010). Teaching teachers to use prompts, opportunities to respond, and specific praise. *Teacher Education and Special Education, 33,* 300−318. doi:10.1177/0888406409359905

Skinner, B. F. (1971). *Beyond freedom and dignity.* New York, NY: Knopf.

Stahl, S. A. (1999). Different strokes for different folks? *American Educator, 23*(3), 1−5.

Sternberg, R. J., Grigorenko, E. L., Ferrari, M., & Clinkenbeard, P. (1999). A triarchic analysis of an aptitude-treatment interaction. *European Journal of Psychological Assessment, 15,* 1−11. doi:10.1027//1015-5759.15.1.3

Sullivan, M. (1993). *A meta-analysis of experimental research studies based on the Dunn and Dunn learning styles model and its relationship to academic achievement and performance.* Unpublished doctoral dissertation. St. John's University, Jamaica, NY.

Sutherland, K. S., & Wehby, J. H. (2001). Exploring the relationship between increased opportunities to respond to academic re-quests and the academic and behavioral outcomes of students with EBD: A review. *Remedial and Special Education, 22,* 113−121. doi:10.1177/074193250102200205

Sutherland, K. S., Wehby, J. H., & Copeland, S. R. (2000). Effect of varying rates of behavior-specific praise on the on-task behavior of students with EBD. *Journal of Emotional and Behavioral Disorders, 8*(1), 2−8. doi:10.1177/106342660000800101

Tomlinson, C. A. (1999). *The differentiated classroom: Responding to the needs of all learners.* Upper Saddle River, NJ: Pearson Education, Inc.

Tomlinson, C. A. (2003). *Fulfilling the promise of the differentiated classroom.* Alexandria, VA: Association for Supervision and Curriculum Development.

Tomlinson, C. A. (2009). Learning profiles & achievement. *School Administrator, 66*(2), 28−29.

Tomlinson, C. A., Brighton, C., Hertberg, H., Callahan, C. M., Moon, T. R., Brimijoin, K., & Reynolds, T. (2003). Differentiating instruction in response to student readiness, interest, and learning profile in academically diverse classrooms: A review of literature. *Journal for the Education of the Gifted, 27*(2−3), 119−145. doi:10.1177/016235320302700203

Ulke-Kurkcuoglu, B., & Kircaali-Iftar, G. (2010). A comparison of the effects of providing activity and material choice to children with autism spectrum disorders. *Journal of Applied Behavior Analysis, 43,* 717−721. doi:10.1901/jaba.2010.43-717

U.S. Department of Education. (1983). *A nation at risk: The imperative for educational reform.* The National Commission on Excellence in Education, Washington, DC.

Vygotsky, L. (1978). *Mind in society.* Cambridge, MA: Harvard University Press.

Vygotsky, L. (1986). *Thought and language (A. Kozulin, Trans. & Ed.).* Cambridge, MA: MIT Press.

Willingham, D. T. (2005). Do visual, auditory, and kinesthetic learners need visual, auditory, and kinesthetic instruction? *American Educator, 29*(2), 31−35.

Willingham, D. T., Hughes, E. M., & Dobolyi, D. G. (2015). The scientific status of learning styles theories. *Teaching of Psychology, 42,* 266−271. doi:10.1177/0098628315589505

CHAPTER 8

NEVER SAY NEVER: THE APPROPRIATE AND INAPPROPRIATE USE OF PRAISE AND FEEDBACK FOR STUDENTS WITH LEARNING AND BEHAVIORAL DISABILITIES

Lauren W. Collins and Lysandra Cook

ABSTRACT

The use of verbal reinforcement has longstanding support in encouraging desired student responses. For students with learning and behavioral disabilities, the use of verbal reinforcement through behavior specific praise (BSP) and feedback are promising practices for improving academic and behavioral outcomes. While these strategies are relatively straightforward to implement, they are often applied inappropriately. Thus, specific guidelines should be followed to ensure that BSP and feedback are used effectively. The purpose of this chapter is to provide an overview of BSP and feedback related specifically to students with learning and behavioral disabilities, provide theoretical and empirical support for these

Instructional Practices with and without Empirical Validity
Advances in Learning and Behavioral Disabilities, Volume 29, 153–173
Copyright © 2016 by Emerald Group Publishing Limited
All rights of reproduction in any form reserved
ISSN: 0735-004X/doi:10.1108/S0735-004X20160000029007

practices, offer research-based recommendations for implementation, and identify common errors to avoid.

Keywords: Praise; feedback; learning disabilities; emotional and behavioral disorders

Teachers are notorious for investing their own time and resources to build behavior management systems that often include complex or resource-intensive behavioral interventions such as School-wide Positive Behavior Interventions and Supports, functional behavioral assessment based interventions, group contingencies, and token economies. Even though these approaches are effective and appealing to teachers because they can help establish a positive classroom climate and learning environment, practitioners should not underestimate the power of a simple (and free) strategy: the use of effective verbal reinforcement. More specifically, behavior specific praise (BSP) and feedback are effective strategies for providing verbal reinforcement to students (Brophy, 1998) and are often included as components of larger intervention frameworks (e.g., SWPBIS).

Establishing a positive classroom climate with effective behavior management reduces the likelihood of disruptive behaviors (Capizzi, 2009). Generally speaking, a well-managed classroom leads to a more positive learning environment with better behavioral and academic outcomes. More specifically, when classroom management systems are designed to incorporate the use of evidence-based practices, students are more engaged in on-task behaviors, demonstrate more prosocial interactions with peers, engage in fewer disruptive behaviors, and exhibit higher rates of correct responses (Simonsen, Fairbanks, Briesch, Myers, & Sugai, 2008). Behavior specific praise and feedback represent two evidence-based practices that are critical components of an effective classroom management plan.

Traditionally, verbal reinforcement has been considered a behavioral intervention for modifying the behaviors of students exhibiting challenging behavior patterns (Reed, Gable, & Yanek, 2014). However, the relationship between learning and behavior has long been established and educators no longer should adhere to the "two-box" system when considering the educational programming for students with both learning and behavioral disorders (Reed et al., 2014). In other words, it is generally accepted that there is a direct and reciprocal relationship between learning and behavior. For example, a student with a specific learning disability (SLD) may demonstrate maladaptive behaviors that serve the function of escaping from a task demand that she is unable to perform due to deficits in cognitive processing. As a result, she may be removed from the classroom and unintentionally reinforced for the demonstration of the maladaptive behavior (Maag, 2001). Consequently, the student with SLD, who under other circumstances may be a very "well behaved" child, may become more likely to demonstrate aversive behaviors upon receiving tasks that are too academically demanding for her ability level (Gettinger & Seibert, 2002). On the other hand, a student with an emotional or behavioral disorder may demonstrate attention-seeking behavior during instructional time. Again, he may be removed from the instructional setting and given one-on-one attention from an administrator, which reinforces his attention-seeking behavior. However, upon returning to class, it is likely that the student missed instruction and will now be behind academically. Thus, effective verbal reinforcement techniques can promote both improved behavioral and academic outcomes for students with and at risk for learning and behavioral disabilities.

BEHAVIOR SPECIFIC PRAISE AND FEEDBACK AS VERBAL REINFORCEMENT

Behavior specific praise has been defined as "positive declarative statements specifically directed to the target child that describes the child's behavior" (Fullerton, Conroy, & Correa, 2009, p. 121). To put it simply, BSP is a verbal form of teacher attention that is issued immediately following the demonstration of an appropriate behavior or academic response (Lewis, Hudson, Richter, & Johnson, 2004). For example, rather than waiting to say "Good job, Joey" to a student for raising his hand to talk during math class until after class is over, it is more effective to say "Good job raising your hand to ask a question, Joey. How can I help you?" when the student is called on to participate. Or, if Joey has been struggling with two-digit addition, it would be most effective for his teacher to monitor his work in class and say "Joey, you did an excellent job lining up the numbers by place value and adding them correctly" rather than waiting to provide him with praise until after an assignment is over.

Hattie and Timperley (2007) defined feedback as "information provided by an agent (e.g., researcher, peer, book, parent, self, experience) regarding aspects of one's performance or understanding" (p. 81). Feedback is most effective when it is delivered immediately and when it offers correction. For example, rather than saying "You need to stop slamming your book on the desk, Brandon" as he leaves class, a more appropriate response would tell a student what to do instead directly after the behavior occurs, such as "Brandon, when you take your book out of your desk, please gently place it on top so that it doesn't make such a loud noise." Or, rather than saying "No, that isn't correct. Try again, Heather" to a student who incorrectly spells high-frequency words, it is more effective to say "Heather, remember that the word 'was' can't be sounded out. 'Was' is spelled w-a-s. Remember to use the word wall in the classroom if you forget how to spell these tricky words."

The use of BSP and feedback serves as verbal reinforcement in that they provide students with an indication as to whether they should continue or modify a specific academic or social behavior, which increases the likelihood of future success. While we are certainly not suggesting that the use of BSP and feedback is a panacea for all learning and behavior challenges, we maintain that they comprise important components in a comprehensive approach to teaching academics and behavior (Conroy, Sutherland, Snyder, Al-Hendawi, & Vo, 2009). When paired with other instructional strategies, such as direct and explicit instruction and increased opportunities to respond, the use of BSP and feedback is even more effective in achieving desired student outcomes (Vo, Sutherland, & Conroy, 2011).

Inappropriate and Underuse of Praise and Feedback

Despite the considerable potential for BSP and feedback to advance behavioral and learning outcomes, educators often choose not to use them or use them ineffectively. We propose that two primary reasons underlie the infrequent and ineffective use of praise and feedback: (a) purposeful withholding due to what we believe are misguided moral issues stemming from the teachings of Kohn (2001) and others who suggest praise is not just ineffective but immoral and (b) misapplication of the recommended practices. The wide ranging perspectives on and applications of praise and feedback in the educational community have resulted in considerable confusion as to what these practices are, how effective they are, and how they should be applied. For example, the research on praise may appear conflicting. Many studies have shown that praise is associated with an increase in correct responses (Allday et al., 2012; Sutherland & Wehby, 2001), work productivity (Craft, Alber, & Heward, 1998), and on-task behavior (Sutherland, Wehby, & Copeland, 2000). In contrast, other studies indicate a decrease in motivation associated with praise (Anderson, Manoogian, & Reznick, 1976; Harackiewicz, 1979; Swann & Pittman, 1977). We contend that the research literature is not contradictory; rather, the disparate findings can be explained by conflicting definitions and applications of praise. That is, the impact of praise depends on when and how it is used.

Characteristics and Needs of Students with Learning and Behavioral Disabilities

Although verbal reinforcement is appropriate and helpful for all students (Brophy, 1998; Emmer, Evertson, & Worsham, 2003; Shores, Gunter, & Jack, 1993), students with learning and behavioral disabilities may especially benefit because of overarching deficits in executive functions (De Weerdt, Desoet, & Roeyers, 2013). As a result of these deficits, students with learning and behavioral disabilities characteristically have a difficult time with the following academic and behavioral skills: understanding social norms; planning, organizing, and initiating tasks; controlling emotional regulation; sustaining attention to the appropriate stimuli; completing tasks within a given amount of time; transitioning within and between activities; and manipulating information for storage and retrieval (Meltzer, 2010). Moreover, deficits in executive functions lead to a significant impairment in the ability of students with learning and behavioral disabilities to evaluate the appropriateness of their actions (e.g., academic problem solving, behavioral performance).

At least in part due to these deficits in executive function, students with learning and behavioral disabilities experience extremely poor outcomes, both in and out of a school setting. According to the data presented in the 36th Annual Report to Congress (US Department of Education [US DOE], 2014) students with emotional disturbance (ED) experience disciplinary removal (e.g., suspension, expulsion) at the highest rate and students with SLD at the third highest rate among all disability categories. Additionally, only approximately 70% of students with a SLD and 50% of students with ED graduate high school with regular diplomas. More concerning, students in these two subgroups of special education dropout of school more than students receiving special education services under any other disability category (National Center for Learning Disabilities [NCLD], 2014). Roughly 20% and 40% of students with SLD and ED, respectively, dropout of school (US DOE, 2014). The dismal outcomes of these populations do not end upon exiting the public school setting. In fact, students with ED are at extreme risk for drug abuse, arrest, and job termination at the post-secondary level (Kern, Hilt-Panahon, & Sokol, 2009). Despite having similar post-secondary goals as their typically developing peers, students with SLD attend a four-year college or university at approximately half the rate of their general education counterparts (NCLD, 2014).

Given that just under 50% of school aged children who receive special education services qualify under the federal definition of SLD or ED (US DOE, 2014), it is imperative that teachers use strategies that have been found to be effective for these populations. In order to address the challenges that students with learning and behavioral disabilities experience with motivation and in evaluating their own actions, teachers should employ consistent and appropriate use of verbal reinforcement in the form of BSP and appropriate feedback to encourage desirable academic and behavioral responses.

In this chapter, we provide an overview of verbal reinforcement in the classroom, specifically as it relates to encouraging correct student responses for students with learning and behavioral disabilities. First, we discuss the theoretical underpinnings of these methods and explain why and how they are effective for students with learning and behavioral disabilities. Next, we define and describe effective and ineffective uses of BSP and feedback, including examples and non-examples. We conclude with a brief review of research literature examining the effectiveness of each practice.

THEORETICAL UNDERPINNINGS OF VERBAL REINFORCEMENT

The effectiveness of verbal feedback is supported by the principles of behaviorism — the philosophy that supports the "science of human behavior" (Skinner, 2011, p. 3). More specifically, verbal reinforcement can serve as behavioral reinforcement in operant conditioning (i.e., behavior that is influenced by the events, or consequences, immediately following it; Cooper, Heron, & Heward, 2007). From a perspective grounded in behaviorism, the events that occur immediately after a behavior, such as the use of reinforcement strategies, impact the likelihood of the behavior occurring again in the future.

One example of how reinforcement works that many individuals have witnessed outside of a classroom is when a child is throwing a "temper-tantrum" in a store because he or she has asked for a certain toy. At first, the parent denies the request. The child may begin to fuss and whine, but the parent ignores the complaining or offers an explanation to the child as to why he or she cannot have the toy. However, the child's behavior begins to escalate to screaming and crying and, alas, the parent gives in to the request. On the next aisle, the child requests his favorite lollipop. Again, the parent denies the request and this time, the child immediately begins to scream. As a result, the parent hands the child a lollipop (and as quickly as possible checks out of the store). Although this is a somewhat exaggerated and oversimplified example, it describes how a consequence can positively reinforce a behavior. After the child screamed, he received what he asked for. The behavior (screaming) was reinforced when the child obtained a desired object. The next time the child wanted something, he repeated the behavior that previously resulted in a desired outcome.

The same theoretical underpinnings of behaviorism are also applicable for classroom environments. In a classroom setting, the use of BSP and feedback are usually considered to be forms of positive, verbal reinforce-ment. More specifically, these methods are considered social reinforcers, as they provide approval or attention to a student (Alberto & Troutman, 2013). When a teacher offers BSP to a student, he or she is acknowledging that a student demonstrated an appropriate response (e.g., raised his hand) for a particular situation (e.g., he had something to contribute during a class discussion). In the event that a student is not demonstrating an appro-priate response (e.g., he shouts out the answer), a teacher can encourage the appropriate response by providing the student with a type of feedback known as error correction, which is targeted at correcting the response to increase the likelihood of a more appropriate response in the future (Conroy et al., 2009). When the student demonstrates the appropriate behavior following the feedback, the teacher should then respond with BSP. Teachers can also use feedback to reinforce appropriate academic and behavioral responses. This type of instructive feedback can be used to acknowledge a correct response and then provide a student with additional information related to the topic or behavior (Conroy et al., 2009). In both instances, effectively providing positive reinforcement will increase the future occurrence of appropriate behavior. While the pairing of social rein-forcers with other rewards is beyond the scope of this chapter, keep in mind that BSP and feedback can be even more effective when paired with other reinforcers, such as time on the computer or another preferred activity (Alberto & Troutman, 2013).

EFFECTIVE AND INEFFECTIVE APPROACHES FOR PROVIDING VERBAL REINFORCEMENT

The daily instructional routines that occur in both regular and special education classrooms offer numerous opportunities for teachers to offer verbal feedback to all students. For students with learning and behavioral disabilities, it is especially important for teachers to capitalize on these opportunities to encourage appropriate behaviors and accurate academic responses. In lieu of general, non-contingent praise, teachers should implement contingent BSP and immediate, corrective feedback.

Behavior Specific Praise

The use of BSP should be frequent and purposeful. Although a consensus has yet to be reached in regard to the exact amount of BSP statements that a teacher should emit, in general a ratio of at least 4:1 of praise to reprimand statements is desirable. Using about 6 praise statements every 15 minutes is also recommended (Myers, Simonsen, & Sugai, 2011). Research suggests that when teachers increase rates of BSP, on-task behavior of students increases (Allday et al., 2012; Sutherland, Wehby & Yoder, 2002). However, teachers should be cautious not to overuse BSP. As with any intervention, overuse of BSP can lead to satiation (i.e., the effectiveness of the reinforcer is reduced) and decrease its value (Cooper et al., 2007). The use of BSP should also be contingent on student behavior (Lewis et al., 2004). In other words, teachers should not arbitrarily provide BSP statements simply for the sake of providing praise. Each BSP statement should be targeted at a specific student response, particularly for students who are struggling to demonstrate appropriate behavior. One caveat to this rule of thumb is if a functional behavioral assessment has indicated that non-contingent praise (i.e., praise that is not reliant on a student's behavior) will help reduce attention-seeking behaviors. In this case, teachers should follow the interventions as outlined by the student's behavior intervention plan and provide non-contingent praise (Carr, Bailey, Ecott, Lucker, & Weil, 1998).

Immediate and Corrective Feedback

Praise is an effective strategy for reinforcing appropriate behavioral and academic responses, but teachers also need a strategy that is well-suited to correct inappropriate responses in a manner that increases appropriate responses in the future. The use of feedback is one of the most effective strategies teachers can employ to change student outcomes (Hattie & Timperley, 2007). However, depending on how feedback is used, the impact can be a positive or negative change in student performance (Hattie & Timperley, 2007). Therefore, it is critical that teachers understand the essential components of effective feedback. Instead of merely reprimanding students (e.g., "stop it Sergio"), teachers should use feedback that is corrective, positive, purposeful, and immediate when addressing inappropriate social behaviors and academic responses (Conroy et al., 2009). When used to increase correct responding, feedback can help bridge the gap between what students can currently do and what students need to be able to do for specific academic or behavioral tasks (Chappuis, Stiggins, Chapppuis, & Arter, 2011).

Key Principles of Implementation

We will focus on five key components of praise and feedback that have been associated with positive changes in student behavior. The key principles are: positive and nonjudgmental, specific and corrective, sincere and credible, immediate and with proximity, delivered with variety, and evaluate and adjust (Conroy et al., 2009; IRIS Center for Training Enhancements, 2012). Each of these principles is detailed below with specific examples and non-examples, as summarized in Table 1.

Positive and Nonjudgmental

Behavior specific praise and feedback are most effective when they are made as positive, nonjudgmental statements. For praise or teacher feedback to be effective the teacher should recognize the student's accomplishment or behavior in a way that does not compare the student or behavior to others (Brophy, 1998). The positive effects of praise can be undermined

Table 1. Examples and Non-Examples of Academic and Behavioral Reinforcement.

Components of Effective Verbal Reinforcement Practices	Examples	Non-Examples
Positive and nonjudgmental	Academic: "Great job adding key details and descriptive vocabulary to your writing today."	Academic: "Great job writing today. It's about time"
	Behavioral: "Thank you for raising your hand and waiting to be called on."	Behavioral: "Thank you for finally following our classroom rules and not shouting out your answer."
Specific and corrective with details	Academic: "You did an excellent job adding all of the digits correctly. Remember, after adding the ones column, you need to carry the tens and then add that column."	Academic: "That's not the right answer. You did not add correctly."
	Behavioral: "You did a really nice job staying in your seat and keeping your hands and feet to yourself."	Behavioral: "Thank you for not disrupting the class today."
Intentional, sincere, and credible	Academic: "Great job blending sounds together. You read with 100% accuracy today!"	Academic: "You got it all right. You're the smartest first grader I know."
	Behavioral: "You did an awesome job taking turns during recess today. That's an excellent way to play with your classmates."	Behavioral: "You are the nicest friend ever!"
Immediate with proximity	Academic: "Well done! You set up all of your problems correctly, and now you are ready to solve them." (Delivered during seatwork, immediately after the student wrote the problem.)	Academic: "Good work in math yesterday. You got a lot right."
	Behavioral: "Thank you for speaking in an inside voice. Keep up the good work." (Whispered to the student immediately after he asked for permission to use the bathroom.)	Behavioral: "You did a good job last week with your inside voice. Let's try that again today."
Delivered with variety	Academic: Pair verbal statement with written feedback and vary the phrasing.	Academic: Using only verbal or written feedback and/or similar phrasing.
	Behavioral: Pair verbal statement with gestures and vary the phrasing.	Behavioral: Using only verbal or written feedback and/or similar phrasing.

when the teacher undercuts a student's accomplishment in some way. For example, rather than say "Nice job raising your hand, just like everyone else," or "Nice job raising your hand like I've told you a thousand times," the effective teacher focuses on the specific behavior and just says, "Thank you for raising your hand." In regard to feedback, teachers may sometimes include a statement of judgment such as, "I'm really surprised you're still forgetting to carry your ones. Carry the ones and *then* add the tens." It is more effective to stick to providing feedback without an evaluative comment: "Remember to carry the ones and then add the tens." Teachers are humans too; and students' inappropriate behaviors and lack of academic progress can be frustrating. It is perhaps not surprising that teachers sometimes, purposefully or unintentionally, qualify their praise and feedback. However, praise and feedback that is delivered with negative or judgmental comments tend to be much less effective.

Specific and Corrective
BSP and feedback must be specific; ineffective BSP or feedback from teachers is general (e.g., "good job!" or "that's right!"). In daily life, people make general comments all of the time (e.g., "I love it"). However, in a classroom context general praise does not assist the student in identification of what they have done to gain reinforcement from the teacher or how to repeat the behavior in the future. That is, students will not always know what it is they have done that is a "good job" and what they should do in the future to get more reinforcement. Without including specific details of what the student has done to merit praise, non-specific praise can reinforce a student's sense of an external locus of control. In other words, a student will not attribute his success or incorrect response to his or her own behavior. The student may not be aware of the appropriateness of behaviors or accuracy of responses they have displayed and the critical role that their behavior or response played in achieving a successful outcome. Rowe (1974) found that general statements like "good job" or "you are so smart" actually lowered students' confidence in their answers and resulted in fewer responses. Similarly, when students are praised for an inherent trait, such as being smart, it can decrease their locus of control. The student may feel that reinforcement depends on ability rather than effort and will not focus on the work they engaged in to receive the praise. When used correctly BSP will assist the student in identifying the behaviors they displayed and increase the student's internal locus of control and ultimately their ability to self-regulate (Brophy, 1998). BSP has also been shown to increase a student's own positive self-statements (Phillips, 1984).

In some instances, specific praise may not be the most appropriate form of verbal reinforcement because a student may not have exhibited an appropriate behavior or response. In these cases, specific and corrective feedback can be used to increase an appropriate response. However, just like it is often not instinctive for many teachers to provide specific praise, general and non-specific feedback is common in everyday life and may be the type of feedback many teachers naturally provide to their students. When we want a friend to stop distracting us when we're talking on the phone, we probably would just say, "stop it" and assume that they know what we're talking about. However, such general feedback does not tell the person receiving the feedback (a) exactly what to stop (they might think we are asking them to stop chewing gum or to stop gesturing with their hands) or (b) what to do instead (they might stop talking, but could start singing instead). It is more clear and effective to use specific and corrective feedback (e.g., "please stop talking while I'm on the phone, we can talk in a minute when I am finished"). Similarly, teachers should use feedback that specifies the problem behavior and indicates how to correct that behavior or response (Alberto & Troutman, 2013). A teacher using effective feedback offers a corrective statement such as "when we sit on the carpet, we keep our hands folded in our lap so that we aren't touching others" as opposed to a non-corrective statement such as "don't touch the person sitting next to you." This type of feedback will assist the student in identifying errors in his or her behavior or academic response and adjust accordingly. Effective feedback to maladaptive behaviors or inappropriate responses should include the specifics of the desired behavior rather than solely focusing on what the child should stop doing for example "stop running and walk calmly to the carpet" (Connolly, Dowd, Criste, Nelson, & Tobias, 1995).

Sincere and Credible

Ineffective application of BSP and feedback may occur when the teacher delivers statements that are not sincere or credible. Teacher praise and feedback will not have the desired impact or the student may simply dismiss it if the student perceives that it is not truthful (Henderlong & Lepper, 2002). Teaching is a demanding profession and teachers are dealing with constant demands for their attention. When things become rushed and harried, it is perhaps not surprising that teachers' praise and feedback is sometimes delivered quickly and perfunctorily, which may result in the communication being perceived as insincere. Similarly, in an attempt to make students feel good, teachers may deliver praise that is over-the-top and incommensurate with the behavior. Such praise may also fail to ring true and therefore not have the desired effects. The research on when students perceive praise to be insincere is limited, but it has been suggested (O'Leary & O'Leary, 1977) that very global, effusive praise (e.g., "You are the smartest!") carries a higher risk of disbelief than specific praise (e.g., "You did very well using colorful adjectives"). Moreover, in addition to what is said, we suspect that that how praise is delivered can affect its sincerity. For example, praise that is delivered in a monotone deadpan without eye contact (perhaps delivered in this way because the teacher has her mind on two other tasks and is hurrying to help another student) is less likely to be effective.

Feedback and praise that students perceive as controlling are not effective. Deci, Koestner, and Ryan (1999) compared the effect of controlling praise – which included a direction of something the student should do such as, "Good job on your math assignment; you should write that legibly every day" – to similar praise without the controlling phrase such as, "Good job on your math assignment; it was very accurate and legible." The review demonstrated that specific praise increased later motivation to engage in the praised task, but controlling praise reverses the effect. We suspect that the controlling statements are ineffective in large part because students do not perceive them as sincere or credible and therefore may dismiss them. Deci et al. (1999) proposed what they call the cognitive evaluative theory, stating that underlying intrinsic motivation are the physiological needs for competence and autonomy. They postulated that controlling reinforcement negatively impacts the student's sense of competence and autonomy and therefore decreases intrinsic motivation. We agree that this interpersonal context is critical in determining if a phrase is controlling or sincere and credible.

Immediate and with Proximity
Researchers also have shown that the power of praise and feedback increases when it is delivered immediately following a response, in close physical proximity to the student, and in a manner acceptable to the student (e.g., verbal or nonverbal, public or private; Burnett, 2001; Feldman, 2003; Lampi, Fenty, & Beaunae, 2005). Again, teachers are busy and have many demands to attend to. When a teacher is busy, it might make sense to think "I'll praise Leilani for working well with her group when I get done helping this group out" or "I'll provide feedback to James by yelling across the room because I don't have the time to walk over to him now." However, these types of interactions are likely to be less effective. Numerous studies highlight the positive influence of contingent BSP and feedback in conjunction with teacher physical proximity (Gunter, Shores, Jack, Rasmussen, & Flowers, 1995; Shores et al., 1993). Given that proximity

can be used as a cue to attend to reinforcement, Gunter et al. (1995) suggested moving around the classroom when delivering verbal reinforcement in an effort to use proximity for all students.

Feedback is most effective when it is delivered immediately following an academic or behavioral response (Conroy et al., 2009). During small group instruction, a teacher might notice that a student at an independent work center is roaming around the room rather than engaging in the assigned task. While it might not be feasible for a teacher to stop her small group lesson and redirect the student, it would be most effective if the teacher addresses the behavior as soon as she finishes working with the small group (as opposed to waiting until the next day when she begins small group instruction). A teacher employing the principles of effective feedback would walk over to the student and say, "Antonio, remember to stay in your seat during independent work. If you have trouble on the assignment, you can raise your hand and ask for help."

Delivered with Variety
Although the emphasis of this chapter is on the use of BSP and feedback as forms of verbal reinforcement, it is also important to remember that these strategies should be used with a variety of other delivery methods. It is easy to fall into routines. Teaching and delivering praise and feedback are no exceptions. A teacher may fall into the habit of delivering praise in the exact same way (e.g., "Nice job [name], I really liked the way you [behavior]"). Although this technically follows the guidelines for providing effective praise and may initially be effective, after the students hear the same line multiple times a day, everyday, it is bound to lose its impact. To make messages stick, it is helpful that they have an unexpected or surprising element to them (Cook, Cook, & Landrum, 2013). There are many types of verbal, written, and physical movements that can be used in conjunction with the effective forms of feedback and/or BSP described previously that can help vary the delivery of reinforcement. Research supports the use of a variety of types of BSP to avoid overuse and satiation (Brophy, 1998). When students are praised every time they sit up straight, wait in line, listen, or engage in routine behaviors, they may experience satiation and no longer respond in a positive manner, especially as they become proficient in the behavior (Brophy, 1981; Emmer et al., 2003). In cases of behaviors that are highly resistant to change, praise should be used in conjunction with other types of reinforcement systems, such as a token economy with tangible rewards (Duncan, Kemple, & Smith, 2000; Kerr & Nelson, 2002).

Evaluate and Adjust

As with any intervention teachers must evaluate and adjust as needed in response to student behavior. Adapting and adjusting evidence-based practices is a significant obstacle in providing effective instruction (Leko, 2015). When teachers receive training in highly effective, evidence-based practices (e.g., BSP, corrective feedback), they often only know one way to implement them (i.e., how they were trained). However, students have unique needs and may need practices adapted for them to be effective. For example, a student with autism may need corrective feedback more consistently or delivered with a different tone than a student with a learning disability. Similarly, older students may respond differently (Brophy, 1998; Emmer et al., 2003) or have different preferences for types of teacher praise than younger students (Elwell & Tiberio, 1994). In addition, students with more deviant forms of school behaviors or with long histories of negative forms of attention from adults at school may respond adversely to occasional expressions of approval from teachers (Brophy, 1998).

Because no practice works in the same way for every learner, teachers need to formatively assess the impact of any instructional approaches, including BSP and corrective feedback, to determine whether it is being effective in increasing the occurrence of desired behavior or if the practice needs to be adapted to improve its effectiveness (Torres, Farley, & Cook, 2012). This ongoing evaluation may, for example, involve collection of observational data on students' general or specific behavior to confirm that appropriate behavior does, in fact, increase when quality praise is contingently delivered in response to a targeted behavior. On the basis of data, experiences with particular students, and self-reflection teachers may find that different aspects of praise (e.g., frequency, public or private, paired with tangible reinforcers) may be differentially reinforcing to students. Many studies document ways teachers can increase their rates of praise (Kalis, Vannest, & Parker, 2007; Sutherland & Wehby, 2001) and improve the quality of their praise statements (Partin, Robertson, Maggin, Oliver, & Wehby, 2009).

SUMMARY OF RESEARCH SUPPORTING EFFECTIVE IMPLEMENTATION

In this section, we briefly summarize the research literature on BSP and corrective feedback related to learner outcomes.

Behavior Specific Praise

The effectiveness of teacher praise is supported by more than 45 years of empirical research. Early research indicated that, when compared to effects of ignoring and the use of rules, praise, even when used in isolation, was the most important component in a comprehensive classroom management system (Madsen, Becker, & Thomas, 1968). Teacher use of BSP has been found to improve time on task, prosocial behavior, and accuracy of academic responses of individual students as well as reduce overall classroom disruptions (Conroy, Sutherland, Snyder, & Marsh, 2008; Niesyn, 2009). It is likely that one of the primary reasons that the use of BSP yields such salient results in classroom management and instruction is that it increases appropriate academic responses and student engagement, which are generally accepted as key predictors of academic achievement, as well as student behavior.

Two meta-analyses have examined the effects of external rewards, including verbal reward or feedback, on intrinsic motivation (Cameron, Banko, & Pierce, 2001; Deci et al., 1999). Although verbal reinforcement was not the primary focus of either review it was included in both. Both teams of authors contended the other meta-analysis is seriously flawed and each reached two very different conclusions regarding the overall effects of external rewards on intrinsic motivation. However, both found that verbal praise served to increase intrinsic motivation and self-reported interest. Deci et al. (1999) explored the effects of verbal rewards (i.e., positive feedback) on free-choice behavior. They examined 148 studies and calculated a composite d of 0.33 (CI $=$ 0.18, 0.43) indicating that positive feedback significantly enhances intrinsic motivation. Cameron et al. (2001) examined 145 independent studies and concluded that verbal rewards significantly enhanced both free-choice intrinsic motivation ($d +$ [a weighted effect size] $=$ 0.31, CI $=$ 0.20, 0.41) and self-reported task interest ($d + =$ 0.32, CI $=$ 0.22, 0.43).

Feedback

Hattie and Timperley (2007) conducted one of the most noteworthy and comprehensive meta-analyses on feedback to date. Research on feedback has been conducted in a variety of settings. The average effect size for the use of feedback in a classroom setting across 12 meta-analyses was 0.79 for all participants and 1.24 for students receiving special education services, making feedback one of the most influential interventions to increase student performance. More specifically, feedback was most effective when it was delivered in audio, verbal, or computer assisted form and was corrective and included information about how a student could improve his or her performance on a task.

Like praise, the use of effective feedback has been suggested to improve both student behavior and academic responding more than ineffective methods of feedback (Conroy et al., 2009). For example, in a comparison of the effects of delayed and immediate feedback on sight-word recognition of students with developmental disabilities, Barbetta, Heward, Bradley, and Miller (1994) reported that when compared to delayed feedback, providing immediate feedback in the form of error correction improved student outcomes when assessed later in the same day, the following day, and the following week. Barbetta and colleagues suggested that immediate feedback provided students with more opportunities to respond correctly during instruction, thus improving their performance, even when assessed a week later. Teacher feedback has also improved student performance in the area of mathematics, especially when paired with praise (Luiselli & Downing, 1980).

FINAL THOUGHTS

While the use of verbal reinforcement, and specifically BSP and feedback, is highly effective and easy to implement at no cost to teachers, certain guidelines should be followed to maximize the likelihood that implementation of these strategies will lead to improved student outcomes. To most appropriately deliver BSP and feedback to students with learning and behavior disabilities, teachers should be nonjudgmental, specific and corrective, sincere and credible, immediate and proximal, and varied in their delivery. As with all strategies, effective teachers should be reflective by evaluating the effectiveness of these strategies as well. We encourage teachers to collect and analyze data related to target behaviors of the classroom as a whole as well as for individual students with learning and behavioral disabilities who may require more intensive application of these strategies or supplemental interventions. Based on formative assessment data, teachers should continue or adjust their use of BSP and feedback to maximize student success in both behavioral and academic outcomes.

REFERENCES

Alberto, P. A., & Troutman, A. C. (2013). *Applied behavior analysis for teachers* (9th ed.). Upper Saddle Ridge, NJ: Pearson.

Allday, R. A., Hinkson-Lee, K., Hudson, T., Neilsen-Gatti, S., Kleinke, A., & Russel, C. S. (2012). Training general educators to increase behavior-specific praise: Effects on students with EBD. *Behavioral Disorders, 32*, 87–98.

Anderson, R., Manoogian, S. T., & Reznick, J. S. (1976). The undermining and enhancing of intrinsic motivation in preschool children. *Journal of Personality and Social Psychology, 34*, 915–922. doi:10.1037/0022-3514.34.5.915

Barbetta, P. M., Heward, W. L., Bradley, D. M., & Miller, A. D. (1994). Effects of immediate and delayed error correction on the acquisition and maintenance of sight words by students with developmental disabilities. *Journal of Applied Behavior Analysis, 27*(1), 177–178. doi:10.1901/jaba.1994.27-177

Brophy, J. (1981). Teacher praise: A functional analysis. *Review of Educational Research, 51*, 5–32. doi:10.3102/00346543051001005

Brophy, J. (1998). *Motivating students to learn.* Boston, MA: McGraw Hill.

Burnett, P. (2001). Elementary students' preferences for teacher praise. *Journal of Classroom Interaction, 36*, 16–23.

Cameron, J., Banko, K. M., & Pierce, W. D. (2001). Pervasive negative effects of rewards on intrinsic motivation: The myth continues. *The Behavior Analyst, 24*, 1–44.

Capizzi, A. M. (2009). Start the year off right: Designing and evaluating a supportive classroom management plan. *Focus on Exceptional Children, 42*(3), 1–13.

Carr, J. E., Bailey, J. S., Ecott, C. L., Lucker, K. D., & Weil, T. M. (1998). On the effects of noncontingent delivery of differing magnitudes of reinforcement. *Journal of Applied Behavior Analysis, 31*, 313–321. doi:doi:10.1901/jaba.1998.31-313

Chappuis, J., Stiggins, R. J., Chapppuis, S., & Arter, J. A. (2011). *Classroom assessment for student learning: Doing it right-using it well* (2nd ed.). Chicago, IL: Pearson.

Connolly, T., Dowd, T., Criste, A., Nelson, C., & Tobias, L. (1995). *The well-managed classroom.* Omaha, NB: Boys Town.

Conroy, M. A., Sutherland, K. S., Snyder, A., Al-Hendawi, M., & Vo, A. (2009). Creating a positive classroom atmosphere: Teachers' use of effective praise and feedback. *Beyond Behavior, 18*(2), 18–26.

Conroy, M. A., Sutherland, K. S., Snyder, A. L., & Marsh, S. (2008). Classwide interventions effective instruction makes a difference. *Teaching Exceptional Children, 40*(6), 24–30.

Cook, B. G., Cook, L. H., & Landrum, T. J. (2013). Moving research into practice: Can we make dissemination stick? *Exceptional Children, 79*, 163–180. doi:10.1177/001440291307900203

Cooper, J. O., Heron, T. E., & Heward, W. L. (2007). *Applied behavior analysis.* Upper Saddle River, NJ: Pearson.

Craft, M. A., Alber, S. R., & Heward, W. L. (1998). Teaching elementary students with developmental disabilities to recruit teacher attention in a general education classroom: Effects on teacher praise and academic productivity. *Journal of Applied Behavior Analysis, 31*, 399–415. doi:10.1901/jaba.1998.31-399

De Weerdt, F., Desoet, A., & Roeyers, H. (2013). Working memory in children with reading disabilities and/or mathematical disabilities. *Journal of Learning Disabilities, 46*, 462–472. doi:10.1177/0022219412455238

Deci, E. L., Koestner, R., & Ryan, R. M. (1999). A meta-analytic review of experiments examining the effects of extrinsic rewards on intrinsic motivation. *Psychological Bulletin, 125*, 627–668. doi:10.1037/0033-2909.125.6.627

Duncan, T. K., Kemple, K. M., & Smith, T. M. (2000). Reinforcement in developmentally appropriate early childhood classrooms. *Childhood Education, 76,* 194–203. doi:10.1080/00094056.2000.10521162

Elwell, W. C., & Tiberio, J. (1994). Teacher praise: What students want. *Journal of Instructional Psychology, 21,* 322–328.

Emmer, E. T., Evertson, C. M., & Worsham, M. E. (2003). *Classroom management for secondary teachers* (6th ed.). Boston, MA: Allyn and Bacon.

Feldman, S. (2003). The place for praise. *Teaching PreK-8, 5*(6), 341–352.

Fullerton, E. K., Conroy, M. A., & Correa, V. I. (2009). Early childhood teachers' use of specific praise statements with young children at risk for behavioral disorders. *Behavioral Disorders, 34,* 118–135.

Gettinger, M., & Seibert, J. K. (2002). Best practices in increasing academic learning time. In A. Thomas (Ed.), *Best practices in school psychology IV* (4th ed., Vol. 1, pp. 773–787). Bethesda, MD: National Association of School Psychologists.

Gunter, P. L., Shores, R. E., Jack, S. L., Rasmussen, S. K., & Flowers, J. (1995). On the move: using teacher/student proximity to improve students' behavior. *Teaching Exceptional Children, 28,* 12–14.

Harackiewicz, J. M. (1979). The effects of reward contingency and performance feedback on intrinsic motivation. *Journal of Personality and Social Psychology, 37,* 1352–1363. doi:10.1037/0022-3514.37.8.1352

Hattie, J., & Timperley, H. (2007). The power of feedback. *Review of Educational Research, 77*(1), 81–112. doi:10.3102/003465430298487

Henderlong, J., & Lepper, M. R. (2002). The effects of praise on children's intrinsic motivation: A review and synthesis. *Psychological Bulletin, 128,* 774–775. doi:10.1037//0033-2909.128.5.774

IRIS Center for Training Enhancements. (2012). *Encouraging appropriate behavior.* Retrieved from http://iris.peabody.vanderbilt.edu/module/beh1/

Kalis, T. M., Vannest, K. J., & Parker, R. (2007). Praise counts: Using self-monitoring to increase effective teaching practices. *Preventing School Failure, 51,* 20–27. doi:10.3200/psfl.51.3.20-27

Kern, L., Hilt-Panahon, A., & Sokol, N. (2009). Further examining the triangle tip: Improving support for students with emotional and behavioral needs. *Psychology in the Schools, 46,* 18–32. doi:10.1002/pits.20351

Kerr, M. M., & Nelson, C. M. (2002). *Strategies for addressing behavior problems in the classroom* (4th ed.). Columbus, OH: Merrill Prentice Hall.

Kohn, A. (2001). Five reasons to stop saying "good job." *Young Children, 56*(5), 24–30.

Lampi, A., Fenty, N., & Beaunae, C. (2005). Making the three Ps easier: Praise, proximity and precorrection. *Beyond Behavior, 15,* 8–12.

Leko, M. M. (2015). To adapt or not to adapt: Navigating an implementation conundrum. *Teaching Exceptional Children, 48,* 80–85. doi:10.1177/0040059915605641

Lewis, T. J., Hudson, S., Richter, M., & Johnson, N. (2004). Scientifically supported practices in emotional and behavioral disorders: A proposed approach and brief review of current practices. *Behavioral Disorders, 29,* 247–259.

Luiselli, J. K., & Downing, J. N. (1980). Improving a student's arithmetic performance using feedback and reinforcement procedures. *Education and Treatment of Children, 3,* 45–49.

Maag, J. W. (2001). Rewarded by punishment: Reflections on the disuse of positive reinforcement in schools. *Exceptional Children, 67,* 173–186.

Madsen, C. H., Jr., Becker, W. C., & Thomas, D. R. (1968). Rules, praise, and ignoring: Elements of elementary classroom control. *Journal of Applied Behavior Analysis, 1*, 139–150. doi:10.1901/jaba.1968.1-139

Meltzer, L. (2010). *Promoting executive function in the classroom*. New York, NY: The Guilford Press.

Myers, D. M., Simonsen, B., & Sugai, G. (2011). Increasing teachers' use of praise with a response-to-intervention approach. *Education and Treatment of Children, 34*, 35–39. doi:10.1353/etc.2011.0004

National Center for Learning Disabilities. (2014). *The state of learning disabilities* (3rd ed.). Retrieved from http://https://www.ncld.org/wp-content/uploads/2014/11/2014-State-of-LD.pdf

Niesyn, M. E. (2009). Strategies for success: Evidence-based instructional practices for students with emotional and behavioral disorders. *Preventing School Failure, 53*, 227–234. doi:10.3200/psfl.53.4.227-234

O'Leary, K. D., & O'Leary, S. G. (1977). *Classroom management: The successful use of behavior modification*. Oxford: Pergamon.

Partin, T. C. M., Robertson, R. E., Maggin, D. M., Oliver, R. M., & Wehby, J. H. (2009). Using teacher praise and opportunities to respond to promote appropriate student behavior. *Preventing School Failure, 54*, 172–178. doi:10.1080/10459880903493179

Phillips, R. H. (1984). Increasing positive self-referent statements to improve self-esteem in low-income elementary school children. *Journal of School Psychology, 22*, 155–163. doi:10.1016/0022-4405(84)90035-9

Reed, L., Gable, R. A., & Yanek, K. (2014). Hard times ... uncertain future: Examining issues facing those working in the field of EBD. In P. Garner, J. Kauffman, & J. Elliott (Eds.), *The SAGE handbook of emotional and behavioral difficulties* (2nd ed.). London: Sage.

Rowe, M. B. (1974). Relation of wait-time and rewards to the development of language, logic and fate control: Part II–rewards. *Journal of Research in Science, 11*, 291–308. doi:10.1002/tea.3660110403

Shores, R. E., Gunter, P. L., & Jack, S. L. (1993). Classroom management strategies: Are they setting events for coercion. *Behavioral Disorders, 18*, 92–102.

Simonsen, B., Fairbanks, S., Briesch, A., Myers, D., & Sugai, G. (2008). Evidence-based practices in classroom management: Considerations for research to practice. *Education and Treatment of Children, 31*, 351–380. doi:10.1353/etc.0.0007

Skinner, B. F. (2011). *About behaviorism*. New York, NY: Vintage Books.

Sutherland, K. S., & Wehby, J. H. (2001). The effect of self-evaluation teaching behavior in classrooms for students with emotional or behavioral disorders. *Journal of Special Education, 35*, 161–171. doi:10.1177/002246690103500306

Sutherland, K. S., Wehby, J. H., & Copeland, S. R. (2000). Effect of varying rates of behavior-specific praise on the on-task behavior of students with EBD. *Journal of Emotional and Behavioral Disorders, 8*(1), 2–8. doi:10.1177/106342660000800101

Sutherland, K., Wehby, J., & Yoder, P. (2002). Examination of the relationship between teacherpraise and opportunities for students with EBD to respond to academic requests. *Journal of Emotional and Behavioral Disorders, 10*, 5–14. doi:10.1177/106342660201000102

Swann, W. B., Jr., & Pittman, T. S. (1977). Initiating play activity of children: The moderating influence of verbal cues on intrinsic motivation. *Child Development, 48*, 1128–1132. doi:10.1111/j.1467-8624.1977.tb01281.x

Torres, C., Farley, C. A., & Cook, B. G. (2012). A special educator's guide to successfully implementing evidence-based practices. *Teaching Exceptional Children*, *45*(1), 64–73. doi:10.1177/004005991204500109

United States Department of Education. (2014). 36th annual report to congress on the implementation of the individuals with disabilities education act. Office of Special Education and Rehabilitative Services, Washington, DC. Retrieved from http://www2.ed.gov/about/reports/annual/osep/2014/parts-b-c/36th-idea-arc.pdf

Vo, A. K., Sutherland, K. S., & Conroy, M. A. (2011). Best in class: A classroom-based model for ameliorating problem behavior in early childhood settings. *Psychology in the Schools*, *49*, 402–415. doi:10.1002/pits.21609

CHAPTER 9

DO SCHOOL-WIDE POSITIVE BEHAVIORAL INTERVENTIONS AND SUPPORTS, NOT EXCLUSIONARY DISCIPLINE PRACTICES

Rhonda N. T. Nese and Kent McIntosh

ABSTRACT

All educators will inevitably face unwanted student behavior that they need to address. A ubiquitous response to unwanted behavior is exclusionary discipline practices, including time-out, office discipline referrals, and suspensions. However, extensive research has demonstrated that these practices are associated with negative outcomes, including increased likelihood of further unwanted behavior, decreased achievement, and racial/ethnic discipline disparities. In this chapter, we provide a preventative alternative to exclusionary practices, school-wide positive behavioral interventions and supports (SWPBIS). SWPBIS is an evidence-based framework for implementing systems to reduce unwanted

Instructional Practices with and without Empirical Validity
Advances in Learning and Behavioral Disabilities, Volume 29, 175–196
Copyright © 2016 by Emerald Group Publishing Limited
All rights of reproduction in any form reserved
ISSN: 0735-004X/doi:10.1108/S0735-004X20160000029009

behavior and increase prosocial behavior, decreasing the need for exclu-
sionary practices.

Keywords: Suspension; school discipline; school safety; positive
behavior support; school-wide positive behavioral interventions
and supports

The importance of social behavior has increasingly been regarded as a
critical and necessary variable related to a range of important outcomes.
School success hinges not just on intellectual ability, but on social competencies such as self-regulation, positive interactions with adults, and
conscientiousness. These skills, as well as social interactions and attention,
affect readiness for learning and are thus critical for averting students from
trajectories toward chronic problem behavior and other undesirable learning outcomes (Dishion & Snyder, in press). For example, Bennett, Brown,
Boyle, Racine, and Offord (2003) found that teacher-perceived social competencies amongst kindergarten students were predictive of adult outcomes
such as education, employment, crime, substance use, and mental health.
Thus, addressing student problem behavior early and often has significant
social and learning outcomes for students.

Studies have found that schools with proactive and preventive
approaches to addressing student behavior have lower rates of discipline
referrals and dropout, more instructional time provided to all students, and
thus higher rates of academic success (Bradshaw, Waasdorp, & Leaf, 2012;
Eddy, Reid, & Curry, 2002). Unfortunately, many schools struggle with
implementing preventative and evidence-based practices for addressing
behavior concerns, and too often turn to punitive and reactionary forms of
punishment, such as suspensions and expulsions, as a common response.
Although suspensions may be justified for violent offenses, they are often
used for non-threatening problem behaviors, such as chronic absence or
minor disruptions (Newton et al., 2014). For these common behaviors,
there are effective strategies that teachers and administrators can use to
address the causes of problem behaviors and prevent them from occurring
in the future.

The purposes of this chapter are twofold. First, we describe the overuse
and ineffectiveness of exclusionary practices, such as suspensions, in

schools and the detrimental impact they have on social and academic outcomes for students. Second, we provide an introduction to school-wide positive behavioral interventions and supports (SWPBIS), a systems-level approach for establishing the social culture and individualized behavior supports needed for schools to be a safe and effective learning environments for all students. We will present the theoretical foundation of SWPBIS, the research that has documented its effectiveness for improving student outcomes over the last two decades, and how SWPBIS can be utilized as an alternative to exclusionary practices in schools.

INEFFECTIVENESS OF EXCLUSIONARY PRACTICES

Exclusionary discipline practices can be defined as removing students from typical instruction (or social environment) for a period of time in response to unwanted student social behavior. Exclusionary practices include a range of intensities, including brief time-out from classroom instruction, cross-class ("buddy room") time-outs, sitting in the hall, reflection rooms, seclusion rooms, office discipline referral, detention, suspension, or expulsion (Lin et al., 2013). Brief time-outs, the mildest forms of exclusion, are often used in response to minor misbehavior. At the other end of the spectrum, expulsions are often used as mandated responses to a limited number of state-identified offenses, such as possession of weapons or drugs. Regardless of the type, the effective result of each of these practices is that a student is removed from instruction and interactions with teachers and peers.

Rationale for Exclusionary Practices

Exclusionary practices are often implemented for one or more of the following three reasons (Morgan, Farkas, & Wu, 2012). First, they are used as reactive strategies to decrease the frequency of unwanted behavior. The intent is that exposure to exclusionary discipline will effectively punish the behavior (Sterling Turner, & Watson, 1999). Second, they may be implemented to respond to safety concerns. For example, a student may receive an out-of-school suspension after a violent incident until the school team can build an appropriate safety plan, preferably as part of a full behavior support plan, to implement upon the student's return. Third, related to the previous reason, school personnel may use exclusion to prevent further disruption of the learning environment for other students.

Presumed Mechanisms of Exclusionary Practices

The primary behavioral principle by which exclusion is intended to work is negative punishment, or removal of reinforcement from interesting activities or interacting with teachers and peers (Ryan, Sanders, Katsiyannis, & Yell, 2007). The exclusion prevents students from accessing attention during the period of exclusion. The premise is that the undesired student behavior will cease once the attention for unwanted behavior is removed (i.e., removing fuel from the fire) or that removal from class is aversive enough that it prevents future unwanted behavior because students would prefer to remain in class with their peers than be removed.

Concerns regarding Exclusionary Practices

Although exclusionary practices are ubiquitous in schools (Losen & Gillespie, 2012; Zabel, 1986), there are serious concerns regarding their use that are worth considering. These issues are especially troubling regarding out-of-school suspensions, although they also pertain to use (and especially overuse) of less severe forms of exclusionary discipline. It is important that schools collect systematic data regarding the use and length of exclusionary discipline events – both for individual students and the school population as a whole – to identify and correct these challenges, as well as minimize their use in general. These challenges are described in the following sections.

Reinforcement of Unwanted Behavior
In keeping with the principle of negative punishment, effective use of exclusion requires that the immediate environment be reinforcing for the student (Sterling Turner & Watson, 1999). If the student does not enjoy the activity or interactions with peers or the teacher, exclusion is unlikely to reduce unwanted behavior and may serve to reinforce it (Maag, 2001). For example, if a student finds a particular activity aversive, she or he may use unwanted behavior to avoid or escape it. In this way, exclusionary practices can backfire, resulting in *more* unwanted behavior. If the immediate staff member excludes the student from instruction (e.g., time-out, office

discipline referral), the student's unwanted behavior is negatively reinforced, meaning that the student is more likely to use unwanted behavior in the future. As such, school personnel who regularly use systems for exclusion need to build systems to make the classroom and general school environment more positive and reinforcing for students (Ryan et al., 2007).

Iatrogenic Effects on Academic Skills
Another drawback of exclusionary practices is that they remove students from the instructional environment, which may decrease unwanted behavior but prevent access to academic instruction (McIntosh & Goodman, in press; U.S. Departments of Education and Justice, 2014). As a result, students who are regularly exposed to exclusionary discipline receive restricted opportunities to build academic skills. For example, a recent study showed that use of a cross-class time-out intervention significantly reduced teacher ratings of problem behavior but also reduced academic achievement as well (Benner, Nelson, Sanders, & Ralston, 2012). Over time, as students fall further behind their peers academically, academic instruction becomes more aversive, triggering more unwanted behavior to escape instruction through exclusion. This set of interactions creates an ongoing coercive cycle, in which students and teachers are continually reinforced for using unwanted behavior and exclusionary discipline, respectively (Dishion & Snyder, in press; McIntosh, Horner, Chard, Dickey, & Braun, 2008).

Accordingly, it is recommended for school personnel to conduct functional behavior assessments when students are excluded repeatedly (Sterling Turner & Watson, 1999). Such information can be used to build a support plan to disrupt these cycles and reduce, rather than reinforce, unwanted behavior.

Association with Poor Long-Term Outcomes
In addition to reinforcing unwanted behavior and decreasing academic achievement, there are many documented distal negative effects of exclusionary discipline. Although it is difficult to prove causation, there is ample research evidence showing the harmful effects of exclusion, particularly out-of-school suspensions, on outcomes such as grade retention, dropout, and adult incarceration (American Academy of Pediatrics Council on School Health, 2013; Fabelo et al., 2011; Noltemeyer, Ward, & Mcloughlin, 2015). For example, a single out-of-school suspension in ninth grade is associated with a 50% increase in dropping out and a 19% decrease in enrollment in postsecondary education (Balfanz, Byrnes, & Fox, 2015). Even when controlling for school and individual risk factors

(e.g., antisocial behavior, deviant peer group membership), receipt of out-of-school suspensions is a significant predictor of future antisocial behavior (Hemphill, Toumbourou, Herrenkohl, McMorris, & Catalano, 2006; Lee, Cornell, Gregory, & Fan, 2011). There is also evidence that the severity of the exclusionary practice is related to severity of long-term outcomes. For example, out-of-school suspension is more strongly related to negative out-comes than in-school suspension (Noltemeyer et al., 2015). Unfortunately, these effects are not seen only for students receiving the exclusion; schools with high rates of out-of-school suspension have lower school-wide achievement and lower perceptions of school safety by the student body as a whole (American Psychological Association, 2008).

Overuse of Exclusion for Non-Violent Offenses
Because of the strong associations between exclusionary practices and negative outcomes, it seems clear that they should be limited to severe inci-dents, violent offenses in particular. However, there is evidence that exclu-sion is used for a range of less severe student behaviors. A recent study (Losen, Martinez, & Okelola, 2014) found that 34% of out-of-school suspensions were issued for non-violent behaviors, such as disruption or willful defiance. Unfortunately, as with students, exclusion can be reinfor-cing for school personnel as well. The option to remove a student from class for the rest of the period or school for multiple days can be powerfully reinforcing.

To place the use of out-of-school suspension into perspective, a longitu-dinal study (Schollenberger, 2015) found that 1 in 3 students have been suspended at one point in their K-12 schooling. If suspensions served a deterrent effect on future behavior, perhaps their use at these high rates could be justified. However, Massar, McIntosh, and Eliason (2015) recently found that among students that were suspended in August, September, or October, 72% received further discipline later in the year, indicating there was little evidence of a deterrent effect for suspensions, which is consistent with previous research (Atkins et al., 2002).

Racial Disparities in Use of Exclusion
A final concern is that exclusionary discipline is provided disproportio-nately to students of color, and Black students in particular (McIntosh, Girvan, Horner, & Smolkowski, 2014). According to national data from secondary schools (Losen, Hodson, Keith, Morrison, & Belway, 2015), 7% of White students were suspended, but 11% of Hispanic/Latino students, 12% of American Indian students, and 23% of Black students

were suspended. In addition, 18% of students with disabilities were suspended. These risks are compounded — one in 5 districts in the country suspended over 50% of its Black male students with disabilities (Losen, Ee, Hodson, & Martinez, 2015). Although some might perceive that racial disparities can be explained by poverty or racial differences in rates of misbehavior, a range of studies have shown that race remains a significant predictor, even when controlling for these variables (Anyon et al., 2014; Bradshaw, Mitchell, O'Brennan, & Leaf, 2010; Lee et al., 2011; Wallace, Goodkind, Wallace, & Bachman, 2008). There is emerging research that racial disparities in exclusion persist, even though exclusion policies and procedures are supposedly "race neutral," because of bias in disciplinary decision making, particularly for more subjective behaviors (Skiba, Michael, Nardo, & Peterson, 2002; Smolkowski, Girvan, McIntosh, Nese, & Horner, 2015).

What Is Needed in Place of Regular Exclusionary Practices

Given the levels of unwanted behavior seen in schools and the harmful effects of overuse of exclusionary practices, it is important to provide educators with alternatives to removing students from the classroom. Exclusionary practices are reactive in nature — they are implemented in response to unwanted behavior, not as a means of preventing it, and they do not teach students the behaviors to use in place of unwanted behavior. When using exclusionary practices, experts recommend including more proactive, instructional approaches to complement them (Lin et al., 2013; Sterling Turner & Watson, 1999). As such, it is valuable to examine instructional practices that could reduce the need for and use of exclusionary discipline practices in schools.

SCHOOL-WIDE POSITIVE BEHAVIORAL INTERVENTIONS AND SUPPORTS AS AN ALTERNATIVE TO EXCLUSIONARY DISCIPLINE

SWPBIS was initially developed in the late 1980s as a systematic approach for establishing the social culture and behavior expectations needed for schools to be safe and effective learning environments for all students. With its roots in applied behavior analysis and behavioral theory, SWPBIS emphasizes that behavior is learned through modeling and teaching, and that environmental factors influence when and how a behavior is likely to occur (Sugai & Horner, 2009). Therefore, new prosocial behaviors can be taught and reinforced while inappropriate behaviors are minimized through a systematic plan of teaching and reinforcement, with additional environmental changes to increase the likelihood of prosocial behavior. Adapted from the three-tiered public health model of interventions, SWPBIS outlines a continuum of supports from prevention to intensive intervention to provide students with the supports they need to be successful in school. SWPBIS is not a curriculum or manualized program; it is a framework designed to improve the adoption, implementation, and sustained use of evidence-based practices related to behavior, classroom management, and school discipline (Sugai & Horner, 2009). These outcomes are achieved by emphasizing an integration of measureable outcomes, data-based decision making, evidence-based practices, and support systems for school and district-level implementers.

A number of resources are available describing SWPBIS and its critical features in extensive detail (OSEP Technical Assistance Center on Positive Behavioral Interventions and Supports, October 2015; Sailor, Dunlap, Sugai, & Horner, 2009). While this chapter strives to provide a comprehensive examination of the use of SWPBIS for the purposes of reducing exclusionary discipline in schools, we encourage readers interested in the broader uses of SWPBIS for improving student and school outcomes to read the following:

- Horner and Sugai (2000).
- Sailor et al. (2009).
- Sugai et al. (2010).

Research Foundations

A wealth of empirical research conducted over the last 20 years has documented the positive effects of implementation of SWPBIS on student outcomes and organizational health. Specifically, SWPBIS has been associated with decreases in office discipline referrals, suspensions, and expulsions (Bradshaw, Mitchell, & Leaf, 2010); and increases in academic achievement (McIntosh, Bennett, & Price, 2011), students' social and emotional competencies (Bradshaw et al., 2012), and school safety (Horner et al., 2009). In both randomized controlled trials and experimental single case studies, researchers have found that these improvements have been achieved through SWPBIS enhancing academic engagement and teacher efficacy, and reducing the use of exclusionary discipline practices (McIntosh, Ty, Horner, & Sugai, 2013).

Characteristics of SWPBIS

In additional to its grounding in behavioral theory, SWPBIS has five distinct characteristics that make it a systematic framework for implementation of effective practices. These characteristics are (1) the use of a three-tiered prevention model, (2) a focus on explicit instruction of appropriate behaviors, (3) the selection and use of evidence-based behavior supports, (4) a systems perspective driven by local capacity, and (5) the use of data for decision making.

Three-Tiered Prevention
The most defining characteristic of SWPBIS is the emphasis on prevention of problem behaviors before they occur. Unlike traditional school discipline practices, which are characterized by reacting to incidents, SWPBIS stresses the importance of establishing a continuum of behavior supports designed specifically to (a) teach socially appropriate behaviors to all students, (b) prevent the development of new problem behaviors, and (c) reduce the recidivism of existing problem behaviors (Walker et al., 1996). This continuum is organized within a three-tiered prevention model (see Fig. 1). At Tier I, also referred to as universal supports, behavior interventions are provided to all students across all school settings. Tier I supports are implemented to clarify school-wide expectations and to demonstrate for all students what appropriate behavior "looks like." Tier II, or targeted supports, provides more intensive behavior supports for students whose behaviors are not responsive to Tier I interventions. Those students may receive efficient interventions, such as small group instruction or regular check-ins with a staff member. Finally, Tier III or individualized supports are provided to students whose behaviors are not responsive to Tier I or Tier II interventions. These students are given highly individualized and intensive behavior supports to address significant behavior concerns. Specific supports at all three tiers and how they can be used in place of exclusionary discipline practices will be further discussed in this chapter.

SCHOOL-WIDE PBIS

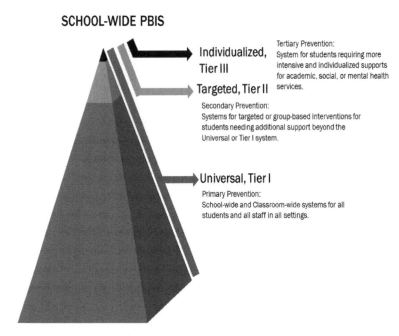

Individualized, Tier III

Tertiary Prevention:
System for students requiring more intensive and individualized supports for academic, social, or mental health services.

Targeted, Tier II

Secondary Prevention:
Systems for targeted or group-based interventions for students needing additional support beyond the Universal or Tier I system.

Universal, Tier I

Primary Prevention:
School-wide and Classroom-wide systems for all students and all staff in all settings.

Fig. 1.   SWPBIS Three-Tiered Prevention Model.

Explicit Instruction

Providing explicit instruction on appropriate behaviors is another defining feature of SWPBIS. It is not assumed that students come to school knowing what is expected of them, how to behave, and how to appropriately engage in class; within SWPBIS, those behaviors are first taught before they are expected. School personnel teach behaviors that lead to increases in social and academic success, such as how to ask for assistance from a teacher, how to behave safely in the hallways, and how to be respectful of others in the classroom.

Evidence-Based Behavior Supports

Although no single intervention or technique is endorsed as the fix-all strategy within SWPBIS, priority is given to the selection and use of behavior supports that have empirical evidence of their effectiveness for improving outcomes for students. Not only it is advised that schools and districts select evidence-based practices, but it is vital that those practices are examined for their social and contextual relevance within the culture of the school and grade levels in which they will be used.

Systems Perspective
To maximize the likelihood that SWPBIS is implemented fully and with supports to keep the practices sustained through challenges often experienced by schools, district and states are encouraged to take a systems perspective toward implementation. A systems perspective emphasizes the establishment of local training and coaching expertise, agreements and commitments among key stakeholders, high levels of implementation readiness and fidelity, and continuous implementation and outcome evaluation (Sugai et al., 2010).

Data for Decision Making
The continuous collection and analysis of data is necessary for determining the extent to which behavior supports are being implemented as intended and whether those practices are improving student outcomes (Sugai & Horner, 2009). The collected data serve to improve the behavior supports available to students and are thus analyzed frequently to assess their effectiveness and feasibility.

Using SWPBIS in Place of Exclusionary Practices

With its emphasis on preventive strategies, such as teaching, modeling, and reinforcing appropriate behaviors rather than waiting for misbehavior to occur before responding, SWPBIS provides multiple effective strategies at all three tiers of the triangle that can be used in place of exclusionary discipline practices. In this section, we outline feasible strategies that may be used at each tier of the SWPBIS framework to prevent as well as address inappropriate behaviors without overreliance on exclusion.

Tier I: Teaching Appropriate Behavior to Prevent the Need for Exclusion
Tier I interventions are developed around the needs of the whole school, delivered to the whole school, and serve to foster a positive social culture for all members of the learning community, including students, staff members, and families (Colvin, Kame'enui, & Sugai, 1993; George, Kincaid, & Pollard-Sage, 2009). Tier I interventions are preventive in nature; if they are implemented well, the majority of students will be successful (Fairbanks, Sugai, Guardino, & Lathrop, 2007). They are important

foundations for (a) providing teachers with the skills to address minor mis-behavior within the classroom, (b) supporting the majority of students, (c) preventing the development of chronic problem behavior that could result in exclusionary discipline, and (d) identifying and providing more specia-lized behavior supports for students with high-intensity problem behaviors (Sugai & Horner, 2009; Sugai et al., 2000).

Tier I Practices. Before Tier I interventions can be implemented, appropri-ate and inappropriate student behaviors need to be clearly defined. The goal of defining behaviors is twofold: (1) to clarify for students and adults what acceptable and unacceptable behaviors look like, and (2) to reduce inconsistency and subjectivity amongst teachers when identifying a beha-vior as unacceptable. Consistency is key – without it, what one teacher considers disrespectful may not be considered disrespectful by another teacher. Differences in personal definitions can send mixed messages to students, and can often result in disproportionate discipline being delivered to different students for the same behavior (Skiba et al., 2002). For that reason, behaviors must be operationally defined so that referrals to the office are appropriate, and that the behavior matches the consequence to be delivered (George et al., 2009).

Once appropriate behaviors have been clearly defined, it is still necessary to teach them. It is not enough for school-wide behavior expectations to be posted in the classroom or in a hallway; students need to receive instruction on these behaviors, as they are the prerequisite skills necessary for success in school. Just like learning a new academic skill, students benefit from repetition of teaching behavior routines and expectations, and therefore it is more effective to teach the expectations several times throughout the school year. A common Tier I support for providing behavior instruction is what some schools refer to as the "Rules Rodeo." This routine is a process for taking groups of students around campus and explicitly demonstrating what appropriate behavior looks like in different locations, such as the gym, cafeteria, bathroom, and hallway. Staff at each of these locations lead students through teaching and modeling the expectations. Teachers also conduct direct teaching on what those school-wide expectations look like in their classroom.

Teaching of behavior expectations is not just important for student success, it is a vital part of teacher development. Ongoing staff training is essential for building fluency in implementing Tier I components. The more that staff members practice and are reminded of the Tier I proce-dures, the more likely the components will be delivered (George et al.,

2009). Additionally, administrators depend on teachers to utilize effective classroom management strategies to prevent problem behaviors from occurring and to use appropriate practices to intervene when they do. Teacher training on how to most effectively address minor problem behaviors in the classroom allows teachers to establish their role as the classroom leader, while reducing the amount of instructional time students would miss if minor problem behaviors were being addressed outside of the classroom.

Reinforcing appropriate behaviors with behavior-specific praise, possibly supplemented with tangible reinforcement, is one of the best strategies for increasing the likelihood that the behavior will continue (Akin-Little, Eckert, Lovett, & Little, 2004; Lepper, Henderlong, & Gingras, 1999). As such, developing a school-wide reinforcement system to provide students access to positive feedback about their behavior is a critical component of Tier I interventions in that it focuses student and staff attention on appropriate behaviors, supports a positive school climate, and highlights the value of appropriate behaviors within the school culture (Florida's Positive Behavior Support Project, 2004; George et al., 2009). For reinforcement to be accessible to all students, the criteria for earning it must be clearly defined for students. Additionally, reinforcement of appropriate behaviors needs to be provided frequently, unexpectedly, and across multiple settings for their effectiveness to be optimized.

Developing and implementing an effective system for responding to problem behaviors is another necessary component of Tier I supports. School SWPBIS teams are encouraged to clearly outline the steps of the school's discipline process in a visual format so that it may be used in teaching the rest of the staff, training new staff, and dissemination to students and families and posted in classrooms for reference (George et al., 2009). A hierarchy of consequences, including teaching strategies as well as mild corrections, is then developed to assist teachers and administrators with choosing the appropriate response when problem behaviors arise. This process should also be communicated to students and families so that everyone is aware of both the strategies teachers will use in the classroom to respond to inappropriate behaviors, and the potential consequences that school personnel may use if problem behaviors continue.

One of the greatest benefits of collecting and analyzing data frequently is that it allows for teams of staff members to assess the extent to which Tier I supports are being adequately implemented and if they are having the expected effect on student behavior. With optimal implementation of Tier I supports, a small percentage of students ($\sim$1–20%) will be identified as those in need of additional intervention. Such patterns of response may be a result of learning histories that make general school-wide interventions less effective for their behavior, or perhaps limited previous exposure and practice with school-wide expectations (Horner, Sugai, Todd, & Lewis-Palmer, 2005). Regardless of the reason, these students should continue to receive Tier I supports along with their peers in addition to more intensive and individualized interventions.

Using Tier I SWPBIS to Reduce Exclusion. With a focus on prevention, the use of Tier I supports might reduce the use of exclusionary discipline by providing instruction on appropriate behaviors before students engage in the types of behaviors that could result in removal from the classroom. Tier I supports also provide instruction to staff on what types of behaviors should be managed in the classroom and strategies to address unwanted behavior without exclusion. Finally, by analyzing school-wide discipline data, Tier I teams are better equipped to identify the misuse of exclusionary practices early and often and are thus more likely to recommend reteaching for staff on how best to address problem behaviors when they arise.

Tier II: Focusing on Skill Building

Students in need of Tier II supports receive interventions that are more intensive in terms of effort and frequency of implementation than Tier I supports, but these supports can be applied to a subset of the larger population of students by staff members who have more frequent interactions with them (Hawken, Adolphson, MacLeod, & Schumann, 2009). Although some implementation differences exist, Tier II supports are directly connected to Tier I interventions by the content that is taught (e.g., instruction and practice in the school-wide behavior expectations). However, Tier II supports focus on building skills that students may be lacking by providing teaching and reinforcement of those skills on a daily basis. In many ways, Tier II strategies can be seen as methods to provide more access to or strengthen Tier I supports.

Tier II Practices. Numerous Tier II interventions have been empirically documented as being effective tools for improving student behavior with students from different age groups, including *Check In/Check Out* (Fairbanks et al., 2007; Hawken, Bundock, Kladis, O'Keeffe, & Barrett, 2014; Maggin, Zurheide, Pickett, & Baillie, 2015), and *Check and Connect* (Christenson, Stout, & Pohl, 2012). These programs have several core features in common. First, they teach self-management strategies such as picking up a self-management card, checking in with your own teachers, and recording your own scores. They also include contact with an adult mentor in the school. Third, they include direct skills instruction of behaviors that are aligned with the school-wide behavior expectation. Finally, they all have a family participation component, which may come in the form of daily and weekly feedback on their student's progress, and suggestions on how to encourage their child's participation (Sugai & Horner, 2009).

Student progress through Tier II interventions are monitored regularly by a team of staff members with more specialized behavior knowledge, and modifications to interventions are quickly implemented when data shows that a student is not meeting behavior goals. Adjustments might include, for example, making modifications to the frequency of daily assessments, the difficulty of set behavior goals, or the schedule and type of reinforcements delivered to students for demonstrating appropriate behaviors (Hawken et al., 2009). Additionally, adequate implementation of Tier II supports might reveal that a student is in need of more individualized Tier III interventions.

Using Tier II SWPBIS to Reduce Exclusion. Tier II supports are necessary in a system geared toward reducing exclusionary discipline practices because they are provided to students who have been identified as regularly engaging in unwanted behaviors, but their behaviors are either lower in intensity and frequency or they are exhibiting new patterns that were not seen previously. These students, without proper supports, are more likely to have their unaddressed behaviors escalate over time, thus leading to higher rates of exclusion from the classroom and harsher discipline. Data systems help to identify these students early. For example, one common practice is to provide Tier II supports to any student who has received two or more discipline referrals within the first two months of the school year. This method of identification allows for students who may be at risk for developing chronic behavior problems to receive the supports they need early, before patterns of repeated exclusion emerge.

Tier III: Individualizing Supports for Students at the Greatest Risk
If a student's behavior is unresponsive to adequately implemented Tier I and II interventions, a shift to more individualized Tier III interventions is appropriate. These interventions tend to be more individualized to the specific conditions that are associated with the problem behavior and are thus considered function-based (Scott, Anderson, Mancil, & Alter, 2009).

Function-based supports refer to careful consideration of environmental factors that occasion (antecedent) and maintain (consequence, function) instances of problem behavior when developing behavior support plans (Sugai & Horner, 2009).

Tier III Practices. Key steps in the function-based support process include (1) selecting an appropriate replacement behavior, which is a behavior that is more socially acceptable than the problem behavior, (2) determining how the replacement behavior will be taught, (3) creating routines to increase the likelihood of success with the new behavior, (4) determining appropriate consequences for replacement behaviors and problem behaviors, and (5) monitoring the behavior support plan (Scott et al., 2009). However, taking a function-based approach when developing behavior support plans takes skill and coordination. Beyond simple plans, the team requires access to individuals with behavior expertise and who are knowledgeable about using data and collaborative planning (Sugai & Horner, 2009). Depending on the size of the school or district, this team may require supports from external sources, such as school psychologists and behavior specialists, to have access to the level of specialized expertise needed to implement Tier III interventions (Scott, 2013; Scott et al., 2009). In some cases, Tier III supports may include school-based mental health services or wraparound care, which often involve family support, medical expertise, and child welfare. In these approaches, student and family strengths, goals, and resources are emphasized as a means of addressing student behavior challenges (Sugai & Horner, 2009).

Using Tier III SWPBIS to Reduce Exclusion. As research has demonstrated, students in need of Tier III behavior supports are amongst those most likely to experience exclusionary discipline in response to their behaviors. Thus, Tier III interventions are critical for keeping these students in school and engaged in learning. Tier III support includes functional behavior assessment to assess the extent to which exclusionary practices may be reinforcing unwanted behavior and to teach students the skills needed to get their basic needs met without the need for exclusion. The individualized nature of Tier III supports also allows for professionals within the school, family, and community to collaborate on the supports that will allow the student to be most successful. Additionally, this type of teaming of supports provides stakeholders with the opportunity to monitor student progress more closely. Information shared amongst key stakeholders allows for regular communication on student performance, and specifically, on any intervention modification or concerning behaviors that need to be addressed. These steps are ideally taken before a student is disciplined. Tier III supports also have a central focus on individualized instruction for students, and those supports may be provided in lieu of or in conjunction with an administrator-designated consequence, reducing the likelihood that a student would be removed from the learning environment without any supplemental instruction being provided in the interim.

CONCLUSION

Although school discipline systems are necessary for maintaining safe school environments where students can learn and thrive, research has demonstrated that exclusionary discipline practices are not capable of ensuring school safety. Even worse, such practices lead to racial and socioeconomic disparities, academic failure, school dropout, and are direct contributors to the school-to-prison pipeline (American Academy of Pediatrics Council on School Health, 2013). Schools and districts are encouraged to weigh all options when considering exclusionary discipline as a consequence for inappropriate behavior. Such practices should be withheld for the most serious of offenses, as they are justified for behaviors that threaten the safety of members of the school community. However, even in instances where safety is a concern and a student is removed from the classroom or school, behavior instruction can teach the student why violent behavior is unacceptable and what alternative behaviors are appropriate for school. Additionally, students who are removed from class must also be provided academic support, as exclusion from class will only increase a student's likelihood of school failure.

Fortunately, as a prevention-oriented school discipline reform framework, SWPBIS has documented evidence of its effectiveness for improving student behavior and supporting a safe and healthy school climate. Many of the behavior challenges often seen by school personnel can be averted through implementing tiered instructional supports to all students, such as those described in this chapter, as well as providing teachers with the skills to address minor misbehavior within the classroom. Above all, the goal of utilizing these strategies, or any alternative to exclusionary discipline, is to provide students with the necessary life skills to solve problems on their own while allowing them to remain a member of a positive school community.

ACKNOWLEDGMENTS

Preparation of this chapter was supported by the Institute of Education Sciences, U.S. Department of Education, through Grant R324A120278 to University of Oregon. The opinions expressed are those of the authors and do not represent views of the Institute or the U.S. Department of Education. The authors declare no potential conflicts of interest with respect to the research, authorship, and/or publication of this chapter.

REFERENCES

Akin-Little, K. A., Eckert, T. L., Lovett, B. J., & Little, S. G. (2004). Extrinsic reinforcement in the classroom: Bribery or best practice. *School Psychology Review, 33*, 344–362.

American Academy of Pediatrics Council on School Health. (2013). Policy statement: Out-of-school suspension and expulsion. *Pediatrics, 131*, e1000–e1007. doi:10.1542/peds.2012-3932

American Psychological Association. (2008). Are zero tolerance policies effective in the schools? An evidentiary review and recommendations. *American Psychologist, 63*, 852–862.

Anyon, Y., Jenson, J. M., Altschul, I., Farrar, J., McQueen, J., Greer, E., ... Simmons, J. (2014). The persistent effect of race and the promise of alternatives to suspension in school discipline outcomes. *Children and Youth Services Review, 44*, 379–386.

Atkins, M. S., McKay, M. M., Frazier, S. L., Jakobsons, L. J., Arvanitis, P., Cunningham, T., ... Lambrecht, L. (2002). Suspensions and detentions in an urban, low-income school: Punishment or reward? *Journal of Abnormal Child Psychology, 30*, 361–371.

Balfanz, R., Byrnes, V., & Fox, J. (2015). Sent home and put off-track: The antecedents, dis-proportionalities, and consequences of being suspended in the 9th grade. In D. J. Losen (Ed.), *Closing the school discipline gap: Research for policymakers* (pp. 17–30). New York, NY: Teachers College Press.

Bennett, K. J., Brown, K. S., Boyle, M., Racine, Y., & Offord, D. (2003). Does low reading achievement at school entry cause conduct problems? *Social Science & Medicine, 56*, 2443–2448.

Benner, G. J., Nelson, J. R., Sanders, E. A., & Ralston, N. C. (2012). Behavior intervention for students with externalizing behavior problems: Primary-level standard protocol. *Exceptional Children, 78*, 181–198.

Bradshaw, C. P., Mitchell, M. M., & Leaf, P. J. (2010). Examining the effects of schoolwide positive behavioral interventions and supports on student outcomes: Results from a randomized controlled effectiveness trial in elementary schools. *Journal of Positive Behavior Interventions, 12*, 133–148. doi:10.1177/1098300709334798

Bradshaw, C. P., Mitchell, M. M., O'Brennan, L. M., & Leaf, P. J. (2010). Multilevel explora-tion of factors contributing to the overrepresentation of black students in office disciplinary referrals. *Journal of Educational Psychology, 102*, 508–520.

Bradshaw, C. P., Waasdorp, T. E., & Leaf, P. J. (2012). Effects of school-wide positive behavioral interventions and supports on child behavior problems and adjustment. *Pediatrics, 130*, e1136–e1145. doi:10.1542/peds.2012-0243

Christenson, S. L., Stout, K., & Pohl, A. (2012). *Check & connect: A comprehensive student engagement intervention: Implementing with fidelity* (2nd ed.). Minneapolis, MN: Institute on Community Integration, University of Minnesota.

Colvin, G., Kame'enui, E. J., & Sugai, G. (1993). Reconceptualizing behavior management and school-wide discipline in general education. *Education and Treatment of Children, 16*, 361–381.

Dishion, T. J., & Snyder, J. (Eds.). (in press). *Handbook of coercive relationship dynamics: Basic mechanisms, developmental processes, and intervention applications.* New York, NY: Oxford Press.

Eddy, J. M., Reid, J. B., & Curry, V. (2002). The etiology of youth antisocial behavior, delinquency, and violence and a public health approach to prevention. In M. R. Shinn, H. M. Walker, & G. Stoner (Eds.), *Interventions for academic and behavior problems II: Preventive and remedial approaches* (pp. 27–52). Bethesda, MD: National Association of School Psychologists.

Fabelo, T., Thompson, M. D., Plotkin, M., Carmichael, D., Marchbanks, M. P. I., & Booth, E. A. (2011). *Breaking schools' rules: A statewide study of how school discipline relates to students' success and juvenile justice involvement.* New York, NY: Council of State Governments Justice Center.

Fairbanks, S., Sugai, G., Guardino, D., & Lathrop, M. (2007). Response to intervention: An evaluation of a classroom system of behavior support for second grade students. *Exceptional Children, 73*, 288–310.

Florida's Positive Behavior Support Project. (2004). *Children's literature: Tools for teaching school-wide expectations and rules.* Tampa, FL: University of South Florida.

George, H. P., Kincaid, D., & Pollard-Sage, J. (2009). Primary-tier interventions and supports. In W. Sailor, G. Dunlap, G. Sugai, & R. H. Horner (Eds.), *Handbook of positive behavior support* (pp. 375–394). New York, NY: Springer.

Hawken, L. S., Adolphson, S. L., MacLeod, K. S., & Schumann, J. (2009). Secondary-tier interventions and supports. In W. Sailor, G. Dunlap, G. Sugai, & R. H. Horner (Eds.), *Handbook of positive behavior support* (pp. 395–420). New York, NY: Springer.

Hawken, L. S., Bundock, K., Kladis, K., O'Keeffe, B., & Barrett, C. A. (2014). Systematic review of the check-in, check-out intervention for students at risk for emotional and behavioral disorders. *Education and Treatment of Children, 37*, 635–658.

Hemphill, S. A., Toumbourou, J. W., Herrenkohl, T. I., McMorris, B. J., & Catalano, R. F. (2006). The effect of school suspensions and arrests on subsequent adolescent antisocial behavior in Australia and the United States. *Journal of Adolescent Health, 39*, 736–744.

Horner, R. H., & Sugai, G. (2000). School-wide behavior support: An emerging initiative. *Journal of Positive Behavior Interventions, 2*, 231–232.

Horner, R. H., Sugai, G., Smolkowski, K., Eber, L., Nakasato, J., Todd, A. W., & Esparanza, J. (2009). A randomized, wait-list controlled effectiveness trial assessing school-wide positive behavior support in elementary schools. *Journal of Positive Behavior Interventions, 11*, 133–144.

Horner, R. H., Sugai, G., Todd, A. W., & Lewis-Palmer, T. (2005). School-wide positive behavior support. In L. Bambara & L. Kern (Eds.), *Individualized supports for students with problem behaviors: Designing positive behavior plans* (pp. 359–390). New York, NY: Guilford Press.

Lee, T., Cornell, D., Gregory, A., & Fan, X. (2011). High suspension schools and dropout rates for black and white students. *Education and Treatment of Children, 34*, 167–192.

Lepper, M., Henderlong, J., & Gingras, I. (1999). Understanding the effects of extrinsic rewards on intrinsic motivation – Uses and abuses of meta-analysis: Comment on Deci, Koestner, and Ryan (1999). *Psychological Bulletin, 125*, 669–676.

Lin, Y., Morgan, P. L., Hillemeier, M., Cook, M., Maczuga, S., & Farkas, G. (2013). Reading, mathematics, and behavioral difficulties interrelate: Evidence from a cross-lagged panel design and population-based sample of U.S. upper elementary students. *Behavioral Disorders, 38*, 212–227.

Losen, D. J., Ee, J., Hodson, C., & Martinez, T. E. (2015). Disturbing inequities: Exploring the relationship of discipline disparities for students with disabilities by race with gender with school outcomes. In D. J. Losen (Ed.), *Closing the school discipline gap: Equitable remedies for excessive exclusion* (pp. 89–106). New York, NY: Teacher's College Press.

Losen, D. J., & Gillespie, J. (2012). *Opportunities suspended: The disparate impact of disciplinary exclusion from school.* Los Angeles, CA: Center for Civil Rights Remedies at The Civil Rights Project at UCLA.

Losen, D. J., Hodson, C., Keith, M. A., Morrison, K., & Belway, S. (2015). *Are we closing the school discipline gap?* Los Angeles, CA: Center for Civil Rights Remedies at The Civil Rights Project at UCLA.

Losen, D. J., Martinez, T. E., & Okelola, V. (2014). *Keeping California's kids in school: Fewer students of color missing school for minor misbehavior.* Los Angeles, CA: Center for Civil Rights Remedies at The Civil Rights Project at UCLA.

Maag, J. W. (2001). Rewarded by punishment: Reflections on the disuse of positive reinforcement in schools. *Exceptional Children, 67*, 173–186.

Maggin, D. M., Zurheide, J., Pickett, K. C., & Baillie, S. J. (2015). A systematic evidence review of the check-in/check-out program for reducing student challenging behaviors. *Journal of Positive Behavior Interventions, 17*, 197–208.

Massar, M., McIntosh, K., & Eliason, B. M. (2015). Do out-of-school suspensions prevent future exclusionary discipline? In *PBIS evaluation brief*. Eugene, OR: OSEP National Technical Assistance Center on Positive Behavioral Interventions and Supports.

McIntosh, K., Bennett, J. L., & Price, K. (2011). Evaluation of social and academic effects of school-wide positive behaviour support in a Canadian school district. *Exceptionality Education International, 21*, 46–60.

McIntosh, K., Girvan, E. J., Horner, R. H., & Smolkowski, K. (2014). Education not incarceration: A conceptual model for reducing racial and ethnic disproportionality in school discipline. *Journal of Applied Research on Children, 5*(2), 1–22.

McIntosh, K., & Goodman, S. (in press). *Integrated multi-tiered systems of support: Blending RTI and PBIS.* New York, NY: Guilford Press.

McIntosh, K., Horner, R. H., Chard, D. J., Dickey, C. R., & Braun, D. H. (2008). Reading skills and function of problem behavior in typical school settings. *Journal of Special Education, 42*, 131–147. doi:10.1177/0022466907313253

McIntosh, K., Ty, S. V., Horner, R. H., & Sugai, G. (2013). School-wide positive behavior interventions and supports and academic achievement. In J. Hattie & E. Anderman

(Eds.), *International guide to student achievement* (pp. 146–148). New York, NY: Routledge.

Morgan, P. L., Farkas, G., & Wu, Q. (2012). Do poor readers feel angry, sad, and unpopular? *Scientific Studies of Reading, 16,* 360–381.

Newton, J. S., Todd, A. W., Algozzine, B., Algozzine, K., Horner, R. H., & Cusumano, D. L. (2014). Supporting team problem solving in inclusive schools. In J. McLeskey, N. L. Waldron, F. Spooner, & B. Algozzine (Eds.), *Handbook of research and practice for inclusive schools* (pp. 275–291). New York, NY: Routledge.

Noltemeyer, A. L., Ward, R. M., & Mcloughlin, C. S. (2015). Relationship between school suspension and student outcomes: A meta-analysis. *School Psychology Review, 44,* 224–240.

OSEP Technical Assistance Center on Positive Behavioral Interventions and Supports. (2015, October). *Positive Behavioral Interventions and Supports (PBIS) implementation blueprint.* Eugene, OR: University of Oregon. Retrieved from www.pbis.org

Ryan, J. B., Sanders, S., Katsiyannis, A., & Yell, M. L. (2007). Using time-out effectively in the classroom. *Teaching Exceptional Children, 39*(4), 60–67.

Sailor, W., Dunlap, G., Sugai, G., & Horner, R. H. (Eds.). (2009). *Handbook of positive behavior support.* New York, NY: Springer.

Schollenberger, T. L. (2015). Racial disparities in school suspension and subsequent outcomes: Evidence from the national longitudinal survey of youth. In D. J. Losen (Ed.), *Closing the school discipline gap: Research for policymakers* (pp. 31–43). New York, NY: Teachers College Press.

Scott, C. (2013). The search for the key for individualised instruction. In J. Hattie & E. Anderman (Eds.), *International guide to student achievement* (pp. 385–388). New York, NY: Routledge.

Scott, T. M., Anderson, C. M., Mancil, R., & Alter, P. (2009). Function-based supports for individual students in school settings. In W. Sailor, G. Dunlap, G. Sugai, & R. H. Horner (Eds.), *Handbook of positive behavior support* (pp. 421–442). New York, NY: Springer.

Skiba, R. J., Michael, R. S., Nardo, A. C., & Peterson, R. L. (2002). The color of discipline: Sources of racial and gender disproportionality in school punishment. *The Urban Review, 34,* 317–342. doi:10.1023/A:1021320817372

Smolkowski, K., Girvan, E. J., McIntosh, K., Nese, R. N. T., & Horner, R. H. (2015). *Identification of vulnerable decision points predicting racial and ethnic disproportionality in school discipline.* Manuscript submitted for publication.

Sterling Turner, H., & Watson, T. S. (1999). Consultant's guide for the use of time-out in the preschool and elementary classroom. *Psychology in the Schools, 36,* 135–148.

Sugai, G., & Horner, R. H. (2009). Defining and describing schoolwide positive behavior support. In W. Sailor, G. Dunlap, G. Sugai, & R. H. Horner (Eds.), *Handbook of positive behavior support* (pp. 307–326). New York, NY: Springer.

Sugai, G., Horner, R. H., Algozzine, R., Barrett, S., Lewis, T., Anderson, C., … Simonsen, B. (2010). *School-wide positive behavior support: Implementer's blueprint and self-assessment* (2nd ed.). Eugene, OR: University of Oregon.

Sugai, G., Horner, R. H., Dunlap, G., Hieneman, M., Lewis, T. J., Nelson, C. M., … Ruef, M. (2000). Applying positive behavior support and functional behavioral assessment in schools. *Journal of Positive Behavior Interventions, 2,* 131–143.

U.S. Departments of Education and Justice. (2014). *Dear colleague letter: Nondiscriminatory administration of school discipline.* Retrieved from http://www2.ed.gov/about/offices/ list/ocr/letters/colleague-201401-title-vi.html

Walker, H. M., Horner, R. H., Sugai, G., Bullis, M., Sprague, J. R., Bricker, D., & Kaufman, M. J. (1996). Integrated approaches to preventing antisocial behavior patterns among school-age children and youth. *Journal of Emotional and Behavioral Disorders, 4,* 194–209.

Wallace, J. M. J., Goodkind, S., Wallace, C. M., & Bachman, J. G. (2008). Racial, ethnic, and gender differences in school discipline among U.S. high school students: 1991–2005. *Negro Educational Review, 59,* 47–62.

Zabel, M. K. (1986). Timeout use with behaviorally disordered students. *Behavioral Disorders, 12,* 15–21.

CHAPTER 10

DEEP PRESSURE THERAPY DOESN'T REDUCE STEREOTYPICAL BEHAVIOR, FUNCTION-BASED INTERVENTIONS DO

Mickey Losinski and Robin Parks Ennis

ABSTRACT

Repetitive and restrictive behaviors are one of the core components of diagnosing a child with an autism spectrum disorder. These behaviors may take the form of repetitive motor movements or vocalizations, often referred to as stereotypical behaviors. These behaviors can impede the child's educational and social opportunities, and have thus become a target for intervention. A variety of interventions have been used to reduce stereotypical behaviors with varied success. One of the most oft-used interventions is deep pressure therapy (e.g., weighted vests), a practice that enjoys substantial anecdotal but little empirical support. Conversely, interventions based on functional behavior assessment (FBA) have been shown to reduce these behaviors, but may not be used frequently within schools. Therefore, this chapter will provide a brief overview of

Instructional Practices with and without Empirical Validity
Advances in Learning and Behavioral Disabilities, Volume 29, 197–219
Copyright © 2016 by Emerald Group Publishing Limited
All rights of reproduction in any form reserved
ISSN: 0735-004X/doi:10.1108/S0735-004X20160000029010

stereotypical behaviors and compare these two intervention approaches, with a clear preference for FBA-based interventions due to their stronger empirical support.

Keywords: Sensory integration; deep pressure therapy; stereotypical behavior; functional behavioral assessment

Repetitive and restrictive behaviors are a central feature of autism spectrum disorder (ASD) and are a necessary symptom in its diagnosis. These behaviors include four subtypes: (1) repetitive or stereotyped movements (stereotypy), (2) insistence on sameness, (3) restricted interests, and (4) unusual interest in sensory aspects of the environment (American Psychiatric Association [APA], 2013). According to Leekam, Prior, and Uljarevic (2011), these behaviors can be further conceptualized as two sub-categories: higher-level repetitive behaviors and lower-level repetitive behaviors. Insistence on sameness and restricted interests are considered the higher-level behaviors as they represent those behaviors most often noted in students with higher functioning autism. Conversely, the lower-level behaviors (stereotypical movements and unusual interests in the sensory aspects of the environment) are more common in younger, lower functioning children.

The lower-level behaviors, particularly stereotypical motor movements, have been noted in typically developing infants (Goldman et al., 2009; Thelen, 1981) and in the development of children with ASD more broadly. It has been suggested that these repetitive movements may be essential for neuromuscular development in infancy, however, in the case of children with ASD they do not end with this developmental function, but may take on different roles in later development (e.g., communication) and are thus maintained longer (Iverson & Wozniak, 2007; Thelen, 1981). For example, most children with ASD have, at some point in their development, been preoccupied with motor behaviors (e.g., hand flapping, tapping). Thus, the term stereotypical behavior (stereotypy) has been applied as a diagnostic criterion for ASD. In addition, stereotypy can manifest itself in the form of repetitive vocalizations, or vocal stereotypy. Vocal stereotypy can take the form of grunting or humming (Lanovaz & Sladeczek, 2012) and mimicking previously heard words/phrases, also referred to as echolalia (Leekam et al., 2011). In this chapter, we will explore causes and characteristics of stereotypical behavior as well as outline two interventions traditionally used to reduce stereotypy, one with a significant research base (function-based interventions) and one without (deep pressure therapy).

CAUSES OF STEREOTYPICAL BEHAVIORS

Stereotypical behaviors are considered a normal stage in infant development; however, for some children with ASD and other developmental
disorders, the behaviors appear later and persist longer than is developmentally appropriate. According to Thelen (1981), stereotypical behaviors may
serve as a developmental evolution in infants between uncoordinated
muscle movements to coordinated and deliberate movements. To that end,
stereotypical behavior is often seen at an earlier age in infants who meet
developmental milestones sooner (Thelen, 1979). Further, Piaget and Cook
(1952) suggested that while these movements may be used to develop motor
pathways, children might also continue these behaviors to extend the contextual effects of the behaviors. For example, an infant rocking their feet in
a crib may cause objects in the crib to move, thus the behavior becomes
maintained by a desire to create the movement in the objects again. For
children with developmental delays, stereotypies develop later and continue
sometimes indefinitely.

In children with developmental delays or ASD, Rodgers, Glod,
Connolly, and McConachie (2012) suggested that stereotypical behaviors
may be stimulated by increased arousal, sensory stimuli, and heightened
levels of anxiety. For example, it is thought that children with ASD may
have abnormal rates of arousal or anxiety, and engaging in stereotypical
movements may modulate that arousal (Sukholdolsky et al., 2008; Thelen,
1979). Furthermore, the factors associated with stereotypy may correspond
with the intellectual functioning of the child (Frankel, Freeman, Ritvo, &
Pardo, 1978). For example, in their study, Frankel et al. (1978) suggested
that children with lower intellectual functioning tend to display these behaviors more often, and often as a reaction to increased sensory stimuli, while
those with higher intellectual functioning may use the behaviors for self-
stimulatory purposes.

As discussed by Thelen (1979) and Piaget (1981), stereotypical behavior
exists in most normally developing infants and serves a developmental purpose. However, neurological and behavioral disruptions in the normal
developmental life cycle of a child with ASD may delay the onset of stereotypies and therefore alter their developmental function. Thus, the stereotypical behaviors may take on an alternate function, a proposition that is in
contrast to early interpretations of stereotypy (e.g., psychodynamic theory;
Greenacre, 1954) that suggested stereotypical behaviors do not serve a
behavioral function. For example, studies of anxiety suggest that stereotypies
may be a subconscious attempt to deal with anxiety through self-soothing or

pre-occupation with ritual (Leekam et al., 2011; Rodgers et al., 2012; Sukholdolsky et al., 2008). Further, research has also found that stereotypical behaviors can often be suppressed by the individual and may be exacerbated by levels of arousal (Reed, Hirst, & Hyman, 2012). Therefore, these behaviors may be considered to be purposeful and used to modulate sensory input for a variety of behavioral functions (Goldman et al., 2009; Lovaas, Newsom, & Hickman, 1987). Early behavioral research by Hutt and Hutt (1965) suggested that stereotypies were maintained by automatic reinforcement (e.g., self-stimulation); however, more recent research has found a variety of functions to these behaviors. For example, Patterson, Smith, and Jelen (2010) described findings from research suggesting that stereotypies may be maintained by avoidance of tasks or to avoid or gain social interactions. In any case, it is likely that a behavioral function for stereotypies does exist.

The exact causes of stereotypical behaviors in children with developmental delays are not clearly understood. However, neurological and developmental research seem to support the conclusion that for developmentally delayed children a disruption occurs within the first years of life that leads to the stereotypical behaviors both occurring later than in typically developing children and taking on different functions. Further, it has been suggested that the insistence on sameness and repetitive behaviors of children with ASD may result in a cyclical pattern that exacerbates the stereotypical behaviors and other autistic symptoms. For example, the review by Leekam et al. (2011) suggests a link between limited environmental variability and heightened occurrence of stereotypic behaviors and other autistic symptoms (poor communication). Leekam and colleagues suggested that children with ASD may create limited environments through their repetitive behaviors as a means of reducing anxiety, thus intensifying those behaviors and the limited environmental variability. Thus, it is important to intervene early and develop contingencies that reward adaptive (replacement) behaviors and increase environmental stimuli.

EDUCATIONAL CONSIDERATIONS

The effects of stereotypical behaviors on the educational performance of students with ASD include both impaired learning and social development (Kennedy, Meyer, Knowles, & Shukla, 2000; Neely, Rispoli, Gerow, & Ninci, 2015). For example, a student's hand-flapping behavior may interfere with completing their math assignment in a timely. Further, these behaviors may irritate, or amuse, the students around them, thus contributing to the student being stigmatized and obstructing social opportunities (Jones, Wint, & Ellis, 1990). Accordingly, it may become necessary to formally address stereotypical behavior in the Individualized Education Plan (IEP). For example, the Individuals with Disabilities Education Act (IDEA; 2004) states that the IEP team must "in the case of a child whose behavior impedes the child's learning or that of others, consider the use of positive behavioral interventions and supports, and other strategies, to address that behavior" (§1414 (d)(3)(B)(i)).

Research suggests that early intervention for individuals with ASD, particularly for stereotypies, is necessary regardless of the theoretical construct thought to underlie the behavior (MacDonald et al., 2007). Interrupting the cycle related to the flawed developmental adaptation of stereotypies prevents the rise of maladaptive functions to stereotypy. For example, if a child begins flapping his hands at age 2 (later than considered in the normal range) and begins to find this behavior gains the attention of adults, the behavior may persist because it functions to attract adult attention. However, if interventions were carried out at the beginning of this cycle, the stereotypy could be headed off before becoming an ingrained behavior with a maladaptive function.

A variety of interventions have been researched to reduce the extent to which students engage in stereotypical behaviors (Howard, Sparkman, Cohen, Green, & Stanislaw, 2005). These interventions can range from non-behavioral holistic treatment models that focus on a range of autistic behaviors (e.g., TEACCH; Schopler, 1997) to very focused behavioral interventions resulting from an experimental analysis of the context of the behavior (Kennedy et al., 2000). Additionally, researchers have investigated different therapies based on research that suggest a link between stereotypy and anxiety (Rodgers et al., 2012). For example, Miguel, Clark, Tereshko, and Ahearn (2009) investigated the use of psychotropic medications (e.g., Zoloft) within a behavioral intervention to determine its efficacy. Further, researchers have also examined cognitive behavioral interventions to reduce stereotypy by, for example, working on the similarities between some repetitive behaviors and obsessive-compulsive symptoms (Lehmkuhl, Storch, Bodfish, & Geffken, 2008). More recently, researchers have looked into the effects of antecedent exercise to reduce stereotypy (Morrison, Roscoe, & Atwell, 2011).

Within the public schools, reduction of stereotypy often involves one of two approaches: (1) Deep pressure therapy (e.g., weighted vests), a form of sensory integration therapy that lacks empirical support, and (2) interventions based on a functional behavioral assessment (FBA), a method that enjoys a considerable research base. Therefore, the remainder of this chapter will describe these two methods and discuss issues related to using peer-reviewed practices to improve outcomes for students with disabilities.

DEEP PRESSURE THERAPY

Deep pressure therapy (DPT) is rooted in sensory integration therapy (SIT), a broad set of intervention strategies that work on the premise that providing rich sensory experiences reduces a person's reaction to sensory inputs and those behaviors attributed to sensory dysfunctions (Ayres, 1972). According to Lang et al. (2012), SIT continues to be one of the most widely used methods by occupational therapists when working with students with ASD. Deep pressure involves squeezing, rubbing, and/or wrapping in an effort to regulate sensory input (Grandin, 1992). Benefits of DPT for students with ASD or other developmental delays are purported to include reduction of anxiety, stereotypy, and disruptive behaviors and increased attention (Ayres, 1972; Fertel-Daly, Bedell, & Hinojosa, 2001; Olson & Moulton, 2004).

Ayres (1972) described one of the earliest forms of DPT, which called for trained therapists to rub the skin of children with sensory dysfunction. She then described another process consisting of, "putting the child between two mats to make a 'hamburger'. The therapist then presses down on top of the child, pretending to put ketchup, mustard ..." (Ayres, 1972, p. 141). It was suggested that this type of intervention resulted in children being calmer when released. Similarly, Temple Grandin developed a "hug machine" (or Squeeze Machine), an early version of which was depicted in the movie *Temple Grandin* (Bellows et al., 2010). In the movie, Temple (played by Clare Danes) gets inside a device normally used to keep cows still and instructs a colleague to apply pressure to her by pressing in on the sides of the chute. Edelson, Edelson, Kerr, and Grandin (1999) investigated a more refined version of the "hug machine" (resembling a massage table that has been converted into a cattle chute with pads on all sides). In the study, persons with ASD climbed into the chute and, using levers, begin a process of hydraulic compression that was purported to provide deep pressure stimulation. The "Hug Machine" is an extreme form of DPT, with the most common practices involving weighted or compression garments (e.g., vests) and therapeutic brushing.

Weighted or compression vests have a strong presence in schools and are favored by many occupational therapists for use with students with ASD or sensory processing disorders (Olson & Moulton, 2004). Weighted vests typically involve a multi-pocket vest sized to fit the person wearing it. Vests usually have two pockets in front and two on the back where sacks of lead shot or sand are placed. The total weight in the pockets can vary between 5% and 10% of the person's body weight evenly distributed among the pockets. The vests are then worn in two-hour intervals for an unspecified length of time.

Compression vests are a variant of the weighted vest typically made of a stretchable (e.g., neoprene) or inflatable material and are sized to fit the person. Tightness is then controlled through Velcro^{TM} straps or by inflating the material with air and, when fitted correctly, provides uniform pressure to the torso. Like the weighted vests, the compression vests are suggested to be worn in intervals, though there does not seem to be an agreed upon time interval within the literature.

Another frequently used deep pressure treatment for overstimulation, or sensory defensiveness, is therapeutic brushing, the most popular method of which is the Wilbarger protocol (Foss, Swinth, McGruder, & Tomlin, 2003). The Wilbarger protocol follows a highly structured procedure lasting approximately 2–3 minutes and uses a specialized, non-scratching brush. The participant's body is brushed at the hands, arms, back, legs, and feet using firm deep pressure with careful attention to avoid scratching or tickling. Next, compression to major joints (e.g., shoulders, elbows, wrists, hips) follows and may be self-administered by engaging in various isometric exercises (e.g., push-ups, jumping jacks). Finally, if deemed necessary by the clinician, the therapist may perform techniques to reduce oral defensiveness (avoidance of activities using the mouth). For example, the therapist may swipe along the inside of the person's mouth with a finger (Wilbarger & Wilbarger, 2002). Application of the Wilbarger protocol is to occur approximately every two waking hours for a minimum of two weeks.

Theoretical Basis

The theoretical basis for DPT lies in the sensory integration framework and the theories put forward by Ayres (1972). According to Ayres, sensory issues are caused by a number of dysfunctional neurological processes that affect the individual's ability to modulate sensory input. The conceptual basis, then, is similar to that described earlier with regard to causation of stereotypical behaviors of students with ASD wherein neurological processing is disrupted at an early age. Ayres described the result of the disruption as a sensory processing disorder, or sensory integrative dysfunction, which may contribute to a variety of childhood issues including hyperactivity, inattentiveness, disruptive behaviors, delayed speech development, and poor muscle coordination (Ayres, 1972; Grandin, 1992).

Sensory integration therapy seeks to address the dysfunctions by providing systematic sensory inputs based on a diagnosis of problem areas (Ayres, 1972). These problem areas include the vestibular system (the system used for balance in animals), major muscle and joint groups, and epidermis (skin). According to Ayres, through careful administration of sensory inputs to these areas, children "spontaneously forms [sic] the adaptive responses and integrate[s] those sensations" (p. 140). One of the primary components of SIT is to provide sensory inputs via deep pressure (Grandin, 1992), which is thought to alleviate symptoms including attention, distractibility, and tactile defensiveness (hyper-sensitivity to touch). Further, Baranek, Foster, and Berkson (1997) suggested that tactile defensiveness is associated with stereotypical behaviors and that individuals exhibiting stereotypical behaviors should be assessed for co-occurring tactile defensiveness.

If a Favorite Idea Fails a Well Designed Test, It's Wrong

> – Neil DeGrasse Tyson (Bragga, Cannold, & Clark, 2014)

From a theoretical standpoint, the proposition of DPT has a certain amount of face validity for treating stereotypical behaviors. This may be the reason occupational therapists and teachers use it with individuals with ASD and other developmental disorders so frequently (Olson & Moulton, 2004). For example, early accounts by Grandin (1992) suggested deep pressure produces a sense of calm in the individual. This framework lends itself to interventions based on the theory that stereotypical behaviors are linked to anxiety. Thus, one could hypothesize that reducing anxiety will produce a reduction in the occurrence of stereotypical behaviors. Additionally, the theoretical concept that the young child with ASD may create their own restricted environment and engage in a cycle of limited sensory experiences that exacerbate their condition would seem to call for interventions to provide rich environments in order to facilitate adaptation to new stimuli. Both of these constructs might suggest that deep pressure and sensory integration therapies may be effective. However, the presence of face validity and anecdotal reports by occupational therapists, teachers, and parents has not lived up to reports of empirical research.

Relatively few studies investigate the use of DPT as a whole, and even fewer studies examine the effect of DPT on stereotypical behaviors – and each of them is limited by a number of factors. In fact, we identified only three studies that have shown positive results of DPT on the stereotypical behaviors of students with ASD (Deris, Hagelman, Schilling, & DiCarlo, 2006; Fertel-Daly et al., 2001; Moore, Cividini-Motta, Clark, & Ahearn, 2015). The study by Fertel-Daly et al. (2001) is heavily cited in the literature on and marketing of DPT to lend validity to the use of weighted garments and DPT more generally. However, this study had significant issues related to potential sources of bias including no measurement of implementation fidelity; vague description of the intervention agent; and, most concerning, the researcher being the only collector of data, without a second rater. In single-case design research, having a second rater to arrive at inter-observer agreement is vital, and the fact that the person implementing the intervention was the same as the one recording the behaviors without an independent observer casts serious doubts on the validity of the findings (Gast & Ledford, 2014). Finally, this study only resulted in slightly positive findings for three of five participants. When reviewing the literature on weighted vests exclusively, we find them to have effectively reduced stereotypy in only 4 of 19 cases (Losinski, Sanders, & Wiseman, 2016). Further, we identified studies that examined the use of a compression vest (Watkins & Sparling, 2014) and the comparison of·compression vest use to DPT to reduce stereotypical behaviors (Deris et al., 2006). However, none of these studies found positive results, with 0 of 4 participants showing noticeable improvement in stereotypical behaviors. The Wilbarger protocol, or therapeutic brushing, has even less empirical evidence than weighted vests, with only two studies targeting stereotypical behaviors, neither of which achieved significant results (Davis, Du rand, & Chan, 2011; Moore et al., 2015). In all, DPT therapy used to reduce stereotypical behaviors in children was effective in only 4 of 25 cases (Losinski et al., 2016). These results do not suggest that therapeutic brushing is generally effective, especially in light of the tendency of journals to publish only positive findings (Maag & Losinski, 2015).

Given this evidence, DPT advocates could contend that we missed some studies in our review, that DPT is effective to treat other conditions, or both. Advocates could, for example, point to a study by Vandenberg (2001) showing improvements in attention associated with DPT. However, that study utilizes a "quasi-experimental, single-system, AB" (p. 623) methodology that can be best described as an approach to a single-case design that meets few of the conventions and standards for high-quality single-case design research (see Gast & Ledford, 2014; Horner et al., 2005). Edelson et al. (1999) conducted another study that used DPT to reduce tension and anxiety. However, as noted by Goldstein (2003), the design of that study also had serious limitations, and we identified concerns about the implementation of the study. For example, the authors stated, "Unfortunately, both children in one match were mistakenly run in the placebo condition" (p. 147). This mistake, coupled with lack of a measure of treatment integrity, casts serious doubt on the internal validity of the study (Shadish, Cook, & Campbell, 2002).

Attempts to shed light on the suspect nature of sensory integration and DPT are not new. For example, Grandin (1996) criticized the National Institutes of Health (Bristol et al., 1996) for failing to target sensory-based dysfunctions in future research. However, in her support for research in this area Grandin included anecdotal claims of the effectiveness of DPT made by parents, teachers, and her. The empirical research she cited is methodologically suspect and includes potentially biased methods. More recently, Goldstein (2003) had a spirited debate with Edelson, Rimland, and Grandin (2003) regarding the use of these modalities. Goldstein's contention was that empirical research did not support the use of these techniques, while Edelson et al. suggested that he was biased against the intervention. The review by Losinski et al. (2016) agrees with Goldstein's position that these treatment modalities have little to no positive impact on students with ASD, and that any positive findings in the literature were found in studies with suspect quality.

Conflicts of Interest

Despite the sparse empirical support for DPT, the practice and products associated with it are frequently promoted as if they are effective. As with many products and practices in education, researchers often have vested interests in the outcomes of the studies on DPT. Whether those interests are strictly monetary, are rooted in the belief systems of the individual, or further an agenda (e.g., research line), researchers often have a vested interest in achieving positive outcomes (Maag & Losinski, 2015). Unfortunately, the DPT literature is replete with apparent conflicts of interest, where the researcher may have something to gain monetarily or intellectually from the product. For example, the "squeeze machine," based on Grandin's hug machine, is marketed in cooperation with Temple Grandin by Therafin (2015). Thus, a conflict of interest between research and product exists as the only research investigating a product like the squeeze machine involves someone with a vested interest in the study outcomes.

The other modalities of DPT don't appear to have the same level of suspect researcher interests as the squeeze machine. However, as Maag and Losinski (2015) discussed, for-profit organizations often selectively report findings about their products, resulting in consumers being provided with partial and biased information on the effectiveness of these products. For example, the makers of the "snug vest" discuss the literature with regard to parent opinions, and generally omit research findings from direct observation and other valid measures (Snug Vest, 2015). Additionally, they cite research conducted in-house and not published in a peer-reviewed outlet. As for the Wilbarger Protocol, it requires certified training and the use of a very specific brush (Therapressure Brush), which was developed by the researchers and which they promote as an effective tool (Foss et al., 2003). Each of these issues potentially contribute to bias in the research studies, as it is clearly in the sellers' interests to portray their products as effective.

In sum, DPT has developed a devoted consumer base thanks to savvy marketing strategies and anecdotal reports. Though we don't contend there is a vast corporate conspiracy where big business is targeting caregivers of individuals with ASD, nor do we contend they are akin to snake-oil salesman, it is hard to ignore the proliferation of materials attesting to the positive impact of DPT in advocacy websites for students with ASD (e.g., autismspeaks.org) and DPT's use in schools. One of the limitations of many interventions for students with ASD is that the most effective practices are not products, and cannot be purchased from a store, and thus have limited marketability. One such approach, functional behavioral interventions (FBI), enjoys robust empirical support for reducing stereotypy.

FUNCTION-BASED INTERVENTIONS

FBA-based interventions are rooted in behaviorism and applied behavior analysis, a broad set of procedures used to determine the relation between an individual and their environment (Baer, Wolf, & Risley, 1987). Within behavioral theory, when a child engages in stereotypy (or any behavior) on a regular basis, they are receiving some form of naturally occurring reinforcement that motivates them to continue to engage in the behavior (Alberto & Troutman, 2013). This reinforcement can be classified as positive (the presentation of a consequence contingent on the occurrence of the behavior) or negative (the removal of a consequence contingent on the occurrence of the behavior). The type of reinforcement they receive is, in effect, the purpose that the behavior serves and can be referred to as the "function" of the behavior. Umbreit, Ferro, Liaupsin, and Lane (2007) categorized functions into three types: attention, tangibles and activities, and sensory. Individuals may seek positive or negative reinforcement in the form of one or more of these types of consequences. For example, a student may engage in stereotypy to access or receive positive reinforcement in the form of sensory stimulation (e.g., it feels good). Another student may engage in stereotypy to receive negative reinforcement in the form of escape from difficult tasks. Yet another student may engage in the same behavior to access both positive reinforcement in the form of sensory stimulation and negative reinforcement in the form of escape from tasks. Once the function of an individual's behavior has been determined, this information can be used to develop an intervention that teaches the student how to earn reinforcement for one or more appropriate replacement behaviors by adjusting antecedent and consequence contingencies within the student's environment (Maag, 2004; Umbreit et al., 2007).

Theoretical Basis

FBA-based interventions are grounded in three basic assumptions: (1) behavior is affected by context, (2) behavior is purposeful, and (3) behavior can be changed if appropriate replacement behaviors are taught (Maag, 2004). Consequences of a behavior (i.e., reinforcement and punishment) affect the frequency with which a behavior occurs. The availability of these consequences as well as the antecedents that occasion the occurrence of problem behaviors make up its context. The purpose of a behavior (or its function) can be appropriate, but we still must intervene if the form the behavior takes is inappropriate. For example, there is nothing wrong with a student engaging in sensory stimulation to receive positive reinforcement (feels pleasant) unless that student decides to engage in disruptive stereotypical behaviors (e.g., hand flapping) to obtain the stimulation. Finally, functional assessment is grounded in the idea that we can help students to reduce or eliminate inappropriate behaviors by teaching them appropriate behaviors as a replacement. For example, teaching the student to engage in more appropriate self-stimulatory behaviors such as wearing a fidget ring can serve as a replacement to hand flapping. If we seek to eliminate the problem behavior but don't teach an appropriate replacement behavior, students are likely to begin engaging in an alternative problem behavior.

Functional Behavioral Assessment Procedures

The goal of FBA is to develop a functional hypothesis or statement on which to base the development of an intervention to reduce or eliminate a target problem behavior (i.e., stereotypy). FBA methods vary greatly and may involve both direct and indirect data collection methods. Further, direct methods can involve both experimental and nonexperimental procedures. See Table 1 for a description of types of data collection used in FBAs as well as advantages and disadvantages of each.

Functional Analysis

A functional analysis (FA) is a form of direct data collection that involves an experimental manipulation of antecedent and consequence contingencies to determine what conditions occasion and/or maintain an individual's problem behaviors (Cooper, Heron, & Heward, 2007). FA typically involves four conditions: play (control), contingent attention, contingent demand, and alone (Iwata, Dorsey, Slifer, Bauman, & Richman, 1994). See Table 2 for a description of each condition. Outside observers then record the number of occurrences of the problem behavior to determine if one or more conditions result in increased rates of the problem behavior. High rates of problem behavior in a given condition indicate the function of the student's behavior. For example, a student who displays high rates of problem behavior during the demand condition may be motivated by escape from task demands. FAs are more often conducted in clinical settings where clinicians can readily control the antecedents and consequences, although they have been set up in applied settings.

Direct Observation

Behavioral observation or ABC (antecedent-behavior-consequence) data collection is important for documenting patterns of behavior in natural settings. While an FA manipulates contingencies to occasion and reinforce responding, ABC data collection should be done in settings where the individual normally engages in the problem behavior (i.e., the classroom, home) under standard practices (i.e., before implementing an intervention or using current intervention practices). An outside observer records each time the problem behavior is displayed and what happens immediately before (antecedent) and after (consequence). It is important to only record objective data during ABC data collection and interpret the data after the observation. Umbreit et al. (2007) recommended observing anywhere from

Table 1. Functional Behavioral Assessment Data Collection Methods.

Type	Method	Description	Advantages	Disadvantages
Direct	Functional analysis (FA)	An outside observer collects direct observation data during an experimental manipulation of antecedent and consequence contingencies to determine which conditions (play, attention, demand, alone) occasion and/or maintain an individual's problem behaviors	• Only experimental form of FBA data collection • Yields a clear demonstration of the relationship between the behavior and the environment	• Can temporarily increase problem behavior during assessment conditions • Can be time-consuming • Requires behavioral expertise to conduct
	Direct observation	An outside observer records each time the problem behavior is displayed and what happens immediately before (antecedent) and after (consequence) in settings where the individual normally engages in the problem behavior under standard practices	• Involves in vivo analysis of the behavior, which provides a true picture of the environmental contingencies	• Can be time-consuming • Requires behavioral expertise to conduct
Indirect	Interview	A standardized interview protocol is used to identify and operationally define the problem behavior(s) and gather information on when, under what conditions, and with whom the behavior is likely to occur, including what happens immediately before and after the problem behavior. Additional questions related to possible functional hypotheses and previous intervention techniques may be included. Interviews may be conducted with students, teachers, parents, and other service providers or caregivers	• Quickly provides information from a variety of stakeholders • Provides information on the problem behavior related to time, location, activities, and persons involved	• Less precise in identifying the function of the behavior • Information can be subjective

Table 2. Functional Analysis Conditions.

Condition	Antecedent Manipulations	Consequence Manipulations
Play (control)	Student engages in a preferred activity (e.g., toys, game), interventionist provides continuous social attention	Clinician ignores or neutrally redirects problem behavior
Attention	Student is placed in a room with limited stimulation, interventionist engages in an activity independent of the subject (e.g., reads, takes notes) in the same room	Clinician provides attention only when the problem behavior is observed (reprimands, redirects)
Demand	Student is given a task demand (e.g., academic worksheet, manual task), interventionist continuously provides task demands including prompts as needed	Clinician provides a break for the task when problem behavior is observed
Alone	Student is placed alone in a room with limited stimulation	Problem behavior is ignored (no clinical present)

Note: Descriptions adapted from Iwata, Dorsey, Slifer, Bauman, and Richman (1994).

5 to 20 instances of the behavior or until a clear pattern of responding is established.

Interviews
An indirect form of data collection involves conducting functional assessment interviews with caregivers (e.g., parents, teachers) as well as the student. These interviews include clearly identifying and operationally defining the problem behavior(s) and involve questions related to when, under what conditions, and with whom the behavior is likely to occur, including what happens immediately before and after the problem behavior. One such interview protocol, the Functional Assessment Checklist for Teachers and Staff (FACTS; March et al., 2000) also involves discussing possible functional hypotheses with the interviewee and what interventions, if any, have been tried before. If an interview is used, it should be conducted prior to conducting ABC observations, as information from the interview can help the observer better understand the data collected during the observations.

FBAs should involve the use of more than one data collection method, as the accuracy of determining the functional hypothesis is increased with additional types of data collection methods (Maag, 2004; Umbreit et al., 2007). Additional widely used FBA tools include behavioral rating scales and record reviews. While these tools may not provide information directly related to function, they can provide information on the student's behavior in relation to standardized norms (rating scales) and/or on the student's learning history (record review). Many school districts, clinics, and hospitals have developed standard protocols of FBA data collection. Further, researchers have developed methods for conducting FBA and developing function-based interventions (FBIs; e.g., O'Neill et al., 1997; Umbreit et al., 2007). It is important to note that an FBA is considered to be an assessment of a child with a disability and as such requires parental consent before conducting one (see Katsiyannis, Balluch, & Losinski, 2016).

Developing Interventions Based on FBA

Once all FBA data are collected, this information is used to formulate a hypothesis statement about the function of the behavior (e.g., during independent work time, John engages in stereotypy to escape difficult task demands), which serves as the basis for developing a behavior intervention plan. Regardless of which data collection methods are used, the goal is to evaluate the data and look for patterns that signify one or multiple functions (Alberto & Troutman, 2013; Maag, 2004). One method for organizing FBA data to make this determination is the use of a function matrix, where data from each source are entered into a matrix cell reflecting whether the behavior serves to elicit positive or negative reinforcement in the forms of attention, tasks, tangibles, or sensory input (Umbreit et al., 2007). For example, if data from the FA, the ABC observations, and interviews appear in the negative reinforcement/task cell, a likely function of the behavior is to escape task demands. Once this statement has been developed, it can be used as the basis for a functionally indicated behavior intervention.

There are many different formats for developing a behavior intervention plan, and many school districts and service providers have standardized protocols they use regularly. In general, plans include many or all of the following components: clearly defined target and replacement behaviors, antecedent strategies, consequence strategies, monitoring plan, generalization and maintenance plan, crisis plan, training procedures, and resources needed (Alberto & Troutman, 2013). Adjusting antecedent strategies involves modifying the environment to prevent the problem behavior from occurring. This can be done by targeting settings (locations, times of day, peers/adults) that have historically occasioned the problem behavior and make modifications so that the behavior is less likely to occur (Losinski, Maag, Katsiyannis, & Ennis, 2014). Adjusting antecedent strategies may also involve teaching the student to engage in the appropriate replacement behavior if that behavior is not currently in the student's behavioral repertoire. Adjusting consequence strategies involves both providing reinforcement for engaging in an appropriate replacement behavior and withholding reinforcement previously received for engaging in the problem behavior (e.g., Lane et al., 2007). It is essential that these consequences be based on the function determined through the FBA.

An Established Research Base

FBA has been used to develop interventions for students with and at-risk for a variety of different disabilities, including ASD, attention-deficit hyperactivity disorder, intellectual disabilities, and emotional and behavioral disorders (e.g., Kern, Gallagher, Starosta, Hickman, & George, 2006; Lane et al., 2007; Turton, Umbreit, & Mathur, 2011). Specifically, FBIs have been used to improve the behavior of individuals with ASD by reducing or eliminating behaviors such as aggression, elopement, food refusal, pica, property distraction, self-injury, stereotypy, stealing, and tantrums (Love, Carr, & LeBlanc, 2009).

In general, researchers have found that individualized interventions based on FBA data are more effective than those that are not (e.g., Campbell & Anderson, 2008). This is because behavioral interventions often involve the use of reinforcement and/or punishment contingencies and individuals respond differently to each. Thus, having a grounded hypothesis regarding which consequences are more likely to work for an individual greatly increases the odds that we can change the behavior. For example, if we provide consequences for appropriate behavior without knowing what is reinforcing to the student (i.e., the function of their behavior), we are likely to select consequences that are not truly reinforcing to the student (i.e., they don't increase appropriate responding). Conversely, if we provide consequences for inappropriate behavior without knowing what is punishing to the student, we are likely to select consequences that are not truly punishing and can inadvertently reinforce a students' inappropriate behavior. In essence, applying behavioral interventions without assessing the behavior amounts to guessing.

One reason stereotypy has been widely addressed using methods other than interventions based on FBA is experts had generally believed that stereotypy was performed for automatic sensory reinforcement (e.g., Lovaas et al., 1987). However, researchers now suggest that stereotypy may have various functions, such as positive reinforcement from attention (Durand & Carr, 1987), positive reinforcement from tangible items (Ahearn, Clark, Gardener, Chung, & Dube, 2003), or multiple functions (Kennedy et al., 2000). For example, Kennedy and colleagues evaluated the stereotypical behavior of five students with ASD, and found that their behavior was associated with a range of behavioral functions. Two students displayed stereotypy under all response conditions. Two students displayed stereotypy to receive positive reinforcement in the form of adult attention and sensory stimulation as well as negative reinforcement in the form of task avoidance. The fifth student displayed stereotypy for negative reinforcement in the form of task and attention avoidance as well as positive reinforcement in the form of sensory stimulation. Their findings also suggested that this was true regardless of the topography of the stereotypic behaviors. In a follow-up study (Kennedy et al., 2000), one student from the initial study received functional communication training and reinforcement for appropriate responding. This resulted in a significant decrease in or elimination of stereotypy across attention, demand, and play conditions.

Similarly, Bruhn et al. (2015) used FBA to evaluate the function of stereotypical behavior of two students with autism. The function of student 1's (Tommy's) behavior was sensory stimulation. The researchers developed a behavior plan based on an FBA that involved giving Tommy access to and praise for using a stress ball, which practically eliminated his skin scratching behavior. The function of student 2's (Buck's) behavior was inconclusive, as he received various forms of reinforcement for engaging in stereotypical behavior and no clear pattern emerged from the FBA. As a result, Bruhn and colleagues applied three separate interventions based on his FBA to help decrease stereotypical behavior. They found teacher self-monitoring of specific praise statements delivered at 2-min interval while ignoring stereotypical behavior was the most effective and resulted in a significant reduction in stereotypy. These illustrations add to the evidence that FBA-based interventions can be used to decrease stereotypical behaviors, regardless of whether the function is sensory (automatic).

The above examples are indicative of recent research supporting the use of FBIs to reduce stereotypical behaviors, both in the form of motor and vocal stereotypies. Indeed, research syntheses have shown FBIs to be effective in reducing stereotypical behaviors of children with autism and other developmental disabilities (Lanovaz & Sladeczek, 2012; Patterson et al., 2010) especially as compared to interventions based on deep pressure therapies (Losinski et al., 2016). In addition, interventions based on FBAs have been shown to be socially acceptable for both caregivers and students

(Lane & Beebe-Frankenberger, 2004). Socially validity refers to the acceptability of (a) the behavioral goals, (b) the intervention procedures, and (c) the resulting behavior change (Wolf, 1978). Even though FBIs require FBAs to be conducted prior to formulating an intervention, and may be laborious, they provide an efficient means for developing successful interventions, making both the procedures and the outcomes socially acceptable.

CONCLUSIONS

A considerable gap between research and practice exists with regard to the use of DPT. With such little empirical support, its wide use in the field is difficult to comprehend. This is unfortunate considering the growing need for socially acceptable and beneficial interventions for students with ASD who are entering schools in growing numbers. Further, with the trend of schools to use an inclusionary model for students with disabilities it is imperative that we intervene on those behaviors that may impede student learning and/ or make the students a target of harassment by peers. The common use of instructional practices with little or no empirical support, such as DPT, may be due to factors such as the financial backing and marketing of these products to parents and practitioners who yearn for something to "fix" children with ASD. Unfortunately, most research-based practices, like FBA, have limited financial backing and little in the way of marketing outside of academic outlets (e.g., journals, conferences). However, the IDEA mandates that students with disabilities have IEPs based on peer-reviewed research. Therefore, it is imperative that practitioners keep up to date on educational research and evidence-based practices.

REFERENCES

Ahearn, W. H., Clark, K. M., Gardener, N. C., Chung, B. I., & Dube, W. V. (2003). Persistence of stereotypic behavior: Examining the effects of external reinforcers. *Journal of Applied Behavior Analysis, 36,* 439–448.

Alberto, P., & Troutman, A. (2013). *Applied behavior analysis for teachers* (9th ed.). Columbus, OH: Prentice-Hall-Merrill.

American Psychiatric Association. (2013). *Diagnostic and statistical manual of mental disorders* (5th ed.). Washington, DC: Author.

Ayres, A. J. (1972). *Sensory integration and learning disorders.* Los Angeles, CA: Western Psychological Services.

Baer, D. M., Wolf, M. M., & Risley, T. R. (1987). Some current dimension of applied behavior analysis. *Journal of Applied Behavior Analysis, 20,* 313–327.

Baranek, G. T., Foster, L. G., & Berkson, G. (1997). Tactile defensiveness and stereotyped behaviors. *The American Journal of Occupational Therapy*, *51*(2), 91−95.

Bellows, G., Di Loreto, D., Edwards, A., Ferguson, S., Lister, P., Owen, A., … Spence, G. (Producers), & Jackson, M. (Director). (2010). *Temple-Grandin* (Motion picture). United States: HBO Films.

Bragga, B., Cannold, M., & Clark, J. (Producers), & Bragga, B. (Director). (2014). *Cosmos A Spacetime Odyssey* (Television mini-series). United States: National Geographic Channel.

Bristol, M. M., Cohen, D. J., Costello, E. J., Denckla, M., Eckberg, T. J., Kallen, R., … Spence, M. A. (1996). State of the science in autism: Report to the national institutes health. *Journal of Autism and Other Developmental Disorders*, *26*, 121−154.

Bruhn, A. L., Balint-Langel, K., Troughton, L., Langan, S., Lodge, K., & Kortemeyer, S. (2015). Accessing and treating stereotypical behaviors in classrooms using a functional approach. *Behavioral Disorders*, *41*, 21−37.

Campbell, A., & Anderson, C. M. (2008). Enhancing effects of check in/check out with function-based support. *Behavioral Disorders*, *33*, 233−245.

Cooper, J. O., Heron, T. E., & Heward, W. L. (2007). *Applied behavior analysis* (2nd ed.). Columbus, OH: Pearson.

Davis, T. N., Du rand, S., & Chan, J. M. (2011). The effects of a brushing procedure on stereotypical behavior. *Research in Autism Spectrum Disorders*, *5*, 1053−1058.

Deris, A. R., Hagelman, E. M., Schilling, K., & DiCarlo, C. F. (2006). Using a weighted or pressure vest for a child with autistic spectrum disorder. ERIC Document Reproduction Service No. ED490780.

Durand, V. M., & Carr, E. G. (1987). Social influences on "self-stimulatory" behavior: Analysis and treatment application. *Journal of Applied Behavior Analysis*, *20*, 119−132.

Edelson, S., Rimland, B., & Grandin, T. (2003). Response to Goldstein's commentary: Interventions to facilitate auditory, visual, and motor integration: "Show me the data". *Journal of Autism and Developmental Disabilities*, *33*, 551−552.

Edelson, S. M., Edelson, M. G., Kerr, D. C., & Grandin, T. (1999). Behavioral and physiological effects of deep pressure on children with autism: A pilot study evaluating the efficacy of Grandin's hug machine. *American Journal of Occupational Therapy*, *53*, 145−152.

Fertel-Daly, D., Bedell, G., & Hinojosa, J. (2001). Effects of a weighted vest on attention to task and self-stimulatory behaviors in preschoolers with pervasive developmental disorders. *American Journal of Occupational Therapy*, *55*, 629−640.

Foss, A., Swinth, Y., McGruder, J., & Tomlin, G. (2003). Sensory modulation dysfunction and the Wilbarger protocol: An evidence review. *OT Practice*, *8*(12), 1−7.

Frankel, F., Freeman, B. J., Ritvo, E., & Pardo, R. (1978). The effect of environmental stimulation upon the stereotyped behavior of autistic children. *Journal of Autism and Childhood Schizophrenia*, *8*, 389−394.

Gast, D. L., & Ledford, J. R. (2014). *Single case research methodology: Applications in special education and behavioral sciences* (2nd ed.). New York, NY: Routledge.

Goldman, S., Wang, C., Salgado, M. W., Greene, P. E., Kim, M., & Rapin, S. (2009). Motor stereotypies in children with autism and other developmental disabilities. *Developmental Medicine and Child Neurology*, *51*, 30−38.

Goldstein, H. (2003). Response to Edelson, Rimland, and Grandin's commentary. *Journal of Autism and Developmental Disabilities*, *33*, 553−555.

Grandin, T. (1992). Calming effects of deep touch pressure in patients with autistic disorder, college students, and animals. *Journal of Child and Adolescent Psychopharmacology*, *2*(1), 63−72.

Grandin, T. (1996). Brief report: Response to national institutes of health report. *Journal of Autism and Developmental Disorders*, *26*(2), 185−187.

Greenacre, P. (1954). The role of transference: Practical considerations in relation to psycho-analytic therapy. *Journal of the American Psychoanalytic Association, 2,* 671–684.

Horner, R. H., Carr, E. G., Halle, J., McGee, G., Odom, S., & Wolery, M. (2005). The use of single-subject research to identify evidence-based practice in special education. *Exceptional Children, 71,* 165–179.

Howard, J. S., Sparkman, C. R., Cohen, H. G., Green, G., & Stanislaw, H. (2005). A comparison of intensive behavior analytic and eclectic treatments for young children with autism. *Research in Developmental Disabilities, 26,* 359–383.

Hutt, C., & Hutt, S. J. (1965). Effects of environmental complexity on stereo-typed behaviors of children. *Animal Behavior, 13,* 1–4.

Individuals with Disabilities Education Improvement Act of 2004, 20 U.S.C. § 1414 & 1415. (2004). (Reauthorization of the Individuals with Disabilities Education Act of 1990).

Iverson, J. M., & Wozniak, R. (2007). Variation in vocal-motor development in infant siblings of children with autism. *Journal of Autism and Developmental Disorders, 37,* 158–170. doi:10.1007/s10803-006-0339-z

Iwata, B. A., Dorsey, M. F., Slifer, K. J., Bauman, K. E., & Richman, G. S. (1994). Toward a functional analysis of self-injury. *Journal of Applied Behavior Analysis, 27,* 197–209.

Jones, R. S. P., Wint, D., & Ellis, N. C. (1990). The social effects of stereotyped behavior. *Journal of Mental Deficiency Research, 34,* 261–268.

Katsiyannis, A., Balluch, F., & Losinski, M. (2016). Informed consent and functional behavioral assessment: An examination of federal guidance for school personnel. *Beyond Behavior, 25,* 35–37.

Kennedy, C. H., Meyer, K. A., Knowles, T., & Shukla, S. (2000). Analyzing the multiple functions of stereotypical behaviors for students with autism: Implications for assessment and treatment. *Journal of Applied Behavior Analysis, 33,* 559–571.

Kern, L., Gallagher, P., Starosta, K., Hickman, W., & George, M. (2006). Longitudinal outcomes of functional behavioral assessment-based interventions. *Journal of Positive Behavior Interventions, 8,* 67–78.

Lane, K. L., & Beebe-Frankenberger, M. (2004). *School-based interventions: The tools you need to succeed.* Boston, MA: Allyn & Bacon Publishers.

Lane, K. L., Rogers, L. A., Parks, R. J., Weisenbach, J. L., Mau, A. C., Merwin, M. T., & Bergman, W. A. (2007). Function-based interventions for students nonresponsive to primary and secondary prevention efforts: Illustrations at the elementary and middle school levels. *Journal of Emotional and Behavioral Disorders, 15,* 169–183.

Lang, R., O'Reilly, M., Healy, O., Rispoli, M., Lydon, H., Streusand, W., … Giesbers, S. (2012). Sensory integration therapy for autism spectrum disorders: A systematic review. *Research in Autism Spectrum Disorders, 6,* 1004–1018.

Lanovaz, M. J., & Sladeczek, I. E. (2012). Vocal stereotypy in individuals with autism spectrum disorders: A review of behavioral interventions. *Behavior Modification, 36,* 146–164.

Leekam, S. R., Prior, M. R., & Uljarevic, M. (2011). Restricted and repetitive behaviors in autism spectrum disorders: A review of research in the last decade. *Psychological Bulletin, 137,* 562–593. doi:10.1037/a0023341

Lehmkuhl, H. D., Storch, E. A., Bodfish, J. W., & Geffken, G. R. (2008). Brief report: Exposure and response prevention for obsessive compulsive disorder in a 12-year-old with autism. *Journal of Autism and Developmental Disorders, 38,* 77–91.

Losinski, M., Maag, J. W., Katsiyannis, A., & Ennis, R. P. (2014). Examining the quality and effects of interventions based on the assessment of contextual variables: A meta-analysis. *Exceptional Children, 80,* 407–422.

Losinski, M., Sanders, S. A., & Wiseman, N. (2016). Examining the use of deep touch pressure to improve the educational performance of students with disabilities: A meta-analysis. *Research and Practice for Persons with Severe Disabilities, 41,* 3–18.

Lovaas, O. I., Newsom, C., & Hickman, C. (1987). Self-stimulatory behavior and perceptual reinforcement. *Journal of Applied Behavior Analysis, 20,* 45–68.

Love, J. R., Carr, J. E., & LeBlanc, L. A. (2009). Functional assessment of problem behavior in children with autism spectrum disorders: A summary of 32 outpatient cases. *Journal of Autism and Developmental Disorders, 39,* 363–372.

Maag, J. W. (2004). *Behavior management: From theoretical implications to practical applications* (2nd ed.). Belmont, CA: Thomson Wadsworth.

Maag, J. W., & Losinski, M. (2015). Thorny issues and prickly solutions: Publication bias in meta-analytic reviews in the social sciences. *Advances in Social Science Research, 2,* 242–253.

MacDonald, R., Green, G., Mansfield, R., Geckeler, A., Gardenier, N., & Anderson, J. (2007). Stereotypy in young children with autism and typically developing children. *Research in Developmental Disabilities, 28,* 266–277.

March, R., Lewis-Palmer, L., Brown, D., Crone, D., Todd, A. W., & Carr, E. (2000). *Functional assessment checklist for teachers and staff (FACTS).* Eugene, OR: Educational and Community Supports. University of Oregon.

Miguel, C. F., Clark, K., Tereshko, L., & Ahearn, W. H. (2009). The effects of response interruption and redirection and Sertraline on vocal stereotypy. *Journal of Applied Behavior Analysis, 42,* 883–888. doi:10.1901/jaba.2009.42-883

Moore, K. M., Cividini-Motta, C., Clark, K. M., & Ahearn, W. H. (2015). Sensory integration as a treatment for automatically maintained stereotypy. *Behavioral Interventions, 30,* 95–111.

Morrison, H., Roscoe, E. M., & Atwell, A. (2011). An evaluation of antecedent exercise on behavior maintained by automatic reinforcement using a three-component multiple schedule. *Journal of Applied Behavior Analysis, 44,* 523–541. doi:10.1901/jaba.2011.44-523

Neely, L., Rispoli, M., Gerow, S., & Ninci, J. (2015). Effects of antecedent exercise on academic engagement and stereotypy during instruction. *Behavior Modification, 39*(1), 98–116.

Olson, L. J., & Moulton, H. J. (2004). Use of weighted vests in pediatric occupational therapy practice. *Physical & Occupational Therapy in Pediatrics, 24*(3), 45–60. doi:10.1300/J006v24n03_04

O'Neill, R. E., Horner, R. H., Albin, R. W., Sprague, J. R., Storey, K., & Newton, J. S. (1997). *Functional assessment and program development for problem behavior: A practical handbook* (2nd ed.). Pacific Grove, CA: Brooks/Cole.

Patterson, S. Y., Smith, V., & Jelen, M. (2010). Behavioural intervention practices for stereotypic and repetitive behaviour in individuals with autism spectrum disorder: A systematic review. *Developmental Medicine and Child Neurology, 52,* 318–327.

Piaget, J. (1981). *Intelligence and affectivity. Their relationship during child development.* Palo Alto: Annual Reviews.

Piaget, J., & Cook, M. (1952). *The origins of intelligence in children.* New York, NY: International Universities Press.

Reed, F. D., Hirst, J. M., & Hyman, S. R. (2012). Assessment and treatment of stereotypic behavior in children with autism and other developmental disabilities: A thirty year review. *Research in Autism Spectrum Disorders, 6*(1), 422–430.

Rodgers, J., Glod, M., Connolly, B., & McConachie, H. (2012). The relationship between anxiety and repetitive behaviors in autism spectrum disorder. *Journal of Autism and Developmental Disorders, 42,* 2404–2409. doi:10.1007/s10803-012-1531-y

Schopler, E. (1997). Implementation of TEACCH philosophy. In D. J. Cohen & F. R. Volkmar (Eds.), *Handbook of autism and pervasive developmental disorders* (2nd ed., pp. 767–795). New York, NY: Wiley.

Shadish, W. R., Cook, T. D., & Campbell, D. T. (2002). *Experimental and quasi-experimental designs for generalized causal inference.* Belmont, CA: Wadsorth Cengage Learning.

Snug Vest. (2015). *Snug Vest: Clinical support.* Retrieved from http://www.snugvest.com/pages/clinical-support. Accessed on October 26, 2015.

Sukholdolsky, D. G., Scahill, L., Gadow, K. D., Arnold, L. E., Aman, M. G., McDougle, C. J., ... Vitiello, B. (2008). Parent-rated anxiety symptoms in children with pervasive developmental disorders: Frequency and association with core autism symptoms and cognitive functioning. *Journal of Abnormal Child Psychology, 36,* 117–128. doi:10.1007/s10802-007-9165-9

Thelen, E. (1979). Rythmical stereotypies in normal human infants. *Animal Behavior, 27,* 699–715.

Thelen, E. (1981). Rhythmical behavior in infancy: An ethological perspective. *Developmental Psychology, 17,* 237–257. doi:10.1037/0012-1649.17.3.237

Therafin Corporation. (2015). *We manufacture the squeeze machine (some people call it hug machine).* Retrieved from http://www.therafin.com/squeezemachine.htm. Accessed on September 3, 2015.

Turton, A. M., Umbreit, J., & Mathur, S. R. (2011). Systematic function-based intervention for adolescents with emotional and behavioral disorders in an alternative setting: Broadening the context. *Behavioral Disorders, 36,* 117–128.

Umbreit, J., Ferro, J., Liaupsin, C. J., & Lane, K. L. (2007). *Functional behavioral assessment and function-based intervention: An effective, practical approach.* Columbus, OH: Pearson.

Vandenberg, N. L. (2001). The use of a weighted vest to increase on-task behavior in children with attention difficulties. *American Journal of Occupational Therapy, 55,* 621–628.

Watkins, N., & Sparling, E. (2014). The effectiveness of the Snug Vest on stereotypic behaviors in children with autism spectrum disorder. *Behavior Modification, 38,* 412–427.

Wilbarger, J., & Wilbarger, P. (2002). Wilbarger approach to treating sensory defensiveness and clinical application of the sensory diet. Sections in alternative and complementary programs for intervention. In A. C. Bundy, E. A. Murray, & S. Lane (Eds.), *Sensory integration: Theory and practice* (2nd ed.). Philadelphia, PA: F.A. Davis.

Wolf, M. M. (1978). Social validity: The case for subjective measurement or how applied behavior analysis is finding its heart. *Journal of Applied Behavior Analysis, 11,* 203–214.